VOLUNTEER
SLAVERY

Printed in the United States of America

Library of Congress Cataloging-in-Publication Data
Nelson, Jill
    Volunteer slavery : my authentic Negro experience / Jill Nelson.
        p. cm.
    ISBN 1-879360-24-1 : $21.95
    1. Nelson, Jill.   2. Afro-American journalists—Washington, D.C.—Biography.   3. Afro-American women—Washington, D.C.—Biography.   4. Washington post (Washington, D.C. : 1974)   5. Washington, D. C.—Biography.   I. Title.
PN4874.N295A3   1993
070'.92—dc20   92-51078
                                                                              CIP

Excerpt from "Volunteer Slavery" by Rahsaan Roland Kirk used by permission of the estate of Rahsaan Roland Kirk.

Noble Press books are available in bulk at discount prices. Single copies are available prepaid direct from the publisher.

The Noble Press, Inc.
213 W. Institute Place, Suite 508
Chicago, Illinois 60610
(800) 486-7737

VOLUNTEER
SLAVERY

MY AUTHENTIC NEGRO EXPERIENCE

JILL NELSON

The Noble Press,
Inc.

CHICAGO

For Leil and Dad, who made me.

For Misu and Michael, who made me do it.

And for Lynn.

ACKNOWLEDGEMENTS

Eternal thanks for the unconditional support of my brothers, Stanley and Ralph, who early on told me to write it as I lived it.

Thanks are due my homegirls, Lynn, Allyson, Thulani, Chocolate, Lorrie, Marcia, Nicky, Adrienne, and Judyie, magnificent women all: and especially Daisy, who appropriated this book as her nightly bedtime story and kept me writing with regular midnight calls demanding, "Where's my chapter? Where's my chapter? Read me a story!"

Thanks to my friend Robert Lipsyte, who gave the *Post* my name and number in the first place, and to Phillip Dixon, Fred Barbash, John Mintz, and Sandi Polaski, who encouraged me to push the parameters.

Thanks also to the folks at *Essence*, who affirmed my talent and kept me working, to Nick Pastor and Eloise Linden, who listened and heard, to Ray Hicks, and to the MacDowell Colony, for delicious solitude and sustenance. And to my editor, Doug Seibold.

Last, but certainly not least, all praises are due my agent, Faith Hampton Childs, a queen among women, whose belief and tenacity sustained me.

VOLUNTEER
SLAVERY

CHAPTER ONE

"Well, this is the final stage of the *Washington Post* interview procedure," says the editor of the newspaper's new Sunday magazine. "Talking to Ben."

Jay Lovinger and I walk through the cavernous newsroom toward executive editor Ben Bradlee's glassed-in office on the north wall. Around me, hundreds of reporters sit at computer terminals, banging away. A few sneak surreptitious glances at me. No one makes eye contact except the two sisters at the switchboard. I feel like a side of beef hooked on a pulley in a meat refrigerator, circling for the buyer's inspection. It is April, 1986.

"Everyone hired at the *Post* talks to Ben. He is an incredible interviewer," Lovinger says.

"Oh really?" I say. I almost say "Ow really," as a needle of excruciating pain shoots up from the cramped space between my little toe and the one next to it. My feet, in three-inch heels, are killing me.

"So far, everyone really likes you."

"Great," I say. What I really want to say is, "Likes me? Who gives a damn if they like me? This is a writing job, not a personality contest, isn't it?"

"The Metro editors even want you for their staff," he says, as if conferring some much coveted status. "They were intrigued by your perspective."

I'm not surprised. Two white males running the Metropolitan desk in a 70 percent-black city that is also the nation's capital are probably in a constant state of intrigue. Mostly involving how to parlay that job into a better, whiter one.

"If everything goes well with Ben, then we'll talk money," he says as we near the glass office, guarded by a fierce-looking redhead. "Just be yourself," he cautions.

I turn to look at him to see if he's trying to be funny, but of course he's dead serious. I decide not to ask him who else but myself he imagines I am, or could be. Instead, I smooth the folds of my turquoise ultrasuede dress, lick my lips, and wiggle my feet, trying to get the wad of Dr. Scholl's lambswool between my toes—the only thing standing between me and triple minority status: black, female, and handicapped—back into a more functional position.

But by now I am tired of being on. For me, the notion of coming to work at the *Washington Post* is mostly about money, but that's a black thing, which these people wouldn't understand. For twelve years, I have lived happily in New York as a successful yet poor freelance writer. I never thought about working for anyone but myself. Then one night the phone rang, and it was the man who's now escorting me to Bradlee's office.

"Hello," he said. "I'm the new editor of the new *Washington Post* magazine, and we'd like to talk to you about working with us."

After the obligatory yah-yah about purpose, art, and objectives, I cut to the chase: "What salary range are you offering?" The figure, twice what I earned the year before, gets me on a plane to this interview.

"What's Bradlee's interview technique like?" I ask.

"Fascinating. Absolutely fascinating. Don't be surprised if he does most of the talking, he usually does. He'll tell you about himself to find out about you. Even though you may not say much, Ben is incredibly insightful about people. He's an amazing judge of character."

"That's interesting," I say, and relax. This I can definitely deal with. White boy interview technique 101, in which he talks about himself in order to see if I can deal with him, which means he can deal with me. I didn't go to prep school and Columbia Journalism for nothing. My parents will be happy their money wasn't wasted.

"This is Jill Nelson. She's here to see Ben," Lovinger says to the secretary/sentinel.

"Go right in," she says, and smiles.

"Good luck," says Lovinger.

"Thank you," I say, smiling, wondering what I'm getting into. Then I remember that I'm just a piece of meat, dark meat at that. And after all, the blacker the berry, the sweeter the juice. It wasn't until years later that Daisy, one of the few friends I make in Washington, pointed out, "Yeah, but who wants sugar diabetes?" She ought to know. Short and olive-shaped, Daisy is Washington's smallest P.R. maven, a native of Boston who escaped via the East Village of the 1960s and ended up in D.C. Smart, acerbic, and outspoken, she pays homage to no one and has everyone's ear.

I am momentarily stunned when I enter Bradlee's office. I'm expecting Jason Robards from *All The President's Men*, tall, gray, and handsome. Instead I'm greeted by a short, gray, wrinkled gnome.

"Ben Bradlee. Nice to meet you. Sit down," he booms. Well, at least he has Jason Robards' voice. I sit.

"Tell me something about yourself."

Temporarily, my mind is null and void. All I can think to tell him is that my feet are killing me and that, in a static-cling war with my dress, my slip has risen up to encircle my waist. Then an ancient Temptations song pops into my head—"Papa was a Rollin' Stone." For years the words to this song, which I didn't particularly like when it was a hit in 1972, spring into mind when I'm queried about myself by white folks. I suspect many think the song defines the authentic Negro experience.

But truthfully, Papa wasn't a rolling stone, he was a dentist, Mommy was a businesswoman and librarian, we were solidly upper-middle-class. Besides, I remind myself, this is the 1980s. The day of the glorification of the stereotypical poor, pathological Negro is over. Just like the South, it is time for the black bourgeoisie to rise again. I am a foot soldier in that army. So I tell Bradlee, briefly, about my educational and journalistic background. Am I imagining it, or is he really impatient for me to shut up?

"Let me tell you about my magazine," Bradlee says, almost before my lips have closed over my last word.

"I want it to have an identity of its own, but at the same time be a mixture of *Esquire*, *New York* magazine, and *The New York Times Magazine*. I want it to be provocative, insightful, funny, and controversial . . . " He goes on.

I sit there looking at him, halfway listening as he talks and talks, struck by the notion of defining a new magazine by old ones, and old tired ones at that. I try to imagine myself, an African-American female, working and thriving at a publication that's an amalgam of white man at his best, a celebration of yuppie-dom, and all the news that fits, we print. I come up blank.

"I want the fashions to be exciting, new, to portray women who dress with style, like my wife," Bradlee is saying when I tune in again. I know he's married to Sally Quinn, but I'll be damned if I know what she wears. I don't remember reading her name in *W* or the fashion columns. What am I doing here?

"I want it to illuminate what really goes on in this city, to get under Washington's skin . . . "

It's when he says *skin* that I remember why I'm here. I'm black and female. The magazine, to debut in a few months, has no black or female writers. In 1986, I'm about to realize my destiny—or pay off some terrible karmic debt—and become a first. Hallelujah!

"So, have you always lived in New York?"

Again, I snap back. "Yes. Except for three years at prep school in Pennsylvania and a year I lived on Martha's Vineyard."

"Martha's Vineyard. How'd you wind up there?" It is the first time he has seemed sincerely interested in anything I've said. After all, only the best people wind up on the Vineyard.

"My parents have a home there. I've spent summers on the Vineyard since I was a child and just decided to spend a year there and write," I say.

He grins. It's as if he's suddenly recognized that the slightly threatening black guy asking for a hand-out on the street is actually a Harvard classmate fallen on hard times. The bond of the Vineyard makes me safe, a person like him.

"Ahhh," he says, "So you're part of that whole black bourgeoisie scene with the Bullocks and the Washingtons?"

"I guess you could say that," I say, and chuckle. So does he. I don't know what he's grinning about, but the notion of myself as part of the black socialite scene I've spent a lifetime avoiding on and off the Vineyard strikes me as laughable. So does his evocation of the Bullocks, old Washingtonians, and former Mayor Walter Washington, who is married to a Bullock. The Washingtons, after all, don't own, they visit—an important distinction in Vineyard society.

Our eyes meet, our chuckle ends, and I know I'm over. The job is mine. Simply by evoking residence on Martha's Vineyard, I have separated wheat from chaff, belongers from aspirers, rebellious chip-on-the-shoulder Negroes from middle-class, responsible ones.

Vanquished is the leftist ghost of my years writing for the *Village Voice.* Gone are the fears he might have had about my fitting in after a life as a freelance writer, an advocacy journalist, a free black. By dint of summers spent on Martha's Vineyard, I am, in his eyes, safe. I may be the darker sister, but I'm still a sister. I will fit into the *Washington Post* family.

Bradlee launches into a story about his house on the Vineyard, traded in for one in the more social media enclave of the Hamptons. I relax, stop listening, and start counting dollars. Unfortunately, there aren't enough of them to last the length of Bradlee's story. He keeps on talking and I just sit there, smiling. A feeling of foreboding expands geometrically around me. I shake it off and concentrate on willing my brain and feet into numbness.

CHAPTER TWO

By the time my day of infamy, er, interviews is over, Ben has communicated his feelings to the editors—probably by talking about himself—and I've been offered a job on the Sunday magazine. I have no feeling left in my feet, and I'm just about brain dead.

I feel as if thousands of cornea-sized holes have been burned into the back of my dress from the discreet scrutiny of the voiceless reporters who may soon become my colleagues.

Lovinger walks me to the elevator.

"Well, what do you think? We'd really like you to be a part of the magazine."

"I'm interested, but I'd like a few days to think about the offer and talk to my daughter," I say.

"Why? Is there a problem?" He looks at me with a mixture of surprise, annoyance, and panic, as if the thought that I might not want to join this particular family is heretical. He needs me, black and breasted, to complete his staff.

A Jew who grew up in the housing projects of Manhattan, Jay Lovinger's come to the *Post* via *People* magazine and is desperate to make the magazine work, and to prove himself—poor, Jewish, a college dropout—worthy of membership in the *real* white boys club, the WASP one. It isn't enough that he's making big money and working for the number-two newspaper in the country (after *The New York Times*) without benefit of even the most mediocre college education. No, he wants to truly belong. Doesn't he know that without Harvard his efforts are futile?

Belonging isn't what I crave; I'm after money and a larger audience. But as we used to say in the 1960s, I don't like the vibes around here. No one makes eye contact, no one speaks, everyone watches. In nearly eight hours, the only people who've said squat to me besides editors are Joyce and Margo, the sisters at the switchboard. I am not optimistic about the future.

I am so whipped after being on all day that I don't even have the energy to smile superficially. Since ten in the morning I've hobbled from cubicle to cubicle, white male to white male, being interrogated. I feel like a felon up for parole trying to cop a plea with the commissioners.

I've also been doing the standard Negro balancing act when it comes to dealing with white folks, which involves sufficiently blurring the edges of my being so that they don't feel intimidated, while simultaneously holding on to my integrity. There is a thin line between Uncle Tomming and Mau-Mauing. To fall off that line can mean disaster. On one side lies employment and self-hatred: on the other, the equally dubious honor of unemployment with integrity. Walking that line as if it were a tightrope results in something like employment with honor, although I'm not sure exactly how that works.

I keep getting this creepy feeling that the Washington Post is doing me some kind of favor. It's as if, as an African-American, female, freelance writer, I'm a handicapped person they've decided to mainstream. The words to "Look at Me I'm Walking," the theme song of the annual Jerry Lewis Muscular Dystrophy Telethon, pop into my head.

The thought of all those bills being pledged to a good cause makes me think about my favorite cause—me—and my interview with Tom Wilkinson, the money man. As far as I can tell, all he does is talk to people about money and deliver bad news.

"There're not many reporters here who've just been freelancers. This is a tough institution. Most of our people have worked their way up from smaller papers. Do you think you'll be able to fit in, handle the demands of working for a daily newspaper?" he asks me.

"I think freelancers, people who work for themselves, work harder than people who have job-jobs," I say, trying not to sound as exhausted and borderline sullen as I am. My college friend Adrienne, who went off to teach in St. Thomas and never came back, coined the term "job-job." We met in a class on black women writers at City College and first connected when the teacher, an African-American woman, announced that she didn't know what racism was until she was twenty-five. Adrienne and I found this statement both hilarious and outrageous, and said so. We've been tight ever since. "Job-job" is the phrase Adrienne used to differentiate working for someone else from working for yourself. "Have you ever noticed," she'd say, "How the 'J' in job looks just like a hook?"

"We hope you'll come and work here. Everyone liked you," Wilkinson says. Here we go again with the popularity contest. I'm glad I wore the turquoise dress. I smile, cross my legs. Then I recross them.

"Now. Let's talk about salary. How much money did you make last year?" I stare at him. He sits, a thin, intense man in his forties with a weasel-like face, waiting for a response. I do what everyone does in salary negotiations. I lie.

"About $40,000."

"We can offer you $42,500," he spits out.

"Well, the editor mentioned a salary of—"

"$45,000," he interrupts. I feel like a damaged urn under bid at a Sotheby's auction. Get me off the block fast and maybe no one will notice the cracks.

"I was thinking more in terms of—"

"Without newspaper experience, I think that is a good starting salary. Of course, if things work out well, there'll be raises and that sort of thing."

"I understand that," I say, "But I'll be moving both myself and my daughter from New York, she has to go to school and—"

He looks at me with what I think is exasperation, then glances at his wrist. Clearly, I am taking up too much time. I feel myself slipping off that tightrope. I also feel like a troublemaker, a subversive for not being properly grateful for the chance to work at the *Washington Post*, whatever the salary. I also feel out of my league. Mommy and Daddy never fully explained to me that I'd have to support myself when I grew up. They certainly never mentioned salary negotiations.

I have the feeling that even though I'm doing the right thing, I'm also somehow in bad taste, a familiar feeling for African-Americans. It's like I'm the first black woman to become Miss America and instead of feeling thankful I refuse to put on the tiara because the rhinestones are of such lousy quality. Instead of being happy I'm an ingrate.

"All right, $50,000," he snaps. I can almost hear a voice saying, "Going once, going twice, gone." I'm not sure anymore which way is which.

"Fine. But I need a few days to think about it." Now he looks really annoyed, but what the hell? Last year I made about $20,000, so $50,000 would be a hefty raise. So why do I have a feeling of impending doom? I try to talk myself out of it, but I can't think of what to say.

Then I hear my mother's voice from the day before.

"I think it's a great opportunity even though if you move I'll miss you and Misu you'll be making good money and the *Post* is a good liberal newspaper after all they brought down Nixon that son of a bitch you're getting older and have to start thinking about college for your daughter and retirement some security you can't be a vagabond all your life what about health insurance . . . "

Enough. I shut her off. My mind begins to wander to boutiques, malls, bookstores, liposuctionists, all the places I can spend the *Post*'s money. I don't notice Wilkinson standing by the door waiting to usher me out until he says, "Nice meeting you." I want to ask him, "But do you like me, really *like* me?" Instead, I leave.

"Please let me know your decision as soon as possible," Lovinger says as I leave, sticking his long neck and nearly bald head inside the elevator doors. "We'd like you to be a part of what we're trying to do." It's as if I'm being recruited to join a crusade, but no one will tell me its objective.

"I will," I say. The doors close. I fall back against the wall and do some deep yogic breathing. What I'd really like to do is scream. My pantyhose feels like a girdle, slowly cutting off the circulation from feet to waist. I barely manage to cross the street to The Madison Hotel, where my daughter Misu, age thirteen, awaits me.

As I am soon to discover is true of much of Washington, The Madison Hotel is a warped facsimile, an unknowing parody of something that probably never was real. It has cachet because Washington is a city of pretension and nostalgia. Whites yearn for the time when the city was run by a cabal of presidentially appointed commissioners and not a black mayor; for the good old days when D.C. was a cultural backwater but there were no traffic jams; for the bygone era when there was no race problem because genteel segregation reigned. Black people yearn for the 1960s, before the riots, when it really did seem things would change. They yearn for Marion Barry in his first two—sober—terms, for D.C.B.C., before crack. Organizations have their own specific nostalgia; at the *Post*, it is for the boom days of Richard Nixon and Watergate.

The Madison, with its faux tapestry-upholstered loveseats, neo-Japanese flower arrangements, bad food, and obsequious Central

American waiters, is a wannabee's vision of the life of the powerful WASP. Aspiring yuppies, brought to Washington by a job in corporate or political middle-management, lunch at The Madison and declare themselves important, in the know, powerbrokers. This is a town where importance and longevity are connoted by having a capital "The" in front of everything.

"Hi, Misu. I'm back." My daughter sits propped up on one of the two double beds, watching television. She is brown, thin, wears braces. The debris of room service—trays, frilly paper things, silverware, and the smell of grease—surrounds her.

"Sorry I took so long." My daughter, a hotel abuser from way back, shrugs. Being left alone in a room she doesn't have to clean up, with television and room service, is a significant element in her vision of nirvana.

"That's okay, Mom. How'd it go?"

"Okay. But really weird," I say, yanking off my shoes and stockings in one effective but less than fluid movement. I walk into the bathroom, turn on the water, and begin scraping mascara and eyeliner from my face before I'm blinded.

"I don't really think the *Washington Post* is the place for me—" I begin, shouting to be heard above the roar of Madison water.

"I like it here, Mom. I think we should move here," my daughter says.

"Why?" I ask, drying my face. "What do you like about it here?" I try to keep my tone neutral.

"The buildings are small. The people are nice. And it's clean," she says. "If we lived here, we'd live in a house, right? Then we could have a car and lots of cats and a dog and all that stuff, like the Cosbys, couldn't we?"

I open my mouth to point out that the Cosbys don't have cats or dogs, that they have a father, that they live in New York. Then I look at the dreamy expression on my daughter's face, and close my mouth again. Abruptly, it all becomes clear to me.

My daughter is tired of being a leftist. She is tired of eccentric clothes, artists, vegetarian diets, the New York subway, and living in an apartment. The culturally rich and genteel poverty in which she was raised is played out. Deep in her little African-American heart, she yearns to be Vanessa Huxtable, her age cohort in the television Cosby clan. With a perfect room, in a perfect house, with perfect parents and lots of perfectly hip clothes in the closet. She is sick of my Sixties class-suicide trip, of middle-class Mommy's vow of poverty in pursuit of the authentic Negro experience. She is tired, simply, of hanging in there with my trip.

She's got a point. I'm tired, too. Taking the job would not only fulfill some of her fantasies, it would provide me with a ready-made escape from New York, Ed Koch and his soul mate, subway gunman Bernhard Goetz, not to mention my life there. Let's face it. I'm burnt out and dread answering the telephone. I'm dating a mortician who's about to lose his business, which is located in the heart of the area with the most liquor stores and highest death rate in the city. At thirty-four, post-divorce, I am again living with my own Mommy. How much worse could Washington be? Still, I have a stress stomachache and the feeling that I'm about to make the wrong decision for all the right reasons. I had the same feeling the night before I got married.

"It might be fun to live here for a while, Mom. Not forever. What do you think?"

"We'll see," I say, falling back on every parent's favorite meaningless expression in a desperate bid for time. "What'd you do today?"

"Watched television and ordered lunch. You know what I like about Washington? When I ordered my lunch they didn't have shakes on the menu. So when I called I asked the lady, 'Do you have milkshakes?' And the woman said, 'My dear, this is The Madison. We have everything.' Having everything. Isn't that great?"

My fate is sealed. We will move to Washington. I will go to work for the *Washington Post*. We will live the life of the Cosbys, sans Daddy. I feel I owe my daughter stability, bourgeoisdom, charge accounts at Woodies, a chance to join the mainstream. I will be the Cosmo mom, the queen of having it all, and my daughter a Cosby clone. For $50,000 smackeroos, how bad could it be?

Three months later we move to Washington. In the four and a half years I work at the *Post*, my daughter never has another milkshake at The Madison.

CHAPTER THREE

"I don't know why you're going to work for those sons of bitches. The *Washington Post* wasn't the place for me, and it sure as hell isn't for you. I hate them so much I'm just waiting to get old so I can go beat the shit out of old man Bradlee."

David Hardy's words come back to me as I stand in the living room of *Daily News* columnist Earl Caldwell's house. David, who once worked at the *Post*, was unable to attend my farewell party, but the memory of our conversation seems more real than most of the people who now surround me.

"I don't give a goddamn how much they're paying you, it's not enough. They'll buy you and try to steal your soul, too," David yelled. There was so much force in his voice that even now, just remembering, the glass of Stoli in my hand trembles.

"You're too good for them, too good. Don't sell yourself cheap. Don't go to work there."

I stand there and visualize six feet, three inches of fine black man, thinking more about what pretty lips he has than what he said.

"You're too much like me to make it there, I know that," David concluded.

In my mind's eye I can see his handsome honey-colored face, his lovely salt-and-pepper hair. I nod to myself in agreement. I fantasize about the two of us, a team, striding through the newspapers and magazines of New York, slaying racism and sexism wherever we find it, making passionate, political love after a grueling day battling whitey. Then I remember that David's married, has three children, and lives in New Jersey.

I snap back to the party, but I'm not sure what I'm returning to. I look around at the fifty or sixty black journalists in Caldwell's house. About half of them are milling around the food table. The others stand or sit in small groups. I don't see anyone I want to talk to.

I lean against a nearby wall, take another gulp of Stoli straight-up, and survey the crowd, haunted by the memory of David's words. He may be right. The *Washington Post* probably isn't the best place for me, but where is? Certainly not New York. In this room stand my esteemed colleagues, and I barely care if I ever see most of them again. I suspect that once I move outside Manhattan's 212 area code, my usefulness will fade dramatically. Once this happens, it's just a few steps to being forgotten.

This party is being given for me by Caldwell and friends, many of them members of the local chapter of the National Association of Black Journalists, the New York Association of Black Journalists, of which I am president. It is, like most every organization with "National" in the title, all black. This is because the white folks used up "American" in naming professional organizations that were segregated before we got a chance to start our own, or integrate theirs.

Like most every place except work, the party is segregated. Newsrooms would be segregated too, except there are laws against that. But we've got our own little ghetto there, too. Most black folks work on the Metropolitan—read "inner city"—Desk, a.k.a., in the 1960s, the "race riot beat."

If we're either very smart, ultra-assimilated, overeducated, or better still, all of the above, we just might be allowed to write features, or, in a Jesse Jackson year, cover presidential politics. A few of us may even become columnists, but only after years of dedicated service, and only if there's a large, vocal, and potentially threatening colored population in the circulation area.

Then there are the copy editors, graphic artists, and wire service reporters, the invisible Negroes of journalism who seldom, if ever, have a byline. Wherever we work, when we go to NABJ conventions every August it is as much to see each other and acknowledge our visibility as anything else. The other fifty-one weeks of the year we spend trying to make the white folks see us without being too scary, too black.

In this landscape, my job as a magazine staff writer at the *Post* is a big deal, not just for me, but for us. Being black, you learn early on that victory and defeat are collective endeavors.

"So, the *Washington Post*. How'd you manage to get that job?" says a voice. A fat, freckled, nearly white man stands next to me. It is Peter Alan Harper, who works for one of the wire services. I always feel he's on the verge of biting me. When and if that happens, I'm not sure if it'll be a love bite or a gouging.

"They called me."

"Really. They recruited you? But how'd they hear about you?" He says this as if I'm something that had to be unearthed. What I want to say is, "They read my byline, you no-byline wire service asshole. Eat your heart out." But I'm leaving the next day, why make more enemies? I keep my mouth shut.

"So, who's going to take over your job at *Essence*?" I knew he wanted something, and now I know what. He wants to become me at *Essence*, a publication largely by and for black women. Is it my imagination, or can I hear him salivating?

"I don't think anyone is," I say. Hearing this, he looks positively hungry. I don't bother to tell him that in my negotiations with the *Post* I insisted on remaining on *Essence*'s masthead and continuing my freelance career. I also don't tell him or anyone else that when I talked about writing for *Essence*, Bradlee said, "What's *Essence*?"

"Feel free to talk to Audrey about it, Harper." I gesture toward Audrey Edwards, *Essence*'s executive editor. Tall, smart, and powerful, she is more than time enough for Harper. I breathe a sigh of relief as he scampers off in her direction.

"I don't know what NYABJ is going to do without you as president," says Charles Moses, vice president of the New York Association of Black Journalists. At 11:00 A.M. tomorrow when I step on the shuttle to D.C., he becomes president.

"I'm sure you'll do fine. You'll be a good president," I say, although I have my doubts. Though an all-right guy, Moses is one of those men who thinks he's smarter than he is and tries to be slick. A month after I leave New York he throws another going-away party for me, even though I've already gone. He sells tickets to a party without a guest of honor, rents a boat that nearly sinks in a torrential downpour, and pays his mother and aunt $3,000 to cater the affair. Some of the reactions to this that filter back to me in Washington from other NYABJers are "nepotism," "impeachment," and "throw the bum out." But hey, it's the thought that counts.

"You've been a great president. It'll be a hard act to follow."

I laugh, thinking of my friend Judyie's words: "Those people don't want a leader, they want a Mammy." Judyie and I have been friends forever. Our parents, united by their middle-class values, were also close friends. Our mothers say that as a toddler, a year older than Judyie, I followed her development avidly, snuggling against her mother's stomach and whispering to her before she was born. I suspect that, if she answered, she did so as wisely and succinctly as she still does today.

My mammying days are over. I have vowed not to join a single organization in Washington, not to run for any office, not to serve even if groveled to. Leaving New York, I also leave behind my presidency, collective consciousness, and promojites dressed in African garb and stuck in the late 1960s, imploring and guilt-tripping me into doing something for the cause.

On July 14 I go to Washington a new Jill Nelson, one who looks out for numero uno, like most people. If that makes me a bourgeois running-dog lackey, so be it. In my middle-class guilt trip, it's taken me nearly a lifetime to understand that the people dissing me for my bourgeois roots are usually the ones trying hardest to get to it themselves.

In 1970, at the height of the fervor for black nationalism, after a lifetime of privilege and private schools, I became obsessed with having an Afro, that living, ever-growing symbol of blackness, of being down with it, whatever "it" was. My hair, long and closer to straight than nappy, and once considered "good" by Negroes, was now "bad" according to black folks. It refused to curl, kink, or do much of anything except look unruly. After months of anguish, a barber in Harlem suggested I wash my hair with Octagon, a rough laundry soap sold in bar form. I did, repeatedly. While my hair didn't exactly nap up, it curled tightly enough for me to have a passable fro, as long as I stayed in out of the rain, which caused it to straighten into a pixie cut.

So there I was, strutting around with my semi-Afro, studiously garbling the English language because I thought that "real" black people didn't speak standard English, mouthing slogans from the Black Panther Party, and contemplating changing my name to Malika, or something else authentically black.

I even had a boyfriend who lived in the projects, had an African name, and could hardly read. "He's bad, therefore I am," or so I thought, in a perversion of prep-school Descartes. Until one day, lounging in my parents' well-appointed apartment after filling himself up on their food, he said, "You know what makes your 'fro so pretty? It's soft, 'cause you got that good hair."

Nowadays, I keep my hair cut short and try to avoid being either Malika or Mammy.

Moses, standing there expectantly, pulls me back to the 1980s.

"Don't worry about it, Charles," I say, gulping Stoli. "Gotta go."

I wander around the room, crunching celery and gulping vodka. My father and Evelyn, his forty-one-year-old fourth wife, stand in a corner, surrounded by a group of apparently mesmerized people.

"It's a magnificent opportunity. And Jill deserves it. Not just because she is a wonderful writer, but because she is about love. She *is* love. Always has been, since she was a little baby," I hear my father saying. He is tall, gray, and absolutely charming. A dentist turned love doctor, he would be a millionaire if I could figure out how to market his rap. Maybe audio and video tapes, like the Maharishi.

"Nervous?" It is Yannick Rice, secretary of the organization. An employee of the *New York Times*, Yannick is one of those few people who can truly be described as good. I will miss her.

"Kind of. But more like impatient."

"You'll be there tomorrow. I hope it works out for you. Give them hell. I'm sure the *Post* doesn't know who they're getting."

"Neither do I."

"Big bucks," chimes in someone next to me.

"Money isn't everything," I say.

"How much money isn't everything?" asks someone. Is it my paranoia, or are these people more interested in how much I'll be making than what I'll be doing, than me? I feel an unhappy revelation about human nature coming on and sip my drink.

"I guess they got you for less because you're a freelancer," says someone who works for the *Times*.

"Less than what?" I say.

"Less than what they'd have to pay an established newspaper journalist."

"Maybe. But they weren't looking for an established newspaper journalist, they were looking for a magazine writer," I snap. The *Times*man walks away.

"You can be damned sure they don't know who or what they're getting," the memory of David Hardy roars in my ear. Hardy is a modern-day warrior, a shitkicker. He and several colleagues are embroiled in an historic discrimination suit against the New York *Daily News*. It is the first time a newspaper will go on trial to defend itself against charges of a pattern of systematic racism in hiring, promotions, and assignments. The trial will be covered scantly and with great bias by America's newspapers. David and the other plaintiffs will eventually win the case and a monetary settlement, and the *Daily News* will be ordered to change its ways. David Hardy will not, as he says, "Act like a nigger, take my million bucks, and buy a goddamn Cadillac. I'm gonna stay right here at the *News*, watch them, and continue to kick their asses."

Across the room stands a young man of nineteen or twenty, looking awkward. Unlike the other people here, most of whom wear jackets and ties, he is dressed in sneakers and a sweatsuit. His eyes dart about uncomfortably.

"Antonio," I call, walking toward him.

"Ma. I was looking for you." Anthony Davis hugs me. I hug him back harder.

"How are you?" I ask, and really mean it. I have known Anthony for five years, since he was sixteen and falsely accused of killing his high school teacher. I wrote about him and his lawyer, Alton Maddox, in the *Village Voice*, and the charges were subsequently dismissed. Ever since, we've been friends. As I get older and more cynical about the business of journalism, I have come to view Anthony as one of the few instances where something I wrote actually helped to change the status quo, at least in one life.

From the second time we saw each other, Anthony has called me "Ma." I once asked him why. "I don't know," he said. "I guess because that's what you are to me." It's funny, but it doesn't bother me when Anthony calls me "Ma," or when my childhood friend Lynn, who is also here tonight, calls me "Mami" in a throwback from our days of fascination with Puerto Rican men. I guess it's because I know they love me, are friends, aren't looking for a Mammy/Enabler.

"Everything's fine, Ma. Fine. I got something for you. Come here."

We slip into Caldwell's bedroom. Anthony hands me a big box. Inside is a white sweatshirt decorated with a drawing of a rosy pink, playful, contented kitten.

"It reminded me of you. Ma."

I laugh. "I think of myself more as a lioness," I say, blinking back tears.

"I know. But that's not really you. That's just what you want people to see."

"Oh, Anthony."

"Don't cry yet. There's something else in the box."

I reach inside and pull out a small vial of perfume. Its smell is thick, sticky sweet, girlish. I hug Anthony.

"That smell just reminded me of you, Ma. I don't know why. I love you and I'm gonna miss you."

I realize that Anthony Davis, uneducated and agendaless, is one of the few people I'll really miss. I'm saved from total blubbering by a journalistic head popping in the door, saying "Time for the official part of the party." I release my friend Anthony and go to face my colleagues.

The official part of the party consists of a few short speeches and the presentation of a plaque commending my work as president of NYABJ. I stand there as my peers congratulate me and speak of my past and future accomplishments. I look from face to face, at the officers of the organization, other reporters, editors I have worked for. I wonder how many of them will keep in contact with me. When I look at the men, I think with regret about those I've slept with, with relief about those I haven't, and with sadness that, as is usual at journalist soirees, most are unattractive. Those who look interesting are either married or well-used retreads.

Someone is saying, "Jill has given so much to the organization . . . " No one suspects that, because this is my last night in New York, I would like to give even more. That I am apprehensive, alone, that it would be nice to spend my last night in the Big Apple making fierce love to someone.

I look around the room, searching for a suitable male on whom to bestow Mammy's last night of mothering. Michael, my favorite shoe salesman, stands at the back of the room. He is tall, very black, very young, and unquestionably fine. As the speaker to my left talks about my "commitment to excellence among black journalists," I imagine lying naked in bed with Michael, his long legs wrapped around me, being kissed by those full, dark lips. He smiles and waves, fluttering his long fingers. I imagine him spreading my thighs, slowly slipping inside me, being made love to by this pretty, pretty man. I look in his direction, trying to catch his eye again, let him know I need to talk to him when the speechifying is over. He is slipping his arm around a short, skinny woman with her hair braided and beaded, what Adrienne calls "Gypsy curtains." That and the sound of applause snap me back to the real world.

Everyone is looking at me, so it must be time for me to speak. I say something not very memorable, truthful, or profound, along the lines of, "Thank you. I will really miss you all. I hope I will make you proud of me, blah, blah, blah." The last thing I want to do is bore the crowd on closing night, so I keep it short and, maybe, leave them wanting more.

There's some applause and then everyone goes back to eating, drinking, and gossiping, the real point of the party. My friend Lynn sidles up to me. A singer, Lynn has beautiful dark skin that absorbs and refracts color and light. Our friendship is anchored by similar histories, a lifetime of summers spent on Martha's Vineyard, of feeling like outsiders, our fathers both dentists, our mothers both outspoken, take-no-shit working women.

"What a bunch of assholes these people are. No wonder you're moving," she says.

I nod.

"I hope everything works out for you, but I'm gonna miss you, Mami," she says. I believe her.

CHAPTER FOUR

I met the Mortician at a party, drunk on Remy. I think I liked him because it was the holidays and I didn't have a boyfriend, he looked cute, and he was a mortician, not a lawyer. It wasn't until we'd been together a few months that I began to realize that the two were pretty much the same: one fleeced the living, the other robbed the dead.

On our first date, he took me to lunch at a fast food joint and bought me a chicken sandwich. I thought that was very grass roots. As always, I was looking for the authentic Negro experience, which of course my own wasn't, since being bourgeois somehow negated being black.

Since the late 1960s, when I'd risked baldness for an Afro, I'd been trying to understand how and where I fit into African-American culture. I wanted to party with the criminals and go home to a nice, safe apartment in a good neighborhood. I wanted to be able to talk just as comfortably with both a wino on the corner and a CEO, to sniff drugs until early in the morning and pump out a brilliant story the next afternoon. I wanted to be down with the get down, but not of it. I wanted to be a street sister by night, black princess by day.

My first date with the Mortician—a poor man, in Harlem, dining on what my friend Judyie calls the "black national foods," salty, greasy, and fried—fit into this scenario. I was like a perverse anthropologist, looking for the real Negro outside myself instead of just looking in the mirror.

On the real side, I was also looking for sex, which I have always had a tremendous ability to enjoy, regardless of the partner. Of course, it helped that the Mortician was a good lover, and fine. Whenever he did or said something stupid, I'd think about what a pure ego feed it always was to look up into his handsome face when he fucked me. Then I'd seduce him again.

My family treated him with the studied indifference with which they have responded to most of the men in my life. They politely ignored him, as they would a roach crawling across the coffee table in someone else's home. That way, maybe he'd just go away—although if he got too close to a shoe, he was dead. I was thirty-four, with a near-grown daughter, a divorced free agent. I'd never married Misu's father, but had been married in 1983, an alliance that lasted a paltry fifteen months. As to the men I dated, I think my family figured why get involved until they had to, until I got serious? Usually, serious never came.

While the number of infant mortality, alcoholism, drug overdose, hypertension, high blood pressure, and heart attack fatalities in Harlem rose steadily, the funeral home sank. The Mortician spent what little money came in and didn't really work. What few bodies arrived languished in the basement mortuary, waiting for him to hire a professional embalmer. After a while, they started to stink. Then he'd sell them off to another mortician for a cut of the fee. He'd use the money to buy sixty-dollar hits of coke and pints of Bacardi rum.

I may have been guilt-ridden, but I wasn't dumb. It soon became clear to me that this wasn't an authentic Negro relationship, it was a black man's middle-class angst, in which he uses drugs and booze to dog into the ground whatever slight edge his family background gave him, and tries to take his woman with him. I might have been horny, lazy, and confused, but I wasn't into human sacrifice. Or was I? He is my final fling before moving to D.C.

"What are you doing here?"

"I thought I'd come and say goodbye," I say.

"Sure you're not afraid you might get herpes?" the Mortician sneers, opening the door.

"Look, I said I was sorry." But I am also safe, armed with a three-pack of condoms.

"I don't know how you could think I'd do that to you. I'm clean. If you have herpes, someone else gave them to you."

"Well, I don't. So let's just forget it," I say, making sure to brush my breast against his chest as I kiss his cheek. When I pull away, I can see his eyes beginning to go sexual. One thing I love about men and pussy is that it makes them so predictable.

"Come on downstairs, I'm working."

I follow him downstairs to the embalming room, a large, cold-feeling space with corpse-size metal tables along two walls and an array of nozzles and hoses mounted above them. In the middle of the room is a long, rectangular table with a motor underneath it. In the ceiling above is a trap door that opens into the floor of the viewing room, a kind of dumb waiter for bodies. Once they are all dressed up, they have someplace to go; the table rises and zaps them upstairs to wait for their bereaved relatives. The room smells of old flesh, formaldehyde, and damp.

The Mortician looks down into the coffin. I stop and stare at him.

"What are you doing?" I ask, watching his firm, round buns and thinking of holding one in each hand.

"Trying to fix this guy's hair," he says, pointing to the coffin on the elevator table in the middle of the room.

"Come here. I need you to help me," he says, leaning into the coffin, doing something with his hands.

"Help you?" I'm not interested in helping him, especially with a dead body. I came over to help myself.

"You're a woman. Just look at his hair for me," he says. "You don't have to touch anything."

Inside the coffin is a black man of about forty or fifty, though it's hard to tell because he has that timeless, ageless, dead look that dead people have. He's dressed in a powder-blue corduroy suit, red and blue paisley tie, and a fedora cocked ace-deuce on his head. His mouth is open in a smile, and one of his front teeth is capped in gold, giving him a jaunty rakishness. He could have been an old hustler or a devout Christian or the man who ran the liquor store across the street. The only thing I can say for certain about him now is that he is dead. Is this an authentic Negro experience?

"I'm looking."

"Can't you see that his hair's all fucked up?"

I look down again, notice the tendrils of hair creeping out from under the man's hat brim. The hair is brittle, dry, a strange grayish-green color. Instead of flowing down to the man's shoulders, it sticks out from his cheeks as though he'd died by electrocution. I snigger.

"It looks horrible. What happened to him?"

"That's what a dead Jheri Kurl looks like," he snaps. "I can't get it to curl up and lie flat. You think this business is easy?"

I would have burst out laughing, but he has such a pathetic look on his face that I know if I do he'll get mad, and might not be able to get it up.

"Come on. You're a woman, don't you know what to do?" he asks plaintively. I want to point out that I am alive, not dead, have short, pseudo-straight hair and not a Jheri Kurl, and know next to nothing about death's effect on Negro tresses, but I don't. Instead I say, "Have you tried hair spray?"

"Of course I have. I've tried spray, gel, mousse, I even got a can of Sterno and used a hot comb on it, but his hair started to burn and when I yanked the comb away I burnt his cheek and had to re-do the make-up on that side . . . " I notice caked pancake on the man's left cheek, but don't mention it. Instead I say,

"Have you tried Vaseline? It used to do wonders keeping my bangs flat when I was in fifth grade . . . " While I'm talking I dig for the container in my purse.

"Vaseline! I didn't think of that," he yells. Snatching it, he begins to smooth great globs of pale green petroleum jelly into the man's wiry hair. Occasionally his hand brushes against the man's mustache. Neither flinches.

Whether because of some mystic property of the Vaseline or simply because of the weight of the oil, the hair begins to lie flat. Too flat. The man now looks like James Brown after he lost his conk in a cold sweat.

"Twist it around your finger while you're greasing it so it curls," I say. "It's supposed to be a Jheri *Kurl*."

He grunts, but does what I say. Finished, he stands back to survey his handiwork. The guy looks like Ron O'Neill in *Superfly*. Ridiculous.

"Perfect," he says. When he kisses me I put my arms around his waist, open my mouth, play with his tongue. Pushing my pelvis forward, I can feel his penis getting hard. I grind my hips lightly against him, put my tongue in his ear. He groans.

"Let's go upstairs."

"No. Let's do it here," he says, and winks. The dead man's gold teeth glint off the hanging light.

"Here? Where?"

"Right here. Help me move this." He gestures toward the casket, grabbing the handle on one end. I take the other end and we sway across the floor, me slipping in my silver shoes, the Mortician's Vaselined hands sliding on the handle. The dead guy rolls from side to side, but keeps on smiling. We dump the casket on the metal embalming table against the wall.

He puts his hand against my breast and rubs gently. I stand in front of him, arms at my sides, as he caresses me. He unbuttons the front of the dress and slides it off my shoulders. His fingers slip beneath the crotch of my panties. I rub his penis through his pants, trace the head, feel the fat vein on its back pulsate.

"Lie down." He pushes me backward until I am leaning against the cold metal of the elevator table. His mouth now sucks, now gently bites my nipple. I slip my panties off and pull my dress up. He unzips his fly and climbs up on the table. Our movements are those of lust, not love: quick, efficient, and practical. I slip a condom on him.

"You know, you're a real bitch," he says. My nipple is still in his mouth, so when he speaks his words are soft and blurred. I run my hands through his hair and pretend he's whispering sweet nothings. I begin feeling little shivery things twinkling through my body. I push up toward him.

"Wait a minute," he says. He reaches underneath the table and flips a switch. As he pushes inside me, the table starts to rise. I think about jumping off.

"I've always wanted to fuck you here," he says as we slowly ascend. I don't know how he means that. I look at him, but he doesn't look fine anymore, just hostile. I close my eyes and concentrate on getting off. In that way I avoid vertigo, the Mortician's nasty expression, and the leering glance of the dead man with the Jheri Kurl as we move up and down.

CHAPTER FIVE

The next day I move to Washington, my promised land, my own private little *hajj*, only I am journeying to the nation's capital instead of Mecca. My motives are not very spiritual. If there is any religion involved at all, it is "spiritual materialism." I am coming in from the cold of activist journalism leftist politics, and poverty, and moving into the mainstream of so-called objective journalism, and more money than I've ever made before.

Not too long ago, when I showed up at my mother's house in a long skirt, she called me an "anachronism." Over time, I have come to suspect she was right. I've watched colleagues ascend the ladder of financial success and corporate irresponsibility. Meanwhile, I continued to write about black folks like Anthony Davis, work at home, and be poor.

While I was busy anguishing about how to reconcile my bourgeois background and tendencies with my commitment to being a "race woman," my black journalist colleagues were, by and large, unbothered by such dilemmas. They were busy getting over, making money, and trying to get as far away from their roots as politely possible.

I began to feel like a symbol, an icon, not a person. Colleagues could read my articles in the *Village Voice* about real-life black people being fucked and soothe their indifferent consciences. They could count on me standing up, in person and in print, to white folks, and then go back to their jobs and reap the benefits of my efforts. After all, Jill had it covered, for everyone. Why should it matter to them that I made next to no money, had a daughter to raise, zilch in the bank? My life was that way because I wanted it that way, wasn't it?

Well, not anymore. Freelancing gave me the freedom to be a full-time, at-home single parent to Misu. For thirteen years I'd been the parent able to chaperon class trips, host after-school dates, and "be there" for my daughter. Then she'd turned into an adolescent. Not only was she not dependent on me in the same ways, but now she didn't even want to be bothered.

Clearly, it was time for me to change, too. I was finally going to present myself to society, but instead of having the cotillion I'd rejected on political principle in 1970, when I was eighteen, I was going to work for the *Washington Post.*

It wasn't, I reasoned, really selling out, but more like buying in. Who said you had to be poor to understand poor people, to advocate for them? Both Martin Luther King Jr. and Malcolm X lived in houses, didn't they? Flo Kennedy kicked butt, but she always looked great. Even the Reverend Al Sharpton has his hair done religiously. I was tired of living in an apartment, cutting my own hair, wearing the same turquoise ultrasuede dress. I was sick of committing class suicide in the name of righteousness. I finally took to heart the words of evangelist Reverend Ike: "The only thing I have to say about poor people is don't be one of them."

I go to work at the *Post* not simply for the money, but for the power. Even though it is the mid-Eighties and I might be ten years too late, I am finally going to try to "change the system from within," what we all said back when the Sixties turned into the Seventies and got deadly.

"Is the house nice?"

"I think you'll like it." My daughter and I are in a cab coming from the airport.

"I wish I could have seen it before we moved."

"Why? It's nice," I say. Misu sits there, looking out the window at block after block of well-tended yards choking with azaleas.

"You'll like it, don't worry."

"I'm not worried," she says, and then after a pause adds, "It's just that you know how you are, Mom, kinda weird. So am I, but I don't want a weird house this time."

"It's not weird, it's nice." Misu's look tells me she's wondering if I know the difference between weird and nice.

I smile. "You'll see." She nods grimly.

The streets here are named after states, presidents, letters of the alphabet, and flowers, all radiating out in circles. The man who designed the city, L'Enfant, was a Frenchman who wanted D.C. to look like Versailles.

History tells us he had the city laid out in circles to keep the unruly mob from the houses of government. After L'Enfant's death, Washington was completed by its surveyor, Benjamin Banneker, a black man. Whatever L'Enfant's intentions, I suspect Banneker laid out the city so it goes round and round in circles just to mess with the white folks, his own brand of architectural revenge against racism.

At first, no matter where I am trying to go from my house in Northwest Washington, I wind up in Hyattsville, Maryland, or points east. Then, one day, the city clicks. Suddenly it makes its own senseless sense, and I can drive anywhere. The illogical becomes logical, lunacy becomes sanity, and I understand that this is a town where going in circles signals progress. It is a realization I am going to have many times in Washington.

It's pretty here, and coming from New York the livin' is easy. So easy that it's not difficult to get lulled into complacency.

D.C. is so neatly segregated that neither the classes nor the races need intermix after working hours. Divided into four virtually autonomous quadrants, after work there is no need to leave your neighborhood to get whatever you want.

If you are poor and black and live in Southeast Washington, there is no reason to leave your bantustan at all. They call where the black folks live "Far Southeast," and the distance is not just geographical. Across the Anacostia River, it might as well be the Red Sea before Moses. The people here are largely ignored by the mayor, the *Washington Post*, and everyone else, except regarding violent crimes, crack houses, and the obligatory "positive" lip service paid on Martin Luther King, Jr. Day. Unemployment is high, so there aren't that many people crossing the river to go to work. In 1986 the people of Southeast are last in line, still awaiting the arrival of D.C.'s subway, called the Metro. It is a long wait despite the presence of Marion Barry, homeboy mayor, for whom they overwhelmingly voted.

As for poor and working-class white folks, they don't live in Washington, but in the surrounding suburbs of Virginia and Maryland, where they also vote. The Metro has been out there for years.

The taxi passes a house with a supercan in the front yard. These multi-gallon green plastic trash cans, issued to every home by the city, are—

besides racial solidarity—the single most frequent reason people in Northwest Washington, where I live, support the mayor.

"You gonna hear a lot of bullshit from these white folks," my neighbor across the alley tells me a few days later when we meet by our garbage cans. "But Barry's a good mayor."

Like one in twelve residents of Washington, he works for district government. Like more than half of D.C.'s residents, he owns his home. Like just about everyone, he keeps his lawn neatly mowed and plants azaleas.

"Why?" I am eager to learn, to live happily in Chocolate City, with a chocolate mayor, for everything to be sweet.

"Why? How the hell I'm gonna tell you why white folks act like they do? Don't quote me—" I am going to hear that a lot here "—but I believe it's racism. You know how they are. Just can't stand to see a black man in charge."

"Or black woman," I say. He ignores this.

"This is the nation's capitol, all that bull, and these ofays just can't deal with a black man . . . " He keeps on talking. I stand there, not really listening. I can tell by the cadence of his voice, its rise and fall, when to grunt or agree. It is a conversation I have nearly every day with at least one black person. It involves dissing white folks for always fucking with us, and celebrating the latest individual, and therefore collective, comeuppance. This is an authentic Negro experience.

He pauses. We chuckle.

"What specifically do you like about him?" After all, I'm a reporter. As Earl Caldwell told us when I was in journalism school, "If you ain't got it in your notes, you ain't got it."

"Supercans."

"Excuse me?"

"Supercans," my neighbor says, leaning toward me. There are beads of sweat on his forehead.

"Huh?"

"Right here!" He bangs closed the lid of the trash can into which I am stuffing crumpled cardboard boxes. Just in time, I snatch my fingers away. "Supercans," he says, stroking its dull green side.

"Oh. These are from the city. That's nice," I say, but I still don't get it. I guess it shows.

"You see, before we got these, we had a real problem . . . "

"Oh. What kind of problem?"

"Terrible," he says, drumming his fingers against the side of the super-can.

"With dogs?"

"No, with coons! Barry got us these supercans and got rid of the coons!" Depending on how you look at it, this is, I realize over time, an arguable assertion.

The taxi stops in front of the house I have rented. A walkway in the shape of an elongated "S" leads up to a wide, heavy front door. Azaleas, lilies, and peonies line the walkway, tumbling onto the path. A magnolia tree in flower stands on one side of the doorway, a pine on the other. The mingled scent of magnolias and peonies hangs in the air. Beside the door is a black wrought-iron dog with a flat blade across its back, a boot-scraper. The nonracist equivalent of a black jockey holding a lantern, it signals that we have arrived.

"Look out Cosbys!" my daughter whoops and jumps out of the cab, laughing.

I watch her run into the house. As the taxi driver tries to compute the fare based on how many zones we've passed through, I sit there, feeling like Rod Serling.

CHAPTER SIX

That night I dream about my father, but it is really more a memory than a dream.

"Number one! Not two! Number one!" my father intones from the head of the breakfast table. The four of us sit at attention, two on each side of the ten-foot teak expanse, our brown faces rigid. At the foot, my mother looks up at my father, the expression on her face a mixture of pride, anxiety, and, could it be, boredom? I am twelve. It is 1965.

"You kids have got to be, not number two," he roars, his dark face turning darker from the effort to communicate. He holds up his index and middle fingers. "But number—" here, he pauses dramatically, a preacher going for revelation, his four children a rapt congregation, my mother a smitten church sister. "Number one!"

These last words he shouts while lowering his index finger. My father has great, big black hands, long, perfectly shaped fingers with oval nails so vast they seem landscapes all their own. The half moons leading to the cuticle take up most of the nail and seem ever encroaching, threatening to swallow up first his fingertips, then his whole hand. I always wondered if he became a dentist just to mess with people by putting those enormous fingers in their mouths, each day surprising his patients and himself by the delicacy of the work he did.

Years later my father told me that when a woman came to him with an infant she asserted was his, he simply looked at the baby's hands. If they lacked the size, enormous nails, and half-moon cuticles like an ocean eroding the shore of the fingers, he dismissed them.

Early on, what I remember of my father were Sunday morning breakfasts and those hands, index finger coyly lowering, leaving the middle finger standing alone.

When he shouted "Number one!" that finger seemed to grow, thicken and harden, thrust up and at us, a phallic symbol to spur us, my sister Lynn, fifteen, brothers Stanley and Ralph, thirteen and nine, on to greatness, to number oneness. My father's rich, heavy voice rolled down the length of the table, breaking and washing over our four trembling bodies.

When I wake up I am trembling again, but it's because the air conditioner, a luxury in New York but a necessity in D.C., is set too high. I turn it down, check on Misu, light a cigarette, and think about the dream.

It wasn't until my parents had separated and Sunday breakfasts were no more that I faced the fact that my father's symbol for number one was the world's sign language for "fuck you." I know my father knew this, but I still haven't figured out what he meant by it. Were we to become number one and go out and fuck the world? If we didn't, would life fuck us? Was he intentionally sending his children a mixed message? If so, what was he trying to say?

I never went to church with my family. While other black middle-class families journeyed to Baptist church on Sundays, both to thank the Lord for their prosperity and donate a few dollars to the less fortunate brethren they'd left behind, we had what was reverentially known as "Sunday breakfast." That was our church.

In the dining room of the eleven-room apartment we lived in, the only black family in a building my father had threatened to file a discrimination suit to get into, my father delivered the gospel according to him. The recurring theme was the necessity that each of us be "number one," but my father preached about whatever was on his mind: current events, great black heroes, lousy black sell-outs, our responsibility as privileged children, his personal family history.

His requirements were the same as those at church: that we be on time, not fidget, hear and heed the gospel, and give generously. But Daddy's church boasted no collection plate; dropping a few nickels into a bowl would have been too easy. Instead, my father asked that we absorb his lessons and become what he wanted us to be, number one. He never told us what that meant or how to get there. It was years before I was able to forgive my father for not being more specific. It was even longer before I understood and accepted that he couldn't be.

Like most preachers, my father was stronger on imagery, oratory, and instilling fear than he was on process. I came away from fifteen years of

Sunday breakfasts knowing that to be number two was not enough, and having no idea what number one was or how to become it, only that it was better.

When I was a kid, I just listened, kept a sober face, and tried to understand what was going on. Thanks to my father, my older sister Lynn and I, usually at odds, found spiritual communion. The family dishwashers, our spirits met wordlessly as my father talked. We shared each other's anguish as we watched egg yolk harden on plates, sausage fat congeal, chicken livers separate silently from gravy.

We all had our favorite sermons. Mine was the "Rockefeller wouldn't let his dog shit in our dining room" sermon.

"You think we're doing well?" my father would begin, looking into each of our four faces. We knew better than to venture a response. For my father, even now, conversations are lectures. Please save your applause—and questions—until the end.

"And we are," he'd answer his own query. "We live on West End Avenue, I'm a professional, your mother doesn't *have* to work, you all go to private school, we go to Martha's Vineyard in the summer. But what we have, we have because 100,000 other black people haven't made it. Have nothing! Live like dogs!"

My father has a wonderfully expressive voice. When he said dogs, you could almost hear them whimpering. In my head, I saw an uncountable mass of black faces attached to the bodies of mutts, scrambling to elevate themselves to a better life. For some reason, they were always on 125th Street, under the Apollo Theatre marquee. Years later, when I got political and decided to be the number-one black nationalist, I was thrilled by the notion that my father might have been inspired by Claude McKay's poem that begins, "If we must die, let it not be like dogs."

"There is a quota system in this country for black folks, and your mother and me were allowed to make it," my father went on. It was hard to imagine anyone allowing my six-foot-three, suave, smart, take-no-shit father to do anything. Maybe his use of the word was a rhetorical device.

"Look around you," he continued. With the long arm that supported his heavy hand he indicated the dining room. I looked around. At the eight-foot china cabinet gleaming from the weekly oiling administered by Margie, our housekeeper, filled to bursting with my maternal grandmother's china and silver. At the lush green carpeting, the sideboard that on holidays sagged from the weight of cakes, pies, and cookies, at the paintings on the walls. We were living kind of good, I thought. That notion lasted only an instant.

My father's arm slashed left. It was as though he had stripped the room bare. I could almost hear the china crashing to the floor, all that teak splintering, silver clanging.

"Nelson Rockefeller wouldn't let his dog shit in here!" my father roared. "What we have, compared to what Rockefeller and the people who rule the world have, is nothing. Nothing! Not even good enough for his dog. You four have to remember that and do better than I have. Not just for yourselves, but for our people, black people. You have to be number one."

My father went on, but right about there was where my mind usually started drifting. I was entranced by the image of Rockefeller's dog—which I imagined to be a Corgi or Afghan or Scottish Terrier—bladder and rectum full to bursting, sniffing around the green carpet of our dining room, refusing to relieve himself.

The possible reasons for this fascinated me. Didn't he like green carpets? Was he used to defecating on rare Persian rugs and our 100 percent wool carpeting wasn't good enough? Was it because we were black? But weren't dogs colorblind?

I've spent a good part of my life trying to figure out what my father meant by number one. Born poor and dark in Washington, I think he was trying, in his own way, to protect us from the crushing assumptions of failure that he and his generation grew up with. I like to think he was simply saying, like the army, "Be all that you can be," but I'm still not sure. For years, I was haunted by the specter of number two gaining on me, of never having a house nice enough for Rockefeller dog shit, of my father's middle finger admonishing me. It's hard to move forward when you're looking over your shoulder.

When I was younger, I didn't ask my father what he meant. By the time I was confident enough to ask, my father had been through so many transformations—from dentist to hippie to lay guru—that he'd managed to forget, or convince himself he'd forgotten, those Sunday morning sermons. When I brought them up he'd look blank, his eyes would glaze over, and he'd say something like, "Jill, what are you talking about? With your dramatic imagination you should have been an actress."

But I'm not an actress, I'm a journalist, my father's daughter. I've spent a good portion of my life trying to be a good race woman and number one at the same time. Tomorrow, I go to work at the *Washington Post* magazine, a first. Falling asleep, I wonder if that's the same as being number one.

CHAPTER SEVEN

"They say this is Bradlee's swan song, his last achievement before he retires," Walt Harrington, a staff writer on the magazine, tells me my first week at work. "He's already insured his place in history with Watergate, now he wants to create a magazine as good or better than the *Times*'. All the newspaper's resources are focused on us."

So are all eyes. During the two months prior to the magazine's debut, a continual stream of marketing specialists, public relations types, designers, bigwigs, and the simply curious traipse through the newsroom, down the steps, past the "Style," "Home," and "Weekend" sections to the very back of the room, the magazine's domain.

Not all eyes are friendly. Though the management types are enthusiastic, encouraging, and cocksure, most of the reporters are skeptical, cynical, or plain pissed off.

"They've tried before with the magazine, and it's always been second-rate. Why try to compete with *The New York Times*?" a colleague says.

"They're putting millions of dollars into the magazine and have frozen everyone else's budget when we need more reporters in Style," whines a Style writer.

"If it's supposed to be a local magazine, how come the editor and half of the writers are from New York?" asks a particularly cynical member of the Weekend staff.

A lot of people just say "Welcome aboard, and good luck," in tones that sound more like they are stewards on the *Titanic* than colleagues.

Those of us who work on the magazine think we are hot shit, and act like it. After all, management treats us like demigods, the money and collective energy of the *Post* is focused on us, and the residents of Washington eagerly await the first issue. We even have a jingle on the radio heralding our arrival. How can we fail?

It seems we can't. The magazine's twenty staff members are the young turks of the newsroom. We can do no wrong in the eyes of management, the only people who matter, and everyone else is too scared to mention it if we do. However, even through the heavy dose of premier issue parties, pats on the back, and lush expense account spending, there are indications that the skeptical comments of most of my coworkers at the newspaper are founded in something more substantial than sour grapes.

Overall, things couldn't be better, or so I think. I am working in what is effectively a one-newspaper town, since the *Washington Times* is owned by the Reverend Sun Myung Moon and dismissed by "real" journalists. I am the only black staff writer, and will be writing about a city that is nearly three-quarters black. It is an authentic Negro's dream monopoly, and no matter how I rearrange the components, I can't imagine the equation adding up to anything but success.

I am living a fantasy, a dream. I have gambled on living by the word, not the sword, and won. I am convinced I will have a successful career at the *Post*, a comfortable life in Washington, that from here on in my living will be easy. I am getting, as my Aunt Florence would say, "my just deserts." I conveniently forget that when she said that, she usually had a knife in hand and was being sarcastic.

Once I start working, Jay Lovinger, who had wooed me so zealously, pretty much ignores me, as if it is enough that I am merely there and I don't have to worry about *doing* anything. This puzzles me at first. I am enthusiastic, I have an agenda, I am good at what I do, and I am the only person on staff who has ever written exclusively for magazines—except Peter Carlson, who worked at *People*, but as far as I am concerned that doesn't count. Lovinger had said that in addition to being a staff writer, I will also be "D.C. assignments editor," with the power to assign stories about D.C. for the magazine. (It is not until I have been at the *Post* six months and been unable to assign a single story that I realize I've been duped—there ain't no such thing as a "D.C. assignments editor.") But in the meantime, I concentrate on producing good stories.

"I'd like to do a profile of Oprah Winfrey," I say, ambushing him in the hallway as he comes in from lunch and falling into step beside him.

"Who's Oprah Winfrey?"

Lovinger has a weird sense of humor and I start to laugh, but when I look at him I see he's serious. Doesn't this guy read the newspaper he works for? The impending ratings battle between Phil Donahue and Oprah is a top story in televisionland.

"She's a young, black talk show host who's about to go head to head with Donahue and may beat him in the ratings," I say.

"Well, we're looking for local stories." I'm ready for that one, I've done my homework.

"She started out in Baltimore, was very popular here in Washington, and her show is going to knock a local woman's program, "The Carol Randolph Show," off the air."

"Who's Carol Randolph?" What's he been doing here the past six months? I know more about what's going on locally after two weeks than he does. That's scary. I shrug off the fear and remind myself this is nirvana, not the terrordome.

"A black woman in D.C. with a popular morning talk show. There's a lot of controversy locally and some negative feeling about Oprah, another black woman, forcing her off the air."

"Is Randolph's show any good?"

"Not as good as Oprah's, but she's a home girl and this is a small town."

"Sounds like it might be a good story. Ask the library to pull the clips," he says, and scurries away.

I don't take it personally. I am too busy trying to fit into the *Washington Post* family, transform myself into Claire Huxtable, and get a story in the September 7 premier issue of the magazine. Anyway, maybe Lovinger is just busy, not uninterested. After all, this is the man who hired me, a homeboy from New York. He had to like my writing, didn't he? He'd wanted me to join the staff so badly that he'd started paying me in June, a month before I officially arrived, hadn't he?

It wasn't until some time later that I found out that in late 1980, the *Post* had entered into a consent decree with the Equal Employment Opportunity Commission, which required that the paper make a "good-faith effort" to hire more women. I came to suspect that paying me for a month when I hadn't yet started to work had nothing to do with corporate largesse or appreciation of my talent; it may just have been that putting me on the payroll enabled the paper to include me in the count when they tallied up the numbers to submit to the EEOC. As the months went on, I began to wonder if Jay had ever even read my clips. As far as liking me went, it seemed that the more he got to know me, the less he did. The feeling was mutual.

But these first months at the magazine are good ones. I go to Chicago and interview Oprah Winfrey, and then to Nashville to interview her father, who raised her. When I come back, there is a message to call my friend Bill Lynch, who in 1986 is working as chief of staff for Manhattan Borough President (now Mayor) David Dinkins. Lynch was my political mentor. I call immediately.

"Nelson. How's it going?" he growls when he answers the phone.

"Great. Everyone's been really nice and—"

"Have you called Bill Lucy yet?" he interrupts. Lucy is an old friend and ally of Lynch's, a power in D.C. and beyond, in part because of his position as secretary-treasurer of the American Federation of State, County, and Municipal Employees.

"No. I've been out of town and really busy and haven't had the chance."

"Make time. This is important."

"I know, but—"

"But nothing. D.C. is a political town. The *Washington Post* is the newspaper in town. You can be important there. You have to announce you've arrived."

"To who?"

"To the powerbrokers."

"Why?"

"Because if you don't, they'll mess with you."

"Why would some Negroes I've never met try to mess with me?"

"Negroes? Who's talking about them? I'm talking about the people you work for. The white folks."

"Why? Everything's cool. I haven't done anything. Yet." We both laugh. I'm laughing about all the changes I've been through in the fifteen years Lynch has been coaching me on how to navigate and manipulate the system.

"That's why you need the party. So you don't have to do anything. Not like last time." His tone is gruffly teasing, but he's not kidding. I still worry that he will never forgive me for refusing to write for the *Village Voice* and removing my name from the masthead after they wouldn't publish my post-Hymietown piece on Jesse Jackson. Ever since, I've tried to mind my political P's and Q's.

"What's a party going to accomplish?"

"It's going to let them know you have allies, a constituency. That you're someone to be reckoned—not messed—with."

"Oh, God. I'm sick of politics," I say. "That's why I left New York."

Lynch laughs so loud he sounds like he's in the room with me. "Welcome to Washington, the nation's capital," he says. "Gotta go to a meeting of the Board of Estimate. Call me after you talk to Lucy. Read me the guest list." When he hangs up, I can still hear the echo of his laughter.

The party is set for the first week in September at Bill Lucy's home in Upper Northwest D.C. A tall, thin, handsome native of Memphis, Lucy is low-key, soft-spoken. Unlike most people in Washington, Lucy truly wields power, and does so quietly and effectively. He and his wife, Dot, a warm, cherubic, southern woman, treat me with affectionate good humor and care. When I read Lucy my guest list, he suggests gently, "What about the people at the *Post*?"

"I don't really know anyone here."

"This is Washington. You don't have to know them to invite them."

"Well, I guess we could invite the other writers, Walt Harrington, Peter Carlson, John Ed Bradley, and a few of the editors, Amanda Spake, Jeanne McManus—"

"Well. I was thinking more in terms of key players," Lucy interrupts.

"Well, who's important?"

"The people who make decisions."

"But I haven't seen them to talk to since I got here," I say.

"It doesn't matter. They know you're there. The point of the party is to let them know that we know you're in D.C."

"Why would they come to my party if they don't know me?"

"They know me."

Well, live and learn, I think. What I say is, "Who do you suggest?"

"Bradlee. Downie. Milton Coleman. And what's the editor of the magazine's name?"

"Jay Lovinger."

"Right. We'll invite him, too."

"Bill, do you think they'll come?"

"They'll come. They understand Washington," Lucy says, and, like Lynch, laughs.

CHAPTER EIGHT

Two weeks later I am clipping on the square rhinestone earrings my mother handed down to me when Bill Lynch rings the bell. When I open the door, he is standing on the stoop, sweating in the legendary Washington humidity. Lynch is a fat man. As long as I've known him he has had problems with his skin, as if hormonally he's an adolescent trapped in an adult body. He looks, as always, rumpled and in disarray. His lack of sartorial coordination is both an idiosyncrasy and a strategy. I love Bill as a mentor, strategist, and master political manipulator.

"I'll tell you something, Nelson. One way I learned as much as I know about politics is by going to meetings, sitting, and listening. Even closed strategy sessions," Lynch explained to me years ago. "No one noticed me. If they did, they didn't throw me out. I guess they thought, 'What harm is there letting a fat, sloppy guy stay in the room?' So I stayed. And watched. And listened."

He greeted me in his typically gruff fashion: "Nelson. Sorry I'm late. The damn shuttle and the Borough President. Are you ready?"

"Almost. What shoes do you think I should wear?" I dangle a pair of demure black pumps, some beige sandals, and my silver slippers from the fingers of one hand.

"The silver. They'll remind them that you're a New Yorker." Bill goes upstairs to change into a dry shirt. I slip on the silver shoes and stand at the mirror, admiring myself. I am wearing a neon-blue raw silk dress. The silvery snakeskin of the shoes is picked up by the rhinestone earrings. My hair is short, curly, with lots of silver in it, too. The dress has a two-inch belt that is tightly cinched around my waist. I stare at my reflection, in search of traces of the fat girl I was twenty years ago. One thing about having been overweight and being female is that the image of myself as Little

Lotta lingers long after the blubber has been starved, exercised, and dexedrined into oblivion. I turn around slowly, checking myself from all angles. My big brown legs, one of my major physical assets, look great. The muscles in the back of the calves knot slightly in the three-inch heels. The fat girl is tucked safely inside me, nowhere to be seen. I pat a few stray curls into place and smile at my reflection.

"Let's go, Nelson." Bill lumbers down the stairs. He always calls me Nelson. I take this as a compliment. It makes me feel powerful, savvy, like one of the political boys. "You don't want to be late for your Washington debut."

I laugh. At the irony of coming out in this, the town of my father's birth, at a party given for me by someone I barely know, with a list full of guests I don't know at all. Then I stop laughing and I wonder if anyone will show up. The party from hell where nobody comes, every party girl's nightmare, pops into my consciousness. Then, as it often does in times of panic, the satellite dish in my brain picks up my mother's voice: "If you have free food and liquor don't worry about it people will come you'd better worry about how you'll fit them all in the house and make sure you have enough so they don't get loud act ugly and talk about you afterward because the grit and booze ran out."

Boy, do they come. Like penitents to the Shrine of Turin, like flies to honey, like aging yuppies to the latest spa, they crowd into Bill and Dot Lucy's candlelit back yard.

The guests are typically Washington: a few of the truly powerful, a great many legends in their own minds, lots of people who either think they have access or would like to be powerful but aren't, and a plethora of women with three names. As my friend Daisy says, "What is it in this town? If you're a woman you've got to have three names to be taken seriously."

Bill introduces me to everyone as "Jill Nelson, the guest of honor and the new reporter on the *Washington Post* magazine." At first I try to hold conversations, find out something about them, figuring they might turn out to be sources, contacts, maybe even friends. Before long I realize that after the introductions are made, the amenities observed, most of these people could not care less about me. Their eyes look over and past me, checking out who else is here, observing the level of animation of different conversational groupings, the political, economic, and social importance of who's talking to who, trying to figure out where else to alight once they escape my talkative grasp.

Attempting to hold a conversation at a Washington party is like going someplace crowded with women in the company of a man who's rapidly tiring of you. He may not be ready to dump you yet, but he's damn well gonna check out his options. That's fine with me. I'm a reporter, I like to watch. I sip my Stoli with a twist of lime and observe.

"Where is she? Where's the star?" a voice roars. It is Bradlee. He bounces in, exuding energy and power, a big man trapped in a little man's body. We greet each other and stand making very small talk. The decibel level of the party drops noticeably as the scent of power, real power—not the black power to which so many of us pay lip service, but white power—permeates the warm summer air, slipping into the nostrils of the sixty or so guests. Perceptibly, wordlessly, the party transforms itself. If the guests came to meet me as a favor to Bill Lucy, the arrival of Bradlee, and after him managing editor Len Downie and Metro editor Milton Coleman, has raised the possibility of currying favor with the *Post*, an obsession in this town.

Bradlee moves out of my celestial orbit. Like a flame, he is immediately surrounded by black moths drawn to his light. One minute I am talking to Dorothy Gilliam, the only black female columnist at the *Post*, and the next minute I am alone, damn near trampled by Washingtonians in their rush toward Bradlee's side. By now, my feet are hurting, the vodka is making me tired, and I am getting annoyed. Plus, there is not one attractive man in the room, something I soon learn is typical in Washington.

"My little girl, living in my home town," a voice says and then laughs. It is my father, who has flown in for the party. Ever since I told him I was going to work for the *Post*, he has seemed alternately impressed and amused.

"I never thought I'd see the day when one of my children came to live here." My ebony-colored father's favorite story about D.C. is how the city was so color-struck when he was a dental student at Howard University in the 1940s that he drove to graduation with his car packed to the hilt, received his diploma, got on Interstate 95 headed north for New York, and never looked back.

"This is a funny town," he chuckles, and squeezes me with the arm he has wrapped around my shoulder.

Maybe it's my feet, the vodka, the humidity, or the company, but I can barely keep myself from snapping "Funny? What's so damn funny? The men are ugly, the women all have three names, everyone hands out business cards instead of holding a conversation, and no one makes eye contact." But instead I say, "Funny? No one's laughing."

"Not funny ha-ha, funny peculiar," my father says, and then roars his deep, booming laugh. Just then Bradlee whisks by. I introduce him to my elegant, laughing father.

Later that evening I make a speech, something I seem to be doing with some regularity since I was hired by the *Post* and legitimized as a spokeswoman for the race, or at least part of it. Since the magazine's debut on September 7 is just three days away, I talk briefly, generally. I figure in a few days people can see for themselves what wonders we have wrought.

"Thank you all very much for coming. It is a pleasure to be here. I'm new to Washington, so I hope that you will all stay in touch, call me, let me know what stories you think are important. I think the new magazine is going to be great and I look forward to writing about this city and the people in it. Please call me. My number is 334–7585," I say.

Faces stare blankly, waiting for me to finish. In Washington, people don't listen as much as they schmooze, network, milk the crowd. I keep it short. By then it's nearly ten, the witching hour in Washington, and everyone's ready to leave. It takes me a couple of years and gallons of Stolichnaya vodka to understand why: people in Washington can be divided into two primary categories, those who are workaholics and alcoholics, and those who are workaholic teetotalers. As Daisy says, "This town will drive you sober."

For those who drink seriously, parties are for business, not pleasure. The rule of thumb is this: in public consume white wine spritzers while you work the crowd for contacts and access; leave early, using an early morning meeting, pressing brief, or press briefing as explanation; go home, turn on CNN, and if necessary kick back a few shots of Jack Daniel's.

Bradlee, Downie, and Coleman exit immediately following the formal remarks. In Washington, when the powerful leave they are followed by a mass exodus.

"What happened to Lovinger?" Bill Lucy asks at the end of the evening.

"He didn't come," I say.

"He got his invitation?"

"Yeah. But he told me today he didn't think he could make it."

"Bradlee and Downie, his bosses, and Milton Coleman came, and he didn't? Lovinger is going to have problems."

"Why?" I ask.

"He doesn't understand Washington," Bill says.

"What do you mean?" Fuzzy on too many Stolis, I want to be clear about what he's saying.

"He doesn't understand power," Bill says. He's smiling, but his voice is deep, sonorous, serious, Moses delivering one of the ten commandments. "And that's a big mistake in this town."

I nod, though I'm not quite sure what he means. A few days later, when the first issue of the magazine appears, I find myself forcibly enrolled in a crash course on power, D.C. style.

CHAPTER NINE

"So, what do you think?" My editor, a caucasian woman, thrusts an advance copy of the premier issue of the magazine toward me. The cover-line reads "Murder, Drugs, and the Rap Star." The cover photograph is the face of a young black man, printed in dark browns and grays, fading first into shadow, then into black. The man looks threatening, furtive, hostile, and guilty: Richard Wright's fictional Bigger Thomas, who chopped up a white girl and stuffed her in the furnace, made real and transposed to the 1980s. The ultimate nightmare Negro.

"So, what do you think?" she asks again.

What I want to say is, "I think this looks horrible. It plays into white folks' stereotypes of young black men as inherently dangerous and rap music as fomenting racist insurrection. Plus, the photograph is ugly, it's too dark and evil looking. Is this really going to be the first issue of the magazine black folks in this city have so eagerly awaited? This is not going to get over. Why not use Harrington's piece on George Bush or mine on Oprah Winfrey? Anything but this."

Of course, I don't say that. We are standing in the middle of our section of the newsroom. Is it my imagination, or has the clack of terminals and the wheedling of sources over the telephone suddenly quieted all around me? Am I paranoid, or are my colleagues really straining to hear my response? I choose my words carefully. I don't want to sound the way the brother on the cover looks: hostile, alienated, potentially dangerous.

"I don't love it," I say. I am both diplomat and chickenshit.

"Neither do I. But Don Graham does, Bradlee does, and Jay does. And John Ed is Bradlee's favorite writer." Why? This I never get quite straight, but I hear several variations of one basic story: Ben Bradlee first saw John Ed Bradley kicking butt on the football field at some college in Louisiana, then subsequently discovered Bradley could write; in this Bradlee saw himself as he was—or wanted to be—forty years earlier, and thus brought John Ed to the *Post*.

"What don't you like about it?" I ask.

"I think the story's good, but not for the first issue. I've lived here for a long time and Washington is a black city. I think black people here will be offended by this. I don't think Jay understands that."

"I think you're right. Have you talked to him?"

"I've tried, but it's too late now," she says, "It's printed." She shrugs, dismissing the topic.

Easy for her. She may be a feminist-progressive type who's dated black men, but she ain't black. She can go to beaucoup anti-apartheid rallies, but she'll never be a race woman, never understand what it is to be compulsively, irrevocably, painfully responsible not only for herself, but for her race. By virtue of my skin color, I'm going to take the weight for this if the shit hits the fan. Blacks folks are going to look at me and ask, "Why didn't you do something?"

For my editor, however, the subject is closed. She launches into a critique of my Oprah Winfrey story, recently transformed by Lovinger into a story about Oprah's father. This decision I consider weird, misogynistic, and dumb, but I'm trying to be a team player. I've been working on the story for so long I've damn near got it memorized. A good thing, too, because what I'm thinking about now isn't fat, happy, rich Oprah Winfrey, but the furtive-looking young brother on the cover. It's making my stomach hurt.

I've only lived in Washington a few months, but it's clear that the black folks here take themselves extremely seriously. With the largest black middle-class population of any city in the country, they not only have a strong—and sometimes distorted—sense of their own importance, but the numbers to make a *lot* of noise.

After I'd been in D.C. four years, I have lunch with Ivanhoe Donaldson, a very smart black man who was a deputy mayor under Marion Barry (until he was stupid enough to get caught stealing $190,000 in city funds and was sent to jail). He summed up the power of black Washingtonians thus: "We're like the people of South Africa. We come off the bantustans every day to work. Even though we don't own much of anything and are economically powerless, if we all took the same day off the city would be crippled, could not function. That's the power of black Washington. We don't own anything but we keep things running."

In the beginning, I didn't know any of this. What I had was a job, a house that cost me $1,200 a month, and, after I saw the first issue, a feeling of foreboding in my stomach. As soon as I finish talking to my editor, I read first the cover story and then a column by Richard Cohen sympathetic to a business owner's refusal to buzz young black men into his store. The stories are sandwiched in between shiny color ads exclusively featuring white folks. I call my friend Thulani in New York for a reality check.

"Hey, Thulani, what's happening?"

"Doreena. I'm glad to hear from you," she drawls. Ever since we read an article by Alice Walker in which she moaned about intra-racial color discrimination in the name of a persecuted dark-skinned woman she called Doreena, we have cynically/affectionately called each other that.

"How's everything going?"

"I don't know, but I think it's about to get weird."

"Well, we knew that."

"Yeah, Doreena, but weirder than even we suspected."

"Now that's weird. What's going on?"

I hunch over and wrap my lips around the telephone—slander mode—and begin talking. I speak *sotto voce* because I sit in a wide-open space, flanked on every side by desks, telephones, computer terminals, colleagues.

"The cover is this hideous picture of a dangerous-looking Negro, complete with animal-like flared nostrils."

"Ummm. The Negroes in Washington are not going to be pleased," Thulani says. Even though she's been gone from her hometown of Hampton, Virginia, for twenty years, Thulani remains a daughter of the south. She still drawls, tells intricate, slightly gothic tales about family, and understands the mentality of the southern black, something that I, a stone child of the north, do not.

"I think there's going to be a problem." She can also be the queen of understatement.

"So do I. I wish you had come to work here, too."

"That was one of my smarter decisions." Thulani, a writer and editor at the *Village Voice*, was offered a job the same time I was, without an interview, sight unseen. We both figured it was because the magazine needed a black editor.

"My stomach hurts," I moan.

"Mine's starting to. But before I get sick, what's the story like?"

"Unbelievably horrible. It's like a pseudo-anthropological "Let's-go-into-de-ghetto-and-see-how-the-sociopaths-live" story. I mean, the kid hasn't even gone to trial yet and when you finish reading it you feel like, screw the trial, send him straight to the gas chamber."

"That bad, huh?"

"Worse. It's full of horrid, sepia-tone photographs, one of which is the rapper lying in bed as his girlfriend cuts his toenails. We're talking maximum stereotype overdrive here. After all the build-up, the newspaper and magazine ads promoting this great new magazine, this shit is unbelievable, I mean—" I am talking so fast I run out of breath and have to pause to gulp for air.

"I hate to sound like an editor and interrupt your ranting, but what's good about it, Doreena?" Thulani says.

The word "ranting" reminds me of how we became friends. Thulani was my editor at the *Voice*. Initially, we greeted each other with suspicion. Middle-class black folks, especially those with straight or pseudo-straight hair who are nearer light-skinned than dark, tend to grow up feeling we have something to prove—not just to white folks but to just about everyone, including each other. We greet one another with skepticism, treating each other as potential Eurocentric sell-outs (or, as the Black Panthers used to say, bourgeois running-dog lackey traitors to the race) until proven otherwise. We scrutinize each other for signs that we are trading on our color or class to get over. We examine each other's attitudes about race and self through our own internal microscopes of fear and self-doubt, looking for indications that we have allowed our educational and material success to distance us from "the people." Discovering this, we distance ourselves from each other.

With me and Thulani, this racial scrutiny made us friends. Peering at each other, we found, was more often than not like looking in a mirror. From similar families, with similar histories, both of us were writers, political progressives, and race women, "stone to the bone," as James Brown would say. We became friends because we discovered we could relax the racial vigilance, discard the "correct" position, with each other.

When we were together, our search for the authentic Negro experience was over: we were *it*. We'd talk about whoever we felt like dissing, get petty, whisper secrets, rant and laugh uproariously at confidences that to other ears would be seditious.

Surely we would become greater pariahs than we already are if a tap had been put on our telephone lines as we discussed Thulani's hotel room interview with presidential candidate Jesse Jackson, who was garbed in sweat pants, a shrinking T-shirt, and what she described as "a big fat stomach and a navel as big as a tire." Or my telling T. about a magazine party, complete with a D.J. and mirrored disco ball, at which managing editor Len Downie commented to me, "We've never had this before. I guess it's for you."

Not infrequently, I have picked up the telephone to hear Thulani's voice, midsentence, and understood immediately what she was talking about. It is the same with her. We are united by our similarities of experience and response. We speak the same language. For us, ranting is a way of communicating, shorthand for all that we are, were told we should be, aspire to become.

"Hell-oooo?" Her voice yanks me back to the present.

"Nothing."

"There must be something."

"I'm serious. Nothing. The whole thing is horrible. The pictures, the reporting, the writing."

"What do the editors there say?"

"Most of them love it. Those that don't realize it's impolitic to say anything negative."

"What about the writers?"

"No one cares what we think. They assume we all have sour grapes because our stories aren't in the premier issue."

"That's typical. Well, FedEx me the story. I'll read it and call you tomorrow. When does it come out?"

"Sunday."

"What are your plans?"

"I'm going to stay home in bed and reread *Song of Solomon*."

Thulani laughs. "Good strategy. Can I make a suggestion?"

"Sure. I wish you would."

"Take your phone off the hook." We both laugh.

"I've gotta go. I'm editing a story by a writer who can't craft a clear sentence."

"All right. Call me tomorrow, as soon as you've read it."

"I will. Relax. You got out of New York and got the money you wanted, didn't you? That was your priority. Remember, you're not running things."

"Yeah, you're right," I sigh.

"I'll call you tomorrow."

"Hey, Doreena, I just thought of something good about the story."

"Yes?"

"I didn't write it."

CHAPTER TEN

My phone starts ringing Saturday evening, a few hours after the home-delivery subscribers receive their "throwaways": circulars, coupons, and cartoons. As it turns out, the magazine is soon to become the greatest throwaway of them all.

"Jillie. What is this piece of shit?"

"Hey, Nicky, what's happening?" I recognize the voice of Lillian Nixon Rickman, a forty-year friend of my parents. She and her children, childhood friends rediscovered, have been mainstays of my move to D.C.

"I was calling to ask you that. I just finished reading this damn magazine. What a disappointment after all that build-up. And that article—"

"About the rapper?" I interrupt.

"That ugly boy on the cover? That didn't bother me nearly as much as Richard Cohen's column saying it's okay to lock shop doors and not buzz in black males."

"Oh yeah. I was trying to forget about that."

"What happened to him? He used to be a liberal."

Black folks say this a lot. I can remember being a kid, lying in bed, enveloped in the smell of scotch and the sound of ice tinkling against glass, listening to my parents and their friends talk about "the race." Almost always, the conversation turned to some elected official, corporate magnate, journalist, or entertainer who was less than supportive of the notion of civil rights. Almost invariably someone would ask, "Didn't he used to be a liberal?"

"Did he? When?" In the few months I've been at the *Post*, the liberals in print have been few and far between. Cohen isn't one of them.

"These bourgeois black folks are going to be hot about this magazine.

You should count your blessings you're not in it—" I hear a click signaling another call coming in.

"Go ahead and get that, I'll talk to you later," Nicky says. I switch over. "Hello?"

"What a piece of garbage," Lorrie, Nicky's daughter tells me.

"I know."

"Did they really spend millions of dollars on this?" She laughs.

"Yeah."

"Those are some simple-minded hoogies."

"Uh huh." Lorrie's laughing, but it's hard for me to enjoy the humor in the situation.

"Jillie? Are you all right?"

"Okay. Apprehensive."

"Don't worry about it. You're new in town. Not that many people know you work there."

"That's a comforting thought." And it is, at least until I remember the picture taken a few weeks earlier of the magazine staff in front of the Jefferson Memorial, which is scheduled to run in the third issue. I sit front row center, grinning like a latter-day Sally Hemings, Jefferson's black mistress. Oh yassuh, boss, I'm just a happy darkie. Oh God.

And so it goes most of Saturday night. Everyone who calls me is black. No one has anything positive to say. In their outrage, paranoia reigns. Just about everyone sees the publication of the Cohen and Bradley articles in the first issue as a diabolical, premeditated, racist attack on D.C.'s black community by the *Washington Post*. The consensus is that the newspaper commissioned and printed the two articles—both of which portray black youth (and by extension, some argue, the black community) as criminal—as an intentional and organized slap in the face.

It does not occur to them that the institution that is the *Washington Post* seldom devotes much thought to black people at all, and that the editors and managers aren't diabolical. They just screwed up.

Warning bells about management's inattention to procedure and lack of foresight should have gone off when, two weeks after I started work, I got a call from New York sportswriter Robert Lipsyte. "Jill, you're already working at the *Post*, aren't you?" he asked. "Yeah, sure, why?" I responded. "Because someone just called me to check your reference," he said. We both laughed. But as time goes on, I realize it really wasn't funny, but symptomatic of a larger problem.

By eleven Saturday night, I'm stressed to the max, exhausted, and have what feels like a permanent knot in my stomach. I turn the ringer off the telephone. Even so, I can feel the weight starting to come down on me. Several Stolis straight-up don't make me feel any lighter. They do knock me out, though.

My inclination Sunday is to leave the phone off the hook, get back into bed with a pint of Häagen-Dazs ice cream covered with sliced bananas and chocolate syrup, and read something with no redeeming intellectual value. But I am constitutionally unable to do so. My upbringing as a good race woman, an eternal striver for number one-dom, coupled with my instincts as a reporter, won't allow it. I answer the telephone and bear witness to the irate ravings of assorted members of Washington's black middle-class. I do not say much.

That Monday I go to work hoping that my own perceptions, and those of my callers, are wrong—that the magazine isn't as heavy-handed as it appears, that I'll see those blue skies that brought me here to Washington and the *Post* in the first place. When I get to the office, I find the air thick, voices thin, faces stricken. The telephones ring relentlessly, a massive complaint line for our readers.

I find a note on my desk from Warren Brown, a black business reporter who covers the auto industry. It read, "Jill: Let's See! Loads of Ain't-we-rich-white-'n'-happy advertisements in the 'Maagggazine,' with nary a brown or black face in 'em. And, ah, two stories on the folk, both negative. Are they kidding?"

Initially, we all underestimate black D.C.'s ire. In spite of the incessantly ringing telephones and the grumblings of other staff members, we at the magazine hope that the anger about the first issue will blow over as the week wears on. It doesn't. The premier issue quickly becomes grist for the local radio talk shows, driven by station WOL's owner and morning talk queen, Cathy Hughes. A coalition of forty-seven community organizations, including the Washington Urban League and the Archdiocese of Washington, forms the Washington Post Magazine Recall Committee, led by Hughes. The coalition demands that the *Post* suspend publication of the magazine and initiate talks about what the coalition sees as ongoing negative depictions of the black community in the newspaper. Once it becomes organized and articulated, the anger of the black community becomes news. Local television and print media soon get on the bandwagon, and the national media picks up the story.

Is it my imagination, or does Lovinger slink and scurry around the office more than usual? Me, I walk around with a stomachache, my standard physiological alert to mounting disaster.

When Lovinger isn't in meetings or at home passing kidney stones, he calls us together to tell us that he stands by the story and is confident the brouhaha will soon blow over. John Ed Bradley lounges around the office with red eyes, looking persecuted. My colleagues pat him on the back, squeeze his arm, make jokes, offer sympathy, as if somehow it is the black community that has done him wrong—conveniently ignoring management's phenomenal fuck-up. I envy their arrogance, their inherent belief in the efficacy of whatever they're doing, the smugness that comes from years of simply being caucasian and, for the really fortunate, having a penis.

From a distance, it's easy to start thinking that white folks run things because they're especially intelligent and hardworking. This, of course, is the image of themselves they like to project. Up close, most white folks, like most people, are mediocre. They've just rigged the system to privilege themselves and disadvantage everyone else.

For the average white male newspaperman, those worlds beyond the narrow one he inhabits exist primarily as paths to career development. When it comes to black folks, we exist mostly as potential sociological, pathological, or scatological slices of life waiting to be chewed, digested, and excreted into the requisite number of column inches in the paper.

Knowing this, I should not be amazed by the shock and surprise with which my colleagues greet the public's almost universal loathing of the million-dollar magazine. Still, they must have been wilfully ignorant when it came to considering place and context; I mean, didn't they realize that in addition to being the nation's capital, this is a principally *black* city?

It's not that surprising that it failed to occur to Don Graham, the boy publisher. He may have spent a few years as a cop, worked in the pressroom, and paid lip service to the *Post*'s commitment to "the local community," but he's still a rich kid waiting for his mother to let go of the reins. But where was Ben "Watergate" Bradlee? His heir apparent, managing editor Len Downie? Magazine editor Jay Lovinger? Didn't it occur to any of these male masters of journalism that in Chocolate City a magazine premier focusing on Negroes with criminal intentions wouldn't do it?

For that matter, where was Milton Coleman, assistant managing editor for Metro, the spook gatekeeper at the *Post*? Shouldn't he have picked up on the message the magazine was sending? So much for fail-safe.

In South Africa a hundred years ago, the Voortrekkers called it the "white lager." That's when they pulled their wagons in a circle, hunkered down, and prepared to defend themselves against the encroaching African hordes who had the audacity to fight for their land.

At the *Washington Post* magazine, the caucasians didn't call it anything, but as far as I was concerned, it was the white lager circa 1986. There I was, an African-American woman, caught in the middle of a bunch of circling white wagons.

With each passing day, the response to the magazine got uglier, broader, more organized. What had started as a few people's rumblings soon became an organized roar of outrage. There were meetings in people's homes, churches, and community organizations. In restaurants, grocery stores, or standing in lines, someone was sure to be talking about the magazine. Get in a cab and that's what the cabbies were talking about. Cathy Hughes discussed the issue on her radio show five mornings a week. Someone even produced a recording called "Take It Back" that got some air play.

Overnight, those of us on staff were transformed from prophets into pariahs. Now when the managers came around it was for grim, huddled conferences in the editor's office. Gone were the encouraging words, slaps on the back, confident grins. In their place came stricken, disbelieving glances, that furtive movement of the eyes that comes when people are looking for somewhere to lay blame. I try to stay out of their line of vision. But it's not as easy to avoid my colleagues, many of whom walk around looking angry, traumatized, and like they're about to burst into tears.

Outside the office, I learn not to tell anyone where I work. When asked the most frequently asked question in Washington, "What do you do?" I respond simply, "I'm a writer." Somehow, "writer" connotes failure, someone sitting at home pounding away at a novel that will never be published. The curious are not only satisfied, but bored.

When I say I work for the *Washington Post* I am usually attacked. In

D.C. everyone has a bone to pick with the newspaper. No matter that I am powerless and unpublished. Work for the *Post* and you open yourself up for a wide-ranging critique of that day's product.

The debut fiasco simply acts as a magnet, a focal point for what had previously been individualized little gripes. Thanks to our first issue, the disparate annoyances of thousands have coalesced into a single being of its own, a big fat monster named collective discontent. Cathy Hughes, Ron Walters, D.C. Congressional delegate Walter Fauntroy, and others organize an ongoing Sunday afternoon demonstration in front of the *Post* building. Citizens are urged to buy the magazine, come downtown, and throw it back on the steps of the building. Hundreds come. Quiet as it's kept, most folks weren't thinking about the magazine or the *Washington Post* until they heard about the magazine on the radio or television and were reminded to be insulted.

It's not just one group of black folks who are disgruntled, but lots of sets and subsets. The "native Washingtonian" Negroes would rather read about their glorious past—say, Walter Washington or Dr. Charles Drew—than their marginalized and increasingly irrelevant future. The buppies resent the aspersions that this one written-up black felon casts on their successful, assimilated, upwardly mobile lives.

And it's not even just black folks, the perennially disgruntled, who don't like the magazine, it's just about everyone in the city. Yuppies think the first issue is glum, depressing, and not upscale enough. Government types and powerbrokers wonder why so much space was wasted on some black criminal. Old-money types are looking for light amusement or abstraction. Advertisers are afraid they'll be stigmatized or boycotted for advertising in the magazine.

I sit tight, trying to be cool and not panic as I see my new life of money, middle-class bliss, and fence-straddling begin to fade away. Inside, I watch the wagons pull into a defensive circle. Outside, I hear the drums speak insult and revenge. I try to ignore them both.

"It's all a bunch of bullshit. It was a good article," says Peter Carlson, one of the other staff writers. Carlson is one of those "I'm proud to be a white male with good old American values, even if I am a member of an effete, liberal profession" type of white boys.

"Why do you say that?" I respond.

"Look at all the crap."

"What crap? Like peacefully demonstrating?"

"Those people are ridiculous."

"Why?"

"They're just too sensitive."

"Because black people don't like an article, that makes them too sensitive and ridiculous?"

"They didn't even read it. I bet half of those idiots who have nothing better to do than demonstrate against a magazine didn't read it."

"What makes you say that?"

"Because of their reaction. They didn't read it, they don't understand it, they're overly sensitive."

"Who's they?" I ask.

"Those people." He waves his hand dismissively toward the window.

"Who's they? I mean, you're so busy talking about 'they' this and 'they' that, who's they?"

I feel myself toppling left, off the fence.

"You have a lot of nerve standing around talking about they this and they that."

"I'm sick of all their whining. If they don't like the magazine, they shouldn't read it."

"Maybe 'they' want to like it."

"Oh. So if they don't like it, it's our fault?"

"Who else's fault is it? Theirs?"

"Don't they have anything better to do than demonstrate? Don't they work?"

"What about free speech?"

"What about freedom of the press? I wish I was some damn minority who could blame race for all my problems," he snarls.

"How about a brownie?" interrupts Debbie Fleming, the magazine's production manager and the only other African-American on staff. Great timing. I'm about to jump over the sheetrock half-wall separating our desks and do my level best to strangle Carlson.

"Cool out, cool out, you all. Jill, let's go get a brownie or something to drink." We walk downstairs to the cafeteria, toward a sugar and caffeine rush.

"What the hell is the matter with these white folks? I wanted to punch that guy in the face."

"I know. That's why I jumped in," Debbie laughs. She has a loud, infectious laugh, recognizable anywhere.

"I guess that was a good thing. All we need is a tall black woman beating up a poor defenseless white man. But that shit makes me so mad."

"I know. But it's not worth getting yourself all worked up about."

"What d'you mean?" I ask through a mouthful of brownie and nuts.

"I've been here almost twenty years. I was around when David Hardy still worked here. When Leon Dash still drank. When Janet Cooke won a Pulitzer. Nothing's changed, except the faces of the black people. Why get into it?" She finishes her cookie and reaches for a cigarette.

"But doesn't it make you so mad?" I ask, lighting her cigarette and mine.

"Not really, not anymore. I ignore it. This is my job. My real life is at home with my crazy kids."

"I hear you, but—"

"No buts. Don't let what goes on in here upset you. Remember, it's only a job." She blows out a cloud of smoke.

I start to argue, but don't. I've got no fight with Debbie. Not only is she a sister, she's a good one. From the git go, she's gone out of her way to make me feel welcome, show me around, explain the tricks, glitches, and loopholes of the institution. I am simultaneously puzzled by and attracted to her transcendent nature, her ability to remain calm in the midst of the chaos inherent in a newsroom.

"You're right. I just couldn't take hearing him talk about 'they' this and 'they' that."

"I know what you mean. But at least he was being honest."

"What do you mean?"

"A lot of the people we work with probably feel the same way, they just won't say it around us. At least we know where he's coming from."

Her words make me think of James Brown wailing about me standing up so he can see where I'm coming from. I can visualize James jamming in the newsroom, his tiny patent-leather-shod feet dancing across the rows of computer terminals. Like Maceo, I want to blow.

"What's funny?" Debbie asks. I tell her. We laugh.

"You're a good sister," I say and smile.

"Thanks." She snuffs out her cigarette, I follow suit. "Ready to go back upstairs? I've got to finish formatting a story."

Abruptly, I am grim again. "As ready as I'll ever be."

Debbie laughs. "It's a job, not your life. Plus, its almost time to go home."

I nod. What I want to do is clutch her shoulders, stare into her eyes, and scream, "I don't have a life!" I have a house, a car, a job, and a daughter, but no life. I haven't made any friends here. I have met no men worth using any brain cells to think about. Between the demands made on me by the job, the black community, my daughter, and myself, by the end of the day I'm so stressed that it's all I can do to drive home up 16th Street without crashing into some other stressed-out drone.

Later, driving home, my mind is preoccupied with getting there as quickly as possible so I can have a drink and relax. For the first time in my life I am now able, from any location, to visualize exactly how much vodka is left in the bottle at any given moment. This is not a good thing.

I turn the car radio on full-blast to drown out my thoughts, distracting myself from visions of frosty vodka gimlets. Rahsaan Roland Kirk's tenor sax teases as he sings, "Oh, volunteer slavery/It's something that we all know/Oh, volunteer slavery, oh volunteer slavery."

Singing along, I catch my reflection in the rearview mirror. I look like the rapper on the cover of the magazine. Haunted, furtive, guilty, the type of Negro no shopkeeper will buzz in, the type white guys will build their careers writing about.

But the truth is, I'm not an outlaw rapper. I'm a volunteer slave, a buppie. My price? A house, a Volvo, and the illusion of disposable income. When it's light out, I convince myself that the quality of the work I do justifies where and for whom I do it. It's in the darkness, black like me, that it's hard. I hurry home to drown my self-disgust in Russian vodka and pray for Harriet Tubman's arrival.

CHAPTER ELEVEN

The *Washington Post* building is in downtown D.C., on 15th Street, Northwest. It is a nondescript building of cream-colored brick, with four broad steps leading from the street into a small entryway. To the right is a small office, open to the public, where people place classified ads, renew subscriptions, buy back issues of the paper. To the left is a long glass hallway. One wall faces the street, the other overlooks an antique printing press. At the end of the corridor is another door and a security desk, and beyond these are elevators. Employees must show identification to gain access, visitors must be invited and cleared.

A small plaque on the front of the building notes that until 1947 the site was occupied by "St. Augustine Catholic Church. Oldest black Catholic church in the nation's capital." It does not say what possessed the church to up and move itself half a mile north.

On the second Sunday after the magazine premiers, the street in front of the *Post* building is a sea of African fabric, dreadlocks, kente cloth, red, black, and green, and black faces suffused with righteous indignation. It is the nationalism of the 1960s and 1970s revisited, the return of the pro-mojites—people who wear African fabric, refer to the continent as "The Motherland," smell of musk oil, and favor polygamy—the revolution all over again.

It is a hot and beautiful fall day. Except for the absence of vendors selling earrings, incense, and Senegalese peanut butter stew, this could just as well be a bazaar as a demonstration.

As I walk through the crowd toward the building people smile, call me "Sister," some say "A salaam alaikum" (Peace be with you) instead of "hi." For a moment I am back in the New York of the 1970s, in my twenties again. This is my kind of crowd: black, beautiful, nationalistic, and friendly. In a city where the men with jobs often seem to have hidden their penises away, these men look virile *and* employed.

"Excuse me, my sister. Are you here for the demonstration?" I stop and look up at the speaker, a dark brown man with salt-and-pepper hair, a medallion in the shape of the continent of Africa around his neck.

"Well, actually I'm going—"

"Sister, wherever you're going couldn't be as important as what's happening here."

"But I have to—"

"You don't have to do nothing but live black and die," he says.

"Well, I understand that, but you see, I have to go to work."

"Your job, my job, all of our jobs is to work to liberate our people from oppression by the white man."

"I know, but I've got to earn a living," I say, and try to move away. Being harangued, even by a fine African-American king, is being harangued.

"I understand. But stay a few minutes and listen to the voice of the people." He gestures toward the building, but there are so many people I cannot see what he's pointing at.

Around me the crowd is restive, surging gently, expectantly forward. Smashed together, I can feel the collective energy bouncing from person to person, searching for someplace to manifest itself. It is the energy of anger, powerlessness, the lust for revenge. It can be a very powerful thing.

"Take it back! Take it back! Take it back!" A woman's voice shouts, amplified by a fuzzy, hand-held bullhorn. Her words bounce forward, onto the crowd of several hundred people in front of her. As if in church, they echo her words, call and response.

"Take it back, take it back, take it back," they shout. I push forward until I can see the woman. Cathy Hughes, owner of WOL-AM Radio, host of "The Cathy Hughes Show," one of the biggest mouths and most adept organizers D.C.'s black community has, stands on the top step of the *Post* building. She is a compact, wiry woman with a thin angular face, big, darting eyes, full lips that she licks at regular intervals.

Were she not screeching into a bullhorn, if you just saw her walking down the street, what you'd notice about her is her hair. In a city where hair—good, bad, long, short, big, little, woven, extended, or braided—is of paramount importance, her hair stands out. It sits on top of her head like a living crown, a mass of brownish-blonde tresses, then cascades, curling, like some Afrocentric version of Shirley Temple, to and beyond her shoulders. As she exhorts she shakes her head, tosses her mane, runs her fingers through her hair for emphasis.

"We don't want this. We are not going to take this. This is not right," Hughes shouts, waving the first issue of the magazine in her hand. The audience claps, snorts, chants in agreement.

"That's why we say to the *Washington Post*, TAKE IT BACK!" With each word the woman slashes the air with the magazine. The face of the rapper accused of murder catches and refracts the sunlight, a grim reminder of why all these people are out here.

"Our community cannot and will not tolerate these attacks. We will not sit by while our community is portrayed so negatively, will we?"

"Noooooooooo!" The crowd roars.

"That's why we say, take it back!" With that, she turns slightly and tosses the magazine upward. Like a talisman from a Steven Spielberg movie, a Molotov cocktail, or the bone thrown by the ape in *2001*, the magazine glides slowly through the air, pages rustling. It lands, *whap!* on a two-foot-high pile of identical magazines already heaped in the alcove behind her. The crowd roars approvingly, modern-day gladiators cheering as the Christians are fed to the lions.

I stand there, the reporter, objectively observing.

The woman with the bullhorn poses on the top step, pitching arm in the air.

The crowd flows toward the woman, the pile of rejected magazines behind her. Their collective gaze focuses not on her, but on the offending publication. Several hundred voices are raised in the chant, "Take it back! Take it back! Take it back!"

It is as if the magazine were George Wallace incarnate, Judas Iscariot reborn, the embodiment of everyone who had ever offended any African-American anywhere. We are a people heavily into rhetoric and symbols. If looks could kill, the stack of magazines would go up in flames.

"Now wait a minute! Wait a minute! Let me say this," screams the woman with the bullhorn. Very gradually, the crowd quiets.

"We're out here today, and we're mad."

"Yes we are, we're mad."

"Amen."

71

"Tell it, sister."

"But *dogs* get mad, don't they?" There is laughter from the crowd.

"Yes, dogs get mad. But people get *angry*. And you know what angry people do?"

"Preach sister."

"Tell it like it is."

"All right."

"I'll tell you what angry people do. They *organize*."

"Say it. Say it."

"Break it down, sister."

"So what we're doing now is organizing. We're going to be out here every Sunday until the *Washington Post* apologizes to the black community for this insulting magazine. But that's not all we want. Sorry isn't enough!"

"Tell it! Tell it!"

"Not enough, not enough."

"No, it's too late for sorry. We want more. We want an issue of the magazine dedicated to us, to celebrating the positivity of beautiful black Washington!"

The crowd erupts with applause and cheers. The brother next to me grabs my arm. "That Cathy Hughes," he says, pointing to the woman with the bullhorn. "That's a strong black woman."

"Until that happens, we're going to be out here every Sunday to let the *Post* know we don't want this magazine. To tell them, take it back! Take it back! Take it back!" The crowd picks up the litany, people clap along rhythmically.

The mood is festive, in a pissed-off sort of way. I stand there, transfixed by the energy, not chanting or clapping, just watching.

"This is a great day for D.C.," the man next to me says, yelling to be heard. "Finally these niggers are waking up and realizing we're all still on the plantation." He grabs my arms, folded across my chest, and twirls me around so I am no longer facing forward, but facing him. My arms drop.

"Are you with us, sister?" He peers down at me. Something swinging against my chest catches his eye and mine. Before I can tuck it back inside my shirt, he reaches out and grabs it. My press pass.

"Hey. The *Washington Post.* So you work for those racist dogs. What are you doing out here?"

"I'm on my way to work."

"Uh huh. Just decided to stop off at the demonstration to get some information for the boss, huh?"

"Not really. I'm interested—"

He cuts me off. "Interested? Interested in what? Sister, this is not time to be interested! Like Eldridge said, 'If you're not part of the solution, you're part of the problem.'"

He's screaming. The veins on his forehead and neck bulge. Flecks of spittle land coolly on my hot face. I feel as if I'm having an out-of-body experience. Is it really me being dissed by this promojite relic? Does spit qualify as a potentially dangerous bodily fluid? Did he really quote Eldridge Cleaver, the man who once "practiced" rape on black women so he could get proficient for his real prey, white women? When last heard from, Cleaver had reincarnated himself as a born-again Christian.

"Which are you?" he screeches. Around us, people stop chanting and clapping, turning to see what the ruckus is about. I can feel their eyes on me, on him, on my press pass. This is not a sympathetic crowd.

"I'm a black woman—"

"That don't mean shit if you work for the man," he snarls. "Black is a state of mind, not the color of your skin."

"I know that. What I mean is I understand what the community feels. I feel some of the same things," I say. I've been to dozens of civil rights, anti-war, and nationalist demo's like this one, where one individual comes to personify the problem. But usually it's Bull Connor, Richard Nixon, or Ed Koch—not me.

The man leans in so close to me I can feel his breath on my face. "Feeling isn't enough. What you gonna *do*?"

I want to say, "Get the fuck out of town, go back to New York, and pretend this shit never happened," but I don't. I stand there, pondering his question, wondering what I am going to do. I cannot imagine spending my money each Sunday on the newspaper, extracting the magazine, coming downtown, throwing it on the *Post*'s steps, and then spending a few hours stomping, chanting, clapping, and otherwise getting riled up with a few hundred promojites. On the other hand, being a token spook on the staff of the magazine, seen as an Uncle Tom traitor by the black community and a good, safe Negro by my colleagues, doesn't appeal to me either.

"Sister! What are you gonna DO?" His voice startles me out of my reverie.

"My job. What I came here to do. Write stories that honestly portray the black community." Before I finish speaking, I realize how lame that sounds.

"Ha! You can try it, but don't expect miracles," he sneers. The crowd around us snickers en masse.

"I don't."

"Like I said, if you're not part of the solution, you're part of the problem."

By now I'm sick of hearing him, of being attacked, blamed for something I was powerless to stop or alter. If I were a man I'd punch this guy in the face. "Look. Isn't it better to have someone who cares about the black community inside?" I ask.

"It depends what you do in there."

"What does that mean?"

"If you just sit up there and collect your check, you're not helping anyone but yourself. But if you work with us—"

"What does that mean?"

"Like Watergate, sister. You could be the movement's Deep Throat."

I have a vision of myself dressed in red, black, and green, the nationalist colors, sneaking to a late-night rendezvous at the Florida Avenue Grill or some other soul food restaurant. There, I sit at a table crowded with brothers in dashikis. Being a good promojite sister, I wear dreadlocks or a headwrap, dresses that fall, correctly, below the knee, and never pants. I do not eat swine or drink liquor, but sip herbal tea as I pass on inside info on the latest racist, diabolical plot against the African-American community being hatched by the caucasian running-dog lackeys at the *Washington Post*.

Frankly, the role doesn't sound very challenging. It's one thing to bring down a smart bastard like Richard Nixon, but going undercover to destroy a magazine whose greatest sin is stupidity and bad judgment? The way things are going, it'll self-destruct pretty soon anyway.

The man sucks his teeth, black people's nonverbal equivalent of "fuck you." "You aren't serious, sister, you're not serious." He looks at me pityingly, shrugs. "Think about what I said. You could play an important role in the movement." He turns away.

The people around us sense the dissipation of anger, no longer smell blood. Mirroring his loss of interest, they turn back to the woman with the bullhorn.

Not wanting to appear to turn tail and run, I wander through the scene for a few more minutes. Again, I am pleasantly struck by the crowd's spirit of community, collectivity, and common purpose, however misguided. The bright colors and intricate patterns of African fabrics are a welcome sight for eyes made sore by the grays and blues of business suits. Walking by, people make eye contact, smile, speak, a rarity among the middle-class black people in this town, where too often it seems that acknowledging others somehow diminishes self.

Suddenly, I cannot remember if I am Claire Huxtable, Harriet Tubman, or someone else entirely. I have no idea who I am or where I fit. Am I a freed black who has made it or a slave struggling to free herself and her people? Maybe I'm just an idiot who took a job thinking I was getting over, only to find myself got over upon. Then I hear my mother's voice.

"You know what's the trouble with you you think too much always analyzing everything I've lived nearly seventy years and I'm here to tell you it's not worth it just live be happy and don't worry with it try to be the best person you can do unto others never forget that discretion is the better part of valor and do something about that temper if you don't you'll have an aneurysm before you're forty did you get your paycheck this week they're paying you good money not to write fine go out and buy yourself something nice . . . "

Her voice is enough to snap me back. I walk around to the back entrance of the building, ride up to the fifth floor. When I get off the elevator I see Ben Bradlee and Vincent Reed, former school superintendent and now the *Post*'s H.N.I.C. (head Negro in charge) of community relations, standing by the floor-to-ceiling windows and looking down at the demonstrators.

"This is something, isn't it?" Bradlee says. Reed nods to me. Is it wishful thinking, a hallucination, or behind his smooth face is he really giving me the familiar soul-to-soul "Oh-Jesus-the-white-folks-done-fucked-up-again-and-now-they-expect-us-to-fix-it" look?

I mutter "It's something all right," and continue on to my desk. I spend the afternoon transcribing notes, calling friends to bemoan my fate, and studiously ignoring the nonstop ringing of the phone. Can I really hear the chanting of the demonstrators, five floors and a world away?

In between typing and dialing, I ponder becoming the movement's informant, an African-American female Deep Throat, but not for long. I'm constitutionally unfit for the gig: my throat just ain't deep enough for that. After all, I've been here three months, barely opened my mouth, and already feel like I'm choking.

CHAPTER TWELVE

The Sunday demonstrations last for three months. As we move into the football season the crowds dwindle significantly. In Washington, nothing—not even race—keeps people from their beloved Redskins.

For me, the demonstrations get to be kind of comforting, a bizarre reality check, a buffer between me and my coworkers. I go to work just about every Sunday, at first because no one else does and it's quiet. I have had a hard time adjusting to the wide-open spaces and noise of the news-room. Eventually, I go to bear weird witness: to see, face to face, in person and upfront, the other half of the forces rattling my dream of bourgeois escapism.

Once I know not to wear my press pass, I blend in unnoticed. Listening to Cathy Hughes or Walter Fauntroy, D.C.'s singing, preaching, nonvoting congressional delegate, I am simply one of the people, not an employee of the evil empire.

It is a latter-day version of passing, in which the thing to be disguised is not the color of one's skin, but one's corporate affiliation. If the early 1970s were a time when many black people decided to "join the system and change it from within," by the late 1980s some of us have realized that the system isn't changing, we are—and not necessarily for the better.

In spite of earlier arguments to the contrary, it has become clear that the benefits of joining the system are limited and individual. A few people might be doing some good, but the race is just about where it had been. Only now, the masses of black people are smart enough to see that. Contrary to the rap we give publicly, most of us corporate Negroes aren't helping anyone but ourselves. The *lumpen* are not pleased.

So I tuck my press pass beneath the underwire of my bra and go to the demo's. Standing there I am, for a few minutes, accepted as who I appear to be: an interested, serious sister in jeans with salt-and-pepper hair. The moment I flash my press pass and go inside the building, however, I am someone else: a corporate sell-out, a traitor, an Uncle Tom.

Inside the office I am just about invisible, unless I act out, in which case I am treated like an intimidating, overbearing, frightening-type black. Then, people notice me. In some ways, the corporate culture is like elementary school: the bad kids are the ones who get the most attention. I realize this when, after three months of generally agreeable behavior, I have only one 750-word story published, a silly item for the grab-bag section on a woman who runs a shop selling magical teas and herbs. This is not so amazing in the hectic world of the newspaper culture, where leads are followed, sources interviewed, stories written, and then BAM! made irrelevant by a more important breaking story. But I am new to that culture; I'm a magazine writer who, as a freelancer, seldom had a story rejected. Here at the *Post* I'm batting near zero.

It seems to be enough that I am here, black and female. No one but me feels it necessary that I actually do anything. As long as I can say that I am "working on" something, everyone is cool.

Everyone but me, that is.

My mother calls for an update: "So, how's everything going?"

"Terrible."

"What's wrong? Is Misu all right?"

"Oh yeah, she's fine."

"So, what's wrong?"

"I hate my job."

"Why?"

"I work for a magazine that black people hate, no one in the city will let me interview them, most of the people I work with are horrible—"

"Did you get paid last week?" my mother interrupts.

"Yes, I got paid."

"How much money have you made since you've been there?"

"I don't know—"

"Look at your pay stub." I rummage through my cavernous bag until I find my most recent pay receipt.

"About $20,000."

"You've been paid $20,000 to write 750 words. I'd say that's pretty good money." My mother laughs.

"But what about my writing?"

"What about it? You're still freelancing. If the Washington *Post* doesn't want to publish you and will pay you anyway, what do you care?"

I'm invisible, all five foot eight of me, and even my mother thinks it's all right as long as the money's good and keeps on coming. Me, I'm miserable. Like most writers, I like to see my byline, visualize people all over the city reading my work. I might have been poor when I was in New York, but I was read. Here, I'm just the spook who sits by the door.

Most of the editors spend their days editing copy, taking long lunches, and gossiping about what the paper has to do to get the protestors to cease and desist while at the same time avoiding any suggestion that it has capitulated, bowed to pressure, or made any mistakes. My editor, the feminist, who is supposed to be my advocate, seems to spend much of her time eating raw carrots and celery, making calls to her ailing mother in California, and complaining.

I pretty much do what I want, come and go as I please. It's as if now that I've integrated the staff, I needn't do much else. This is fun for a few weeks, but then it gets tired. After all, I came here to write and be successful. I'm willing to be a token, but not an unused one. I figure everyone, including white men, gets hired because of who they are. It's just that because white men run things, they're able to pretend that when they hire one another, they do so based on merit; when they hire a black person or a woman, they're doing us a favor.

I feel comfortable getting in the door because I'm a spook, but I don't intend to sit by it. Ambitious, bored, and angry, I go talk to Lovinger.

"So, Jill. What can I do for you?" Lovinger is a tall, thin man with one of those faces in which all the features are slightly down-turned. Consequently, he tends to look depressed or in pain, even when he's not.

"Well, I wanted to talk to you about how I'm doing here."

"Fine. I think everything will work out well. It takes a while to get adjusted to Washington and to the Washington *Post*." He leans back in his chair, puts sneakered feet up on his desk. "How do you think things are going?"

"Not great. The protest has really messed me up. Most black people won't talk to me until the demonstrations are over, and those that will make me promise not to publish the piece until the problem is resolved."

Lovinger raises his eyebrows, nods sympathetically.

"It can't go on much longer," he says. "How's your Oprah Winfrey piece coming?"

"It's not. I'm on my twentieth rewrite. Meanwhile, every other magazine and Style have already written about her."

"I know. That's why I thought we should refocus the piece on her father."

"Yeah. Well, that's not going very well either. I can't get along with my editor."

"What's the problem?"

"She rewrites my quotes. She gives me editorial instructions, not suggestions, she's obsessed by Oprah's fat, she's rude and has no respect for me—" I see Lovinger's face and stop midsentence. His naturally pained countenance looks even more so. He appears uncomfortable and slightly intimidated.

I sit there in a skirt, heels, super-sheer stockings, and a blazer, looking corporate. Dressed for success, I don't seem to be having much. I fiddle with the toy on his desk, slivers of metal clinging to a magnet that can be molded into different shapes.

"Ughhhh. I know Amanda isn't the easiest person to work with. She's also trying to adjust to this place. You're black. You're a woman. I think you would benefit from working with a black editor, someone you felt comfortable with. That's one of the reasons I was interested in hiring Thulani Davis." Well, she wasn't interested in being hired. When we talked about it she giggled, shook her head in that lazy way she has, and drawled, "It's all yours."

He continues talking about my need for a black editor. I bite my lip and try not to let my mouth fall open. For black folks, pursing, licking, or biting our lips has less to do with any nervous tics than it does with how much we have to hold in what we really think. Because if my lips part I'm likely to say, "Look, I know I'm black and I know I'm female, that's no revelation. What the hell does that have to do with editing my work? I mean, do we rewrite quotes here or what? That's what I wanna know, that's not a racial or sexual issue, is it? There's nothing wrong with me, I need a good editor."

"Maybe you should talk to Milton Coleman," Lovinger says. "He's black and has been at this place for a long time. He might be helpful."

"How?" I ask. I mean, Coleman is the man who broke all the journalistic rules and derailed Jesse Jackson's presidential campaign in 1984 by quoting Jackson's off-the-record use of the term "Hymietown" to describe New York. Afterward, many in the black community considered him a traitor. Many still do. He is the only person I can think of who black folks—the most forgiving people on earth—refuse to pardon. The *Post* promoted him.

"Just in putting this place in context."

"Okay. But what about my Oprah story?"

"Well, you and Amanda should go have a cup of coffee and talk about what the problems are."

"I've tried talking."

"Try again. Everyone is under a lot of pressure right now. You're new to the city. It took me months to adjust to Washington, especially coming from New York. This is a strange place . . . "

"That's for sure." We laugh, briefly bonded by our mutual sense of exile.

"Your Oprah piece would be a good, positive piece to run soon. See if you two can work it out."

"I'll try." The carrot of having a full-length piece—maybe even a cover story—in the magazine makes me salivate. I am willing to try just about anything.

I go and stand patiently by my editor's desk. She ignores me and continues to complain to someone on the phone. Finally she hangs up.

"Amanda, let's go get a cup of coffee and talk about the story."

"I don't drink coffee. But I can get some hot water for tea."

"Is now a good time?"

"Not really. I'm just so busy," she whines.

"I just talked to Jay and he wants the story finished."

"I have a few minutes."-

Walking downstairs, I try the conciliatory approach. "Listen, I know things haven't been going very well with this piece, but I'd like to work it out."

"Do you want me to be your editor?" she snaps.

"Well, actually, I feel you're about the best editor available," I say diplomatically. The truth is, she's the only editor available.

"Well, you damn well better act like it!" she barks.

We are midway down a long, deserted hallway leading to the cafeteria when she says this. I slow down, look at her mottled, plump, sour-lipped face, and contemplate smacking her. In my whole adult life I have never had another alleged grown-up talk to me in this way. Briefly, I imagine the satisfaction of kicking this superior, bitchy, neo-feminist ass up and down the corridor. Then I remember where I am, who I'm supposed to be.

"Well, you damn well better act like I'm a good writer, too," I say. Over tea, I take my revenge in the passive-aggressive mode popular in corporate America. I chain smoke in the face of Miss Healthy as we go over my manuscript one mo' time.

CHAPTER THIRTEEN

Long before Louis Farrakhan was a minister in the Nation of Islam, before he was the scourge of white America, before he became both the champion and the nemesis of Jesse Jackson's 1984 presidential campaign, he was a calypso singer, albeit not a very successful one.

Today, Farrakhan's calypso days are largely unknown or forgotten, both by those who view him as a racist maniac and those who see him as a savior. But one morning, a year after I came to work at the *Washington Post*, as I climbed the steps into the building, the title of the only Farrakhan song I remember popped into my head, "The White Man's Heaven is the Black Man's Hell."

For the life of me, I can't remember any of the words to the song, but that doesn't matter. For the next three years, every time I mounted those steps, I found myself thinking of the title. It seemed to sum up my relationship with the *Washington Post* rather neatly.

For caucasian journalists, the *Washington Post* is nirvana. Journalists, politicians, and CEOs consider it the number-two newspaper in the country, right after the *New York Times*. For those who either cannot get or do not want a job at the *Times*, either for journalistic reasons or fear of living in New York, the *Post* is indeed heaven.

In this convoluted heaven, Ben Bradlee is God in the guise of a Boston Brahmin. He bounces through the newsroom on the balls of his feet, impeccably dressed in thinly striped shirts and suspenders. His eyes, buried in a lifetime of wrinkles, are sharp, intelligent, miss nothing. Striding through his domain he growls out praise, criticism, or, more frequently, an obscene comment. Short and not handsome, still, his presence is electric. Reporters feel him coming by the crackling of his energy long before they see him. Most preen self-importantly as he passes by. A writer working desultorily on a weekend story begins to type furiously; a casual phone conversation with a friend becomes the loud interrogation of a source; eyes that have been staring mindlessly become clouded, deep, contemplative.

"Don't go see Bradlee unless you're prepared to leave the *Post*," is the saying around the newsroom. Stories abound about righteously indignant reporters entering Bradlee's office with a long list of complaints and exiting with the verbal equivalent of a short pink slip.

Where Bradlee is loquacious, elegant, aristocratic, managing editor Leonard Downie is taciturn, tall, awkward, quintessentially Midwestern working-class. Where Bradlee exudes innately superior judgment, Downie projects concern, empathy, methodic analysis. In a cosmos where political agendas are rampant, back-stabbing epidemic, and dissembling automatic, I learn that Len Downie is one of the few people from whom I can expect a straight answer. I might not always like what he's saying, but what I hear is what I get.

Being hired by the *Post* is for many journalists the pinnacle of their careers. Wooed from some other newspaper because they are stars, enterprising hot shots with great reportorial skills, they came to the *Post* prepared to take their rightful place in the ultimate journalistic constellation, to join the elite club of the country's finest reporters and writers.

Once arrived, they abruptly find themselves tossed into a newsroom filled with several hundred other stars fighting to see who can shine brightest, eclipse each other, continue to ascend, and yet avoid the always imminent danger of crashing and burning.

Many more crash and burn than ascend. However, for most white folks and a lot of black ones, when they are on the inside looking out, failure at the *Post* looks like success just about anywhere else. Because they are *there*, at the *Washington Post*: dim, minor stars, but stars nonetheless, in a cosmology where, thanks to the Newspaper Guild and inept management, getting fired is damn near impossible.

Those for whom there is scant possibility of revitalization are sent to a reportorial Elba, such as one of the outlying bureaus, or assigned a beat considered necessary but essentially unimportant. If they can make a journalistic silk purse out of a reportorial sow's ear, redemption is possible. The hopeless are simply paid regularly and well, and ignored. Their bylines seldom appear in the paper. Those who are truly loathed are assigned to obits, where they await the demise of someone notable, the off chance of landing a corpse with which to write themselves back into orbit.

This, of course, seldom happens. The newsroom is littered with burnt-out stars, virtually immovable masses of reporter-matter that arrived full of talent, eagerness, hope, and promise and then either weren't chosen, weren't lucky, or couldn't hack cutting throats. They huddle at their desks and spend the day making personal phone calls, gossiping, and complaining. Some of this bunch scroll daily through the "intype" file in the vast computer system, reading the unpublished stories of their colleagues. The more sinister among them use this information to steal ideas, undermine their enemies' articles, leak information to the competition. Powerless as individual writers and reporters, they derive a sense of involvement, of belonging, from knowing today what will be in the paper tomorrow. Reading a story over and over as it goes through the punishing electronic labyrinth of the editing process, they soothe their aching egos and take comfort from watching the computerized trail of a colleague's misery.

Seldom does anyone quit. They have reached the mountain top, the white man's heaven. To quit would be to question the fundamentals of the Judeo-Christian ethic: that hard works brings its just deserts, that heaven and hell really exist, that life is fair and the meek shall inherit the earth.

For many of the black folks there, the *Washington Post* is neither heaven nor hell, but some weird, journalistic purgatory, a seemingly endless proving ground on which, just when you think you've won the game, the rules are changed. This is nothing new for African-Americans, corporate or otherwise, but it does tend to make some of us crazy. Whatever field we're in, we have to justify ourselves daily to people who'd rather we weren't around. For black journalists, the situation is particularly tricky, since we're in a profession that professes to tell "the truth" and holds the chimera of objectivity as its central tenet.

Many of us went into journalism prior to Public Enemy's hit record that warned, "Don't Believe the Hype." Too late—we believed it. It was shocking to some of us to realize that journalism is, first and foremost, a business: its first responsibility is not to the truth, or even to readers, but to corporate America. Then we were hit with the cold reality that objectivity means neither what it says in the dictionary—"of, relating to or being an object, phenomenon, or condition in the realm of sensible experience independent of individual thought and perceptible by all observers,"—or what we learned in journalism school. If it's true that the only free press is the one you own, then it's not surprising that, at the *Washington Post* and elsewhere, objectivity is defined by the owners. Since those who run the *Post* are white men, objectivity, far from being "independent of individual thought," is dependent upon their experience—sensible or not.

For most African-American journalists, working in mainstream media entails a daily struggle with this notion of objectivity. Each day we are required to justify ourselves, our community, and our story ideas. The more successful of us refashion ourselves in the image of white men. We go to Ivy League colleges and socialize primarily with white folks. We wear sober, preppy clothes, earth tones, seldom bright colors. If we are women, we straighten our hair or buy extensions—yards of synthetic or dead hair we have sewn on in order to have flowing locks, what Style reporter Jackie Trescott calls "California hair." If we don't, we wear it short and conservative: no afros, dreads, twists, or other politically correct hairstyles welcome. In short, we make ourselves as nonthreatening— as much like white folks—as possible.

If we are men we wear suits, ties, very occasionally a sport coat and jacket. We keep our hair cropped close, or else brush it down, back, and part it in some corny 1950s style. Male and female, we make ourselves visually harmless. We are nonthreatening and never frivolous, always sensible, sensible, sensible. The more risque among us wear Else Peretti knock-off jewelry, a colorful tie, unique shoes, patterned socks. But mostly we downplay ourselves, try to out-white the white folks. This done, we're still far from assured of success. It's even more important that we prove our objectivity, our white maleness. A familiar means of accomplishing this is by writing a front-page piece that exposes, in great detail, the pathology of some element of the black community.

Years ago, an investigation of a major metropolitan police department revealed that in order to prove they were dedicated cops, black police officers were unofficially encouraged to shoot and kill a black suspect. In this way, they gained their—white—stripes and acceptance by their colleagues.

Journalism is not that much different. Allowed in the door because of necessity during the riots of the 1960s, when white reporters—also known on the streets as honkey devils—were afraid to go into de ghetto during the native uprisings, and later by the legal mandates of the 1970s, we are still viewed as interlopers, intruders, subversives within the ranks. Too often, if we truly want to succeed and ascend, it behooves us to castrate ourselves in voice, demeanor, stance.

The Janet Cooke debacle at the *Washington Post* is an example of this syndrome taken to its ultimate conclusion. Cooke, an African-American female reporter on the lowly "District Weekly," wanted nothing more than to succeed on white men's terms. She was smart, pretty, had long hair, dressed appropriately, and socialized primarily with white people. She was also a good reporter who wanted to move up fast, like the white boys do.

So she made up a story about an eight-year-old heroin addict, complete with a negligent mother and her boyfriend, who obligingly shot-up the fictitious "Jimmy." The story went A1. Cooke was nominated for and won a Pulitzer, journalism's highest honor. Then everything began to unravel.

A standard check by an Associated Press reporter writing a story on Pulitzer winners uncovered the fact that, contrary to what she'd stated on her resume (and the information furnished to the media by the *Post*), Cooke hadn't graduated from Vassar, never studied at the Sorbonne, and didn't have a master's degree from the University of Toledo. Alerted to these discrepancies, it wasn't long before the *Post* discovered the "Jimmy" story was fabricated. Cooke resigned, the *Post* returned the Pulitzer, and the Janet Cooke affair has been infamous in journalistic circles ever since.

Much has been written about what Janet Cooke did, very little about why. Clearly, the sister had some severe ethical, moral, and psychological problems that caused her to mistake fiction for journalism, and self-hating journalism at that. But she was also an African-American female journalist at the *Washington Post*. It's not hard to imagine her nightmare: fighting it out with the other stars while the editors, for the most part, either stood by and smugly watched, or else egged their favorite on, she knew she would be outshone, discarded, and forgotten unless she did something—quick—to earn the notice and approval of the powers that be. What better than following the honored tradition of writing an exposé of pathological Negroes? After all, when you're black in corporate America, self-hatred often passes for being well-adjusted, competent, assimilated, and objective.

Clearly, most African-American journalists are not Janet Cookes. They are, like their caucasian colleagues, dedicated, hardworking professionals trying to play by the rules and move up in the system. The difference is that where white reporters have one job, black reporters have several. Not only must we function as reporters, but we are also ambassadors from that colored catch-all, Black America, explaining and justifying not only ourselves but also the mythical, monolithic "black community."

We must be emotional and professional self-censors, constantly aware that when dealing with white editors, our enthusiasm, passion, and commitment are often perceived as intimidation, anger, and lack of objectivity. Human characteristics and personality traits—such as being outspoken, stubborn, proud—are viewed as "racial," and therefore negative.

This is an alien world for me. The response of Mimi, a prep school friend and Georgetown native who is my daughter's godmother, when I told her I was moving to Washington to work for the *Post*, was "Ugh, Washers. You'll never make it there. The *Post* will never figure out what to do with a black WASP like you." Mimi, bless her heart, is nothing if not eccentric. Brilliant, intellectually eclectic, always politically correct, she is one of the few white folks I know who can deal, straight up, with all kinds of people. I tease her that she is really passing for white. Born into the bosom of monied, aristocratic WASPdom with all its craziness, hers is a struggle to disassociate, whereas mine is a struggle for belonging. To what I'm not exactly sure.

Along with David Hardy's, Mimi's is one of the few voices raised against my upwardly mobile move. As with David, I listen but do not hear what she is saying until it is too late.

CHAPTER FOURTEEN

When the magazine controversy finally ends on Friday, December 12, after thirteen consecutive Sunday demonstrations, it does so not with a bang, whimper, or revolutionary change, but with a sell-out. As a veteran of peace marches, civil rights marches, pro-affirmative action marches, and women's liberation marches of the 1960s and 1970s, I am crushed but not surprised. Ideals for dollars is nothing new in the America of the 1980s. Still, I am disgusted and made that much more cynical.

After nearly three months of Sundays marching, protesting, and spending $1.25 on the *Post* in order to throw the magazine back on the steps of the building, the concerned citizens, political leaders, promojites, and assorted individuals in search of a movement win nothing for their time and trouble. On a sunny Friday morning, unbeknown to the masses, Cathy Hughes cuts a deal with Don Graham. Not for a black editor, or more black writers, or anything else substantial: the protest ends in exchange for Graham and Bradlee agreeing to appear several times on Hughes' morning talk show to discuss news coverage.

Rather than gaining the elusive empowerment, freedom, and respect they'd initially demanded, the angry black community is to be assuaged by a few two-and-a-half-hour radio free-for-alls. It is as if Rome, in response to the gladiators' demands for freedom, instead cut a deal allowing the gladiators a few more minutes to strut around the pit before the lions are released.

There are two winners: the *Washington Post* and Cathy Hughes. Hughes would host as guests on her talk show the white men who ran the *Post*, guests sure to improve her ratings. The white men would have to give up a few early morning hours, nothing more. As Bradlee cackles to me at the magazine's Christmas party a few weeks after the protest ended,

"I can't believe we got out of it so easily, but she needs the ratings. I hear her Arbitron's a seven."

For their trouble, D.C.'s black community receives the right to tune into Hughes' show and try desperately to get through on the jammed telephone lines during the call-in segment. Those who succeed can spend a few minutes haranguing Graham or Bradlee, unseen, from miles away, while simultaneously clutching a telephone receiver and that day's *Post*, for which they would have plunked down twenty-five cents.

As for the evil rap star featured on the premier issue's cover, who'd come to personify an image of black youth gone berserk, no charges are filed against him, presumably for lack of evidence. He isn't even indicted.

I am relieved the protest is over. It means that black and progressive folks will now talk to me for attribution, that the file of completed stories I've agreed to hold until the controversy ended can now be published. I figure the wagons of the white lager will come out of their defensive circle, we can all move forward. Not for the first time, I am wrong.

During the height of the protest, Juan Williams, a black male, joined the staff of the magazine. Williams is the perfect Negro, at least in the eyes of white folks, because most of the time he writes—and apparently, believes—what caucasians think black folks should feel and think, which is as they do. Williams is a child of the *Post*, has spent his whole career there, moving up through the ranks.

Williams is a black Republican type, a neoconservative opportunist a la Clarence Thomas. He is also of Panamanian parentage, which explains some of where he's coming from. He typifies the worst stereotype of people of African descent who come to America inadvertently or willfully ignorant of the history of black folks born here. Many such immigrants, because they ostensibly came here voluntarily, view America as a place where, if you work hard, keep your nose clean, and obey the law, anything's possible. They either don't understand or conveniently forget the hand of America, and those of the other superpowers, in their native region's dismal economy. These immigrants often have a hard time relating to and understanding African-Americans, who after centuries of experience with what psychologist Na'im Akbar calls "the chains and images of psychological slavery," do not see America as so beneficent.

Ignorant of our history, these immigrants of African descent pass judgment: African-Americans, they say, are lazy, cynical, always looking for a hand-out. They point to themselves as proof of the American dream come true. Denying the role of race, they mouth the prejudices of white immigrants in blackface. Forget racism, history, the brutalization of the African-American psyche from the middle passage on down, they holler. America is a nation of immigrants, and we are just like the Irish, Polish, Japanese, and Jews who have come here. They conveniently forget that African-Americans, unlike them, unlike any other immigrants, did not come here voluntarily; we are, all of us, the children of slaves.

Initially I don't know anything about Juan Williams except that he appears to be black, is coming to work on the magazine, and seems as uncomfortable with salary negotiations as I am. I also hear that while on leave from the *Post* he wrote the documentary on the civil rights movement, "Eyes on the Prize," which makes him seem progressive. Much later I learn that the film's activist and progressive politics are no reflection on Juan: he didn't write the documentary, but came in after the film was finished to write the book based on the film. Our sole conversation prior to his arrival on staff consists of him confiding to me that he is struggling to get management to pay him $55,000. I tell him to go for it. I've already learned that after Reagan, Marion Barry, and Social Security get their piece, $50,000 isn't nearly all it's touted to be.

In short, I assumed he was a brother.

My friend Adrienne, who left New York to teach in St. Thomas a decade ago and never came back, once told me that on the first day of school, after she talks about rules, homework assignments, and expectations, she writes "ASSUME" in capital letters on the blackboard, "because it's the most important word they learn in my classroom."

"Are you kidding?" I asked.

"No. Then I ask them, 'What does the word mean?' I tell them to look at it and figure out the meaning."

"So you just want them to give you the definition?"

Adrienne laughs. "No. Then I go to the blackboard and circle the ASS, then the U, than the ME. I tell them, never assume, because it makes an ASS out of U and ME," she says triumphantly.

At the time, I thought Adgie had lost it under the tropical sun in a country where you can buy a fifth of Mount Gay rum for $3.00 in any supermarket. I figured she was nervous about teaching and had read some silly book full of pointers for young teachers. But like my mother's adages, I couldn't forget ASSUME. It stuck with me like a bad knock-knock joke from the second grade.

Because we are both of African descent and working in a primarily caucasian institution, because we both experienced the siege mentality of the first months of the magazine and survived, because I am a race woman, I assume Juan Williams and I are natural allies. I should have written ASSUME on the mirror above my bedroom dresser and recited Adrienne's litany every morning.

In early 1987, I begin reporting a piece on New York attorney Alton Maddox. At the time, Maddox is hot. He and C. Vernon Mason are representing the victims of the Howard Beach, Queens, attack, during which three black men had been set upon and beaten by a gang of white youths. One was chased onto a highway, run over, and killed. It was a case that polarized New York, making it clear that racism was alive and well and driving the media into a frenzy. I have known Maddox and Mason for years. Maddox was Anthony Davis' lawyer, the boy I wrote about who was accused of killing his teacher but didn't. I suggested a profile of Maddox to Lovinger.

"He sounds interesting. But what's the local angle?"

"In the black community, everyone knows about Howard Beach. Whether you live in New York, L.A., or D.C., when someone says 'Howard Beach,' you know what they're talking about."

"I don't know. We're trying to focus on stories about Washington."

"As far as African-Americans are concerned, Howard Beach could be anywhere. Plus, it's an exclusive."

"Huh?"

"I know Maddox. I've written about cases he's defended before, he's agreed to talk to me. He hasn't talked extensively to anyone else."

"Really?" Lovinger looks interested. An exclusive, about a black professional, a champion of civil rights? Eureka!

"Yeah. I've already talked to his assistant and he's willing to do it."

"What's he working on now?"

"He's defending the kid accused of slashing the face of Marla Hanson, the model."

"Oh, yeah . . . " Recognition dawns. Marla Hansen has been in *People* magazine.

"So, what d'you think?"

"Go for it."

I spend the next several months hanging out with Maddox in New York, talking to his relatives, childhood friends, and mentors in Newnan, Georgia, the tiny town where he grew up, and interviewing attorneys and civil rights activists about him. As usual on this magazine, which is run by a man who apparently had a miserable childhood, the past obsessively defines the present. Under Lovinger, the formula for a profile is as follows: consume all the information you can about where someone is now; then investigate his hometown, momma, daddy, first girlfriend, the woman who potty-trained him, until you unearth a traumatic event that explains, or can be made to appear to explain, why he became who he is.

I think of this as the psychobabble approach to journalism, but what the hell? I'm trying to make the best of a bad situation, to fit in without selling out, becoming a Tonto or a Samuel Pierce (the head of HUD under Reagan). Besides, I'm one of those people willing to travel just about anywhere.

The Maddox piece is the first major story I work on with my new editor, Jeanne McManus, rather than Amanda "You damn well better act like it" Spake. Feminist, left-leaning, and progressive though she may be, I find Spake impossible to work with. She is brusque, condescending, and whiny, a classic example of the saying, "Those who can, write; those who can't, edit." By the time my story on Oprah Winfrey is finished, I hardly recognize it. The best I can say for it is that it's not offensive. The experience of working with Spake is one I do not intend to repeat. I talk to Lovinger, but he doesn't get it. He seems to think that since she's a white feminist and I'm a black woman, we are organically simpatico. In late 1986, I go see managing editor Len Downie and tell him the problems I'm having. The next day, McManus becomes my editor. It is not until months later that I realize this was a major *faux pas*. I have identified myself as not a team player, a complainer, trouble. The white lager at the magazine realizes that not only am I not Mammy, I may be part of Nat Turner's gang. I come to the attention of Downie, who has a whole newspaper to run and neither the time nor the desire to be involved in local disputes, as yet another problem associated with the problem-riddled magazine. After less than six months at the *Post* I have used one of the most precious chits, gone to management, the last resort. But didn't he say, "Come to see me if there's anything I can do"?

"So, what do you think of the Maddox story?" I ask Jay. It is early April, 1987. I am grinning, because I know it's good.

"I like it, I like it. I think it tells the reader something new," says Lovinger.

"Great."

"I think it's a cover."

"Fabulous."

"Juan doesn't think we should run it."

"Excuse me?"

"Juan doesn't like it . . . " His voice drifts off, but his words hang between us.

"Why has Juan read it?" This reading of other writers' work and attendant prepublication undermining is a staple of life at the *Post*. Don't these idiots have anything better to do than scroll through intype, then approach writers or editors with unsolicited, almost invariably negative commentary?

Lovinger shrugs. "I guess he was curious. He writes a lot about civil rights." More like civil wrongs. "Why doesn't he think you should publish it?"

"He doesn't think it's a good story. He thinks I'm only publishing it because I'm intimidated by you, that you Mau-Mau'd me into it . . . " Jay sits there with his sneakered feet on the desk, looking mischievous. If he's trying to start some shit, he's succeeded.

"What an insult. Is that why you're going to run it?"

He laughs. "No. It's a good story. It'll get a lot of attention."

I get out of Jay's office as quickly as possible and go in search of Juan. I feel like I'm back in grade school and someone has repeated to me someone else's insulting remark about my momma: it's time to kick ass. I've only had one physical fight in my life, though, with a girl who lived near our home when we lived on 148th Street and Riverside Drive, in Harlem, before Daddy got successful and we moved downtown.

Unlike most kids in the neighborhood, we were bused to New Lincoln, a private, progressive school on 110th Street. Every morning the four of us would stand in the courtyard waiting for the yellow school bus and watching the other kids walking to the public elementary school. My brother Stanley, because he was a good athlete, had lots of neighborhood friends, and was able to cross the chasm of class via the violent bonding of

sports. Ralphie, he was a kid then: quiet, shy, with glasses, so nobody really bothered with him one way or the other. Lynn, with her diminutive
body and perfectly pressed pageboy, was so cool, so superior, it was obvious that messing with her wasn't a good idea, though some of the neighborhood boys looked at her longingly. Me, tall, chubby, with bangs and
two long braids hanging down my back, wanting to belong but just not
sure how—I stuck out like a white person with dreadlocks.

Maybe the kids in the neighborhood could feel how much I wanted to
be popular, fit in; maybe they felt my desire and were contemptuous of it.
Maybe they just didn't like my face. The seminal showdown came one
afternoon roller skating with a gang of kids along Riverside Drive.

"Hey, girl. What school you go to?" a big, tall girl called.

"186." That was the local elementary school, on 145th Street. I knew
enough to lie, knew that being honest, saying New Lincoln, would only
distance me from the crowd.

"You sure?" She spun to a stop in front of me, the tips of her skates
grating against the pebbly asphalt.

"Yeah, I'm sure. Don't you think I know what school I go to?"
Somehow, I managed to stop without falling and emit a reasonably feisty
retort. Seeing us face off, the other skaters stopped too, gathering around.

"What grade you in?"

"Fifth. Why?" This is a cinch, I thought, getting bold, feeling myself on
the verge of acceptance. I can, I thought, beat this big, bossy girl at her
own game. "What's it to you?"

"Who's your teacher?" Suddenly, I'm busted. Since I didn't really go to
186, I had no idea who my teacher was. I just stood there looking stupid.

"Who's your teacher, girl? Don't you know?"

"Ughhh . . . " I stalled for time, racking my brain to remember the
name of a fifth-grade teacher, even though I'd probably never heard it.
The girl had moved perceptibly closer, I could just about feel her breath
on my face. So had the other kids. They knew the smell of doom.

"You stupid, don't know the name of your teacher?" Yeah, but he
taught at New Lincoln, not 186. I tried to remember snatches of conversation at the dinner table, friends' houses, about black people's names. Is
it that Johnson, Jones, Nelson are common black names, Borenstein,
Hurd, Guttman aren't? Wasn't there something about Nelson probably
being the name my ancestors took because the slavemaster's name was

Nel, we were the sons of Nel? Is the son on the end the racial giveaway? But didn't we have relatives in Indianapolis named Kuykendahl? I swore to listen more attentively to adult conversation in the future.

"Miss Johnson," I blurted desperately.

"Hah! You're lying. There ain't no Miss Johnson at 186," she said triumphantly. Surrounding us, the other kids voiced a collective "Ooooohhhhh," which translated as, "you're in deep shit now."

"I know you go to school on that yellow school bus. You think you're hinkty, better than us, don't you?"

"No. Of course not," I said politely.

"Then why did you lie?"

"I didn't want you to think I was special because I take the school bus," I said. Dumb move.

"Girl. You think you better than me?"

"No."

"Yes you do." "No, I don't."

"I wanna fight you."

"Look. I don't wanna fight. I'm sorry I lied."

"Sorry ain't enough. We gonna fight."

"Really. I can't, I—" She cuts me off, pivoting on her skates. "Tomorrow. After school. The courtyard in front of your house," she commanded, and skated off. The other kids trailed after her in ragtag formation, leaving me standing there like a dull lump.

I realized there was no God when I not only woke up alive the next morning, but without measles, leprosy, or any other contagious disease that would keep me quarantined for a week, month, year, however long it would take for the tough girl to forget about me. On the bus to school I confided in Stanley, who told me I had to show, had to fight, and gave me a few pointers about punching from the shoulder and going for the face or stomach.

I took as long as possible with my homework, until even my mother, the queen of homework, got tired of having me around and told me to go outside and play until dinner time. On the way down in the elevator, I gave God a last chance to bestow a serious, even fatal disease on my opponent. Again, God failed me. When I got outside, the girl was there, waiting for me, surrounded by a crowd of kids hungry for blood. My blood. We walked around to the side of the building. Stanley was there. I leaned against the rough gray stone. "Go for the head or stomach, head or stomach," Stanley whispered, then stepped back.

The girl stood in front of me, her back to the sun hanging in the west, over the Hudson River, blinding me. I could barely see her head or stomach. I had never fought anyone except my sister or brothers, and our blows were restrained by our fear of our parents. That day, there were no such restrictions. I did not want to fight but knew that I had to, knew that to chicken out was worse than fighting and losing, that to refuse to fight was the kiddie equivalent of believing it when the seasoned con tells the new guy on the cellblock that if he just lets him have it once, he won't bother him anymore. If I didn't fight, I'd be fair game for everyone. I would never belong.

I leaned against the building waiting for the bell to go off, for someone to say, "One, Two, Three, GO!" for the fight to officially begin, for my trainer to come to my corner and give my shoulder a final rub. Suddenly, WHAM! the girl punched me in the nose so hard the back of my skull smashed into the gray stone behind me. I instantly had the most complete, circular, throbbing headache I ever had in my life.

I just stood there in a daze of shock and pain, barely able to see or hear but aware that the girl's lips were moving and so were the other kids', but totally unaware of what they were saying. I was too engrossed in my own pain. I never threw a single punch. Eventually, Stanley led me upstairs. From that day forward, I did not go outside to play often. When I did I stayed in the courtyard, in hollering distance of our kitchen window. Mostly I remained upstairs, reading. My mother, the librarian, was happy, interpreting this as an intellectual breakthrough. I did not tell her that I was figuring out how to use words as offensive and defensive weapons.

Twenty-five years later, I find Juan Williams in his office.

"Did you really tell Jay not to publish my piece on Alton Maddox?" I demand.

"Yes." He looks uncomfortable.

"Why?"

"I was trying to help you."

"Help me? Help me? Juan, how were you trying to help me?"

"I don't think it's a good piece. I think it's one-sided. I think it's a disservice to you to publish it."

"Are you serious?"

"Yes. I think it's a mistake."

"Who cares what you think? You're not the editor of the magazine."

"No, but I've been at the *Post* longer than you or Jay. I know how this place works," he says pompously. You sure do, you vicious, competitive, Uncle Neocon son of a bitch.

"You should mind your own fucking business."

"I was trying to help."

I can't believe that this creep who just tried to dick me out of my first cover story is pretending he did so out of concern for my reputation. I lean in on him, get in his space and face, just like the tough girl did on me. "Listen, Juan, don't fuck with me. You know, you're worse than a Negro who carries white folks' water for them, because your own water is dirtier than theirs could ever be. Don't get into my business again. Because if you fuck with me, I'll destroy you."

I leave him standing in the middle of his office, stunned. I imagine the expression on his face is identical to the one on mine after that punch, twenty-five years ago. I hope his head aches, too.

CHAPTER FIFTEEN

In the end, the Maddox piece is a cover story, but the office politics surrounding it leave a bitter taste in my mouth. I don't think I say more than twenty words to Juan Williams the rest of the time I'm at the *Post*. In less than a year I've cashed in a management chit, confronted two coworkers, and feel as though I've become increasingly isolated.

Even though things are very strange at the job, or maybe because they are, in the spring of 1987 I decide to have a party. I'm beginning to suspect that I'll never fit in at the *Post*, so I set my sights on making friends, meeting men, and joining the social whirl.

The stress of moving, the magazine debacle, and adapting to the workplace have come to define me. During the year I've been in D.C. I've made a few friends, and met a few more potential friends, but neglected to make the time to nurture them. A party seems like a good means to let people know I'm here and doing all right.

But it is too simple, too boring, too un-Nelsons-of-the-Grand-Gesture-like, to have a mere cocktail or dinner party, those old Washington staples. Because I've always wanted to be a producer, and now have a spacious deck and a huge yard, I decide to give a play. A revue, to be exact, titled "The Best of Okra Beenfried," in which journalists I know will perform satirical skits lampooning current events under the watchful eye of my slightly fictional talk show host, Okra Beenfried.

I enlist my neighbor, *Post* columnist Bill Raspberry, to help write the script, and then start casting, a process that has less to do with talent than with who I like, who sort of looks the part, and who is a silly enough grown-up to participate. Raspberry and I write funny lyrics to old songs for the different characters: the two Russian women who seduced Marines Bracy and Lonetree in Moscow; Marion Barry; Gary Hart; Effi

Barry, Lee Hart, and Alice Bond, a trio of wronged political wives; a tele-vangelist; Imelda Marcos, Cory Aquino, and various others. Initially, the only definite casting decision is that George Curry of the *Chicago Tribune* will play Jesse Jackson. After covering our favorite presidential candidate for years, Curry can damn near out-Jesse Jesse.

Halfway through, I realize there's no one to play Okra.

"What about Okra? She holds the whole show together," I whine to Ras' one evening during script revisions.

Raspberry looks thoughtful. Then a sly smile creeps across his impish face. "Do you know Daisy Voigt?" he asks.

Not only have I met Daisy, but she's the perfect Okra: jazzy, talkative, and doesn't mind making a fool of herself. She shows up in an Oprah wig, a red suit *avec* shoulder shawl, and a cordless mike she flips insouciantly.

Fred Brown, a news aide at the *Post*, is choreographer and codirector. Because we are all journalists first and actors last, rehearsals are truncat-ed and haphazard. James McBride and Craig Herndon, my musicians, appear only for the dress rehearsal. Erich Berg, Daisy's son, arrives with huge lighting rigs the morning of the party. The night before, we barbe-cue tons of chicken in the dark, make vats of rum punch. My friend Sandee Gregg arrives with a huge pasta salad.

Misu, who for this first year in D.C. has been attending the very small, very private, very expensive Field School, where she makes terrible grades and seems chronically depressed, actually gets kind of excited by the play, and even starts talking to me again, a little. We've both been so busy being culture-shocked, trying to fit in, and putting on a happy face to welcome our bourgeois ascendancy that we've neglected our first relationship, with each other.

"Why are you having a play?" she asks one night.

I shrug. "No real reason. It just seemed like fun."

She pauses. I sense this isn't what she really wants to talk about. Then she springs it on me.

"I want to go to public school next year."

"Why? You don't like the Field School?" It seemed like the perfect school to me—or perhaps, *for* me.

"I hate it. The kids wear boxer shorts to school and safety pins in their ears. I feel like I'm not crazy enough, so they're trying to make *me* crazy so

I'll fit in. It's a school for disturbed children. Is that why you sent me there?"

I look over at Misu. She looks lonely, sad, almost scared. It's funny how you try to do what's best for your kid, then get so preoccupied with your own shit that you hardly notice it's not working.

"Do I have to go there next year?"

"No. Where do you want to go?"

"Woodrow Wilson."

"Remember Debbie, from the magazine? Her husband's a coach there. I'll talk to her tomorrow. Okay?" I say.

"All right, Mom!" Misu says, and grins. She spends the rest of the evening telling me outrageously funny stories about the current state of progressive education as we finish the party preparations. Listening reminds me how long it's been since I've really heard her.

At the last minute I invite Jay Lovinger to the party, in the hopes that he'll have a good time, think the play's brilliant, and realize that I'm a talented, funny, easy person, not a scary, threatening, difficult one. Even if he doesn't show, I'm looking forward to having a good time giving my social life a boost. Daisy scoffs at this notion. "Are you kidding? They'll come, eat your food, drink your liquor, and you'll be lucky if you get more than one thank-you note. Forget about the invitations."

Miraculously, on Saturday, June 6, the rain holds off, the cicadas lower the decibel level of their incessant droning. The ham in every serious journalist on stage takes over; the play is a smash. Then, having eaten, drunk, and enjoyed the entertainment, half the people rush home after the final sketch, even though James Brown is blaring and the real New York party is about to start. Lovinger approaches me on the way to his car, looking dazed. "Wow. I can't believe it. I can't believe it," he murmurs, shaking his head.

I guess he can't, because my play doesn't signal the dawning of a new day at work. True to Daisy's word, I receive two thank-you notes and no invites. I manage to resist making the play an annual event.

CHAPTER SIXTEEN

In August of 1987, Misu and I fly to Miami for the annual convention of the National Association of Black Journalists. There we meet up with my filmmaker brother Stanley, who is going to show his documentary on Madam C.J. Walker, *Two Dollars and a Dream*, at the convention.

I'm not particular about going. Miami in August isn't on my preferred list, and since I don't meet the *Post* criteria for subsidy—being neither an awards finalist nor an editor/recruiter—I have to pay my own way. But I've promised Misu we'd go, and she's excited, fueled by airline advertisements and "Miami Vice" reruns into thinking Miami's the place to be.

Before we leave, my friend Morris Thompson, a reporter on the national staff who once worked for the *Miami Herald*, says, "Do you know the secret to coping with Miami in the summertime? Tepid showers." He whispers, as though confiding classified info. "Not cold, not hot, tepid. That way, you won't start sweating the moment you leave the bathroom." He then launches into a lengthy, arcane, overly detailed explanation of why this works, complete with scientific jargon, anecdotes about people I've never met, literary quotes, and various and sundry tangential information. Morris always talks like this, but I don't let him lose me. Usually his information is good. I hold on and repeat "tepid, tepid, tepid" as he babbles.

It doesn't work. Tepid showers or not, Miami is hell: too hot, overbuilt, overrun by bleached blondes who look like white folks until they open their mouths and start speaking Spanish. Refugees from the evil regime of Fidel Castro, Miami's Cuban citizens not only look like caucasians, they act like them, too, at least when it comes to black folks. Once again, I yearn for New York's Puerto Ricans, most of whom, even if they're not always down with us Negritos, know damn well they ain't white folks.

Miami mainly consists of a labyrinthine airport that even Theseus would have a hard time finding his way out of, and hotels. Hundreds, maybe thousands of hotels. The more recently constructed ones are monstrous, towering, multi-room structures of steel and glass whose major function—aside from housing hordes of drunken convention-eers—is adding to the global warming effect by refracting and multiply-ing Miami's already stifling heat and light to meltdown proportions.

The city's only saving grace is South Miami Beach, a strip of small, old, art deco hotels replete with odd architectural ornamentation and painted in lush tropical colors. By contrast, the Fountainbleu, where we spend a day on the beach, is a sprawling horror, hotel hell at its worst. The best thing about it is the *trompe l'oeil* mural we see when we first drive up to it from the south. The refreshing look of the ocean here is also an optical illusion. The water is salty, full of seaweed, and tepid. Maybe God's taking Morris' advice, too.

The NABJ convention is packed. It is old home week for old black journalists, make-contact-and-impressions week for the younger set, make-hay week for just about everyone. As Jimmy Borders, an ex-lover and friend from New Orleans cautions me, "Be in your room, with the door locked, by midnight. That's when they trawl the halls, looking for strays." More good advice.

The vortex of the convention is the hotel bar, situated in the middle of the lobby. Is it that all hotels built in the last twenty years have enormous, open-air lobby bars, or does the NABJ board of directors search out one thusly appointed? Dare I ask someone?

At NABJ conventions, the lobby bar becomes a gigantic, almost all-black newsroom, the happening corner of all our teenage memories, a modern-day facsimile of the African village square we all yearn for, or think we ought to. If you're looking for someone, don't bother to ring their room or attend workshops. Just take a seat at the bar and wait. They'll find you. If they don't, dozens of other journalists you know, would like to know, or are trying to avoid, will.

If you're over thirty and have a reasonably good job in a decent city (i.e., one with a sizable black population), you'll likely spend most of your time in the bar, at the major luncheons and dinners, or sightseeing. If you're over thirty and a heavy hitter, i.e. you work for a big white estab-lishment outfit like the *Times* (L.A. or New York), the *Post*, or any newspaper in New York or Atlanta, you might be invited to participate on a panel, at which time you can pontificate, blow your own horn, and if you'd like, actually impart some useful information. It may well be the one and only time you see the inside of a workshop.

If you are a *real* heavy hitter—read, on the board of directors, winner of a big prize (preferably the Pulitzer or any other given by caucasians), or an excellent bid whist player—you will be invited to hang out in the Presidential Suite with the other NABJ bigwigs and strategize, drink liquor, and gossip. If you are under thirty, female, fine, and preferably have long hair and reasonably light skin, you may be invited to accompany one of these aging sluggers to the Presidential Suite. Heavy hitters are too heavy to trawl the halls for strays.

If you're thirty or less, live and work in the media equivalent of Death Valley, and are looking for a job, you will spend much less time at the bar and most of it, when you're not attending workshops hoping to learn something or meet someone useful, at the Job Fair, the corporate slave market of the last days of the twentieth century.

Held in one of the hotel's ballrooms, the Job Fair consists of dozens of curtained booths in which recruiters and editors from newspapers lie in wait for eager beavers. These unfortunates stroll through the room in suitable corporate garb, resumes and neatly xeroxed clips in hand, until they identify their preferred media outlet and set up an interview.

Once seated, they sit nervously as their clips are perused, hoping to pass the muster of some person they likely know absolutely nothing about except that they work somewhere they'd like to work, even though they have no idea what working there is like. The interviewer, as often as not, is a caucasian male who is incompetent but well-liked at the home office, and thus has been given the unimportant and insincere job of minority recruiting as his bailiwick.

The poor young journalists sit hopefully, when likely as not there isn't any hope. A smooth interviewer will allow them to ask a few questions, strut a little of their stuff, before giving them the standard fuck-off line, which goes something like, "I see some good work here, some good work, but I think you need time to sharpen your skills, work on your reporting. The _____ (fill in the blank) is a very competitive place. We're looking for seasoned journalists who can hit the ground running.

You're young, give it some more time. But stay in touch. Let me see what you're doing in a few years."

What they're really thinking is probably more like, "Jesus. I can't stand much more of sitting here and reading these clips. I can't wait until my relief comes and I can go to my room—not that circus of a bar—and have a drink. What a damn waste of time this is. We're not going to hire any of these people unless Bob Woodward in blackface and a short dress shows up, and maybe not even then. Why am I here wasting my time? Oh yeah, because the black caucus at the paper made a stink about us not having enough minority staffers. Pacification of the natives, ha ha ha. Well, that's affirmative action." Being there is enough. Allah forbid they actually have to hire someone.

The Miami convention is the third I've attended. As always, I feel spaced out here. In general, conventions aren't my thing, although I can see myself getting into a conclave of diehard James Brown, Bob Marley, or Thelonius Monk fans, especially if on the last night there was a jammin' concert, instead of an interminable dinner featuring either freeze-dried chicken or beef jerky passing as prime rib.

I don't feel particularly comfortable hanging out with hundreds of Negro journalists, either, since I see myself not as a media person but as something or someone else—I'm not sure what—who stumbled into newspaper reporting for reasons that are either all wrong or embarrassingly naive.

Anyway, my idea of a good time doesn't include telling reportorial war stories, playing Negro Geography and finding out how horrifyingly small the world—and the people in it—really can be, or swarming around with my accidental colleagues in paroxysms of preening self-congratulation and envy for four days.

In some ways the NABJ convention is like a mass psychotic episode, in which over a thousand African-Americans meet annually to purge our collective repressed rage and to affirm one another's visibility. It's like an Alcoholics Anonymous for black journalists, at which we can share the worst about ourselves, the lives we live, the work we do, without fear of professional retribution. At its heart, underneath the bullshit, gossip, liquor and politics, it's a collective primal scream, a huge release from the rigors of working in corporate America.

Most people arrive a bit crazy and leave slightly saner. Sometimes, good advice is given, strategies evolved, alternatives realized in the struggle to maintain, to excel, or just to survive our workplaces. Usually, one leaves feeling less alone, less persecuted, less personally affronted by the rigors of daily racism. If nothing else, misery does love company.

The good part is that it's nice to see those people I do like and respect all in one place—but that's *all* we do, is see each other. There's barely an empty space, a quiet sober moment, to actually talk. Mostly, it's sightings, hugs, squeals, quick catch-ups, promises to hook up later, and then, *nada*. For the price of the airfare, hotel, and meals, it'd be cheaper to call up the twenty people I actually have something to say to and talk to them for ten hours each.

Because we're electing new officers this year, the Miami convention takes the usual horror and frenzy and multiplies it to the tenth power. In addition, the Miami chapter is obsessed, out to prove that in spite of the heat, hostile Cubans, and exorbitant prices, Miami, No Problem. There are so many planned activities I feel like I'm in an expensive private kindergarten for gifted children, except there's no story hour, no nap time, no milk and cookies. No damn peace and quiet.

A bad situation is made even worse by the impending election, to be held on the third day. You'd think these people were running for president of the U.S.A.—or at least an office that pays—with their buttons, slogans, campaign literature, and endless stalking of votes.

DeWayne Wickham is running against Robert Tutman, a cameraman with CBS in Chicago. Tall, bald, with sharp, glittering black eyes, a pointy beard, and a big mouth, Tutman seems truly disgusted by the orgy of consumption that characterizes NABJ conventions, where one luncheon can cost $100,000—underwritten by Massa, of course—and total scholarships to student journalists amount to $24,814 this year. Tutman's best line is, "We don't need to have these lavish banquets, we're journalists. I can afford to pay for my own damn lunch. We need to eat chicken out of brown paper bags and give these young people the money." I'm sure the food would be better, too.

Word on Tutman is that he can't win. He's a maverick, outspokenly critical of the organization. He does not get invited to the Presidential Suite to play cards. He challenges his colleagues' complacent assumptions about the world of journalism. Tutman seems to make many NABJers uncomfortable. He has a good time, laughs loud, doesn't, as a

Wickham supporter confides to me, "act presidential." That's the type of thought process that emerges when black folks get media jobs, Burberry trenchcoats, and cover the White House.

Wickham, who has a public affairs television show in Baltimore and writes a syndicated column for Gannett newspapers, is light, clean, slightly sleazy around the edges. He's always been nice to me, but I suspect it's more because he thinks I might be useful than from any feelings of affection. Emotionally, I'm a Tutman supporter, but pragmatically, the smart money's on Wickham.

Let's face it, this is a conservative organization, heavily populated by wannabees. If Malcolm X rose from the grave and ran against Wickham, he'd lose. Robert Tutman doesn't stand a chance.

If I want to go with the smart money, I'll vote for Wickham. It's the old American trade-off, your integrity for victory, even though once you've made that deal, there's nothing you can be but a loser.

Misu, Stanley, and I get up at five the morning after we arrive to go on a day-long marathon cruise from Miami to Nassau and back. Not only does the boat sound luxurious, complete with casinos, gamerooms, pools, staterooms, numerous bars, and breakfast, lunch, and dinner buffets, but Stanley's film is going to be shown on board, to a captive audience. We rush out of our room, forgetting essentials like suntan oil, towels, and a hairbrush, but we make it. Once we pull away from shore there's a breeze. On the water I find a chaise longue, close my eyes and ears, and pretend I'm on the Vineyard.

This doesn't last long, since the Good Ship Lollipop is swarming with journalists. Misu decides she wants to go in the water, so we pull chairs up to the balcony next to the pool. But it isn't a pool, it's like a twenty-by-fifteen-foot pond infested with paddling, splashing, phlegm-spitting African-Americans. It's too small for swimming and besides, no one wants to get their hair wet. "Going in?" I ask Misu.

She gives me a look of total snobbery. "Would you?"

"No way." We laugh.

"Ugh, gross. You can see that man's jock strap," she says, pointing. Fourteen, she is into aesthetics. Whale-like, one of my esteemed colleagues crosses the pond in two manly strokes, jock visible between folds of flab.

"Man, look at those butts!" my brother interjects. I follow Stanley's eyes downward to a trio of sisters in black, metallicized suits, lying on their stomachs.

"Attractive," I say.

Stanley laughs. "Their butts are so big they could carry a tray of food."

"You're disgusting."

"They can carry my food anytime," Stanley laughs, lasciviously licking his lips.

"Mom. Can I have some money for video games?"

By noon the sun is beating down and the surface of the pool is covered with oil and what Misu calls "loogies," i.e. phlegm globs, and, presumably, diluted by piss. The Butt Sisters, as Stanley dubs them, have made their third bathing suit change of the morning and are snoring softly. The heat has driven most of the people off the decks: the lucky heavy hitters into staterooms, the unlucky masses into any corner of shade they can find.

Misu has discovered the casino and is compulsively feeding my money into slots. My brother is prowling the ship, simultaneously scoping the women and promoting *Two Dollars and a Dream*. Me, I'm sitting on deck burning. Not from the sun but from anger at a brief exchange with an asshole recruiter from *Newsday* who approaches me, initiates a conversation, and then says that he's "heard I made a lot of trouble at the *Washington Post* magazine."

"Not really," I snap. "Jay Lovinger made problems for himself." Shortly thereafter, he oozes away. Since the premier-issue disaster, things at the magazine have only gone downhill. The general consensus seems to be that the magazine is boring, untimely, and obscure. Advertising pages are well below expectations. There's a constant rumor going around that we're losing millions, may fold at any moment.

Between the sun and my temper, I'm boiling. On the way to the bar to get a cool drink I run into DeWayne Wickham, presidential candidate. We greet each other cordially, hug, kiss air.

"So. Jill. Can I count on your vote?"

"I don't know."

"Why not?"

"Wickham, I see all these people running around with buttons, campaign literature, I haven't gotten anything," I joke. "You have to work for my vote."

He gives me a look of exaggerated exhaustion. "Jill, if I had to lick the pussy of every woman in NABJ to get their vote, my tongue would be dry before I got halfway through," he says. And then he laughs. LAUGHS!

Me, I just stand there, half-drunk from the sun, the rum, righteous indignation, not believing my ears. Wickham grins naughtily, like a little boy who's just told a dirty joke to his enamored parents. Before I can recover and rip his balls off with my bare hands, he spies other potential votes and moves away.

Remember that song, "Nassau is Funky"? Well, I think the writers meant that as dirty, not hip. If they didn't, they should have. The beaches are flat, the sand is more like gravel, the water is perfect Morris Thompson tepid, and the souvenirs are crappy. By the time we get back on the boat for the return to Miami, Misu and I are tired, dirty, and crabby. Stanley, as usual, is perfectly mellow.

It's amazing that as close as we are we're so different. My brother hardly ever gets irritable, uptight, impatient—emotions I am often either having or on the verge of having. He seems unperturbed by the heat, the lack of ambiance, the drunk, half-clothed journalists surrounding us. In fact, he is amused.

I used to think my brother's ability to groove on whatever scene he's in came from doing drugs, but he's been sober for years now and hasn't changed. My mother tells a story of finding us at five and six on the living room floor, me sitting on top of Stanley holding a frying pan in one hand, presumably about to bash his brains out. "I'll never forget it," she says in wonderment. "You were mad as hell about something, and he wasn't even screaming." That night I fall into bed sweating and have a series of disjointed, scary dreams involving boats, oral sex, and being hooked by sinister deep-sea fishermen. The next day, I tell Mary Ann French, who works in the D.C. office of the *St. Petersburg Times*, and Marcia Slacum Greene, a Metro reporter at the *Post*, what Wickham said. Both are smart, take-no-shit, self-possessed sisters. They are appalled, insulted, and want to take action. Me, I'm so cynical, it's like I'm more just grossed-out and apathetically disgusted. Since I never expected much of anything from DeWayne Wickham, I'm not surprised that he's said something dumb, crude, and misogynistic. It'll be no sweat for me never to speak to him again and to vote for Robert Tutman.

But after talking with Mary Ann and Marcia, I realize that Wickham's insult wasn't just to me, it was to all of us women, who make up the majority of NABJ members. If I don't confront Wickham in some way, he'll go on thinking that what he said was okay, or even appropriate. As Marcia says, "He'll probably be elected president in a few days, and he needs to know that if that's his attitude toward the women in this organization, it's not appropriate." The three of us decide to pull together a women's delegation and privately confront him.

In 1987, its twelfth year of existence, there had never been a woman president of the National Association of Black Journalists. In 1989, Ruth Allen Ollison of WTTG-TV in Washington will run against *New York Times* reporter Tom Morgan and lose. She makes one fatal mistake: she doesn't bother to attend more than a few meetings of the organization's local affiliate. Just as much damage, however, results from some of the heavy hitters who support her starting a homophobic whisper campaign against her opponent.

So me, Mary Ann, Marcia, Gwen Ifill, Sandee Gregg, Michelle McQueen (all reporters at the *Post*), Peggy Peterman from the *St. Petersburg Times*, and maybe a few other women, assemble in Wickham's suite. He's there with *Newsday* columnist/national editor Les Payne, although none of us can figure out why. Maybe Les sees it as a free speech issue. I'll never know, because he doesn't say anything, just stands there glaring at the women in the room. It's like a scene out of *West Side Story* when the Sharks and the Jets face-off pre-rumble and try to stare each other down. I guess he's there as Wickham's "boy."

One of the women recounts the "If I had to lick the pussy of every woman in this organization" comment and asks Wickham if he said it. He waffles but doesn't deny it, then tries to play it off by saying, "Jill and I have that kind of friendship, we can talk to each other like that."

"No, we don't. I don't have that kind of relationship with my man," I say.

"We joke around like that all the time."

"No, we don't."

I contemplate leaping from my seat and strangling him. I feel like a victim of attempted rape being asked by the defense, "Isn't it true you were wearing hot pants on the day you were allegedly attacked?" To which I would answer, "Yes, but only because, like James Brown says, they make me sure of myself, not because I wanted to be assaulted." Same old blame-the-victim bullshit.

Before the conversation deteriorates into "No we don't, yes we do, no we don't," somebody cuts to the chase, asking Wickham if he realizes now that the comment was offensive. A few other sisters join in with their feelings, all supportive. Several mention the upcoming election and the impact publicizing his remark could have. I swear, black women can be the baddest humans on earth!

"Yes," he finally says, and puts on a recalcitrant face. Then he looks at me. "Jill, if I've offended you, I'm sorry. Do you accept my apology?"

"Okay." I have seen the future and it does not include spending eight to life behind bars for killing this idiot in front of ten witnesses. It does include getting the hell away from Wickham and Payne as fast as humanly possible, and getting around a nice cold Stoli.

Les Payne never says a word, just stands and glares, but the symbolism is enough. The coercive nature of his silent presence—*Newsday* national editor, Pulitzer prize winner, past NABJ president, journalistic icon—is obvious to me. The old boys network in blackface.

The rest of the convention passes in an unhappy blur. I run into Wickham by the lobby bar and he insists on publicly hugging me—a cheap photo op, but I'm too tired to hold a grudge. Later I hear that he's still insisting that we "have that kind of relationship," and that I laughed when he said it.

Wickham is elected president by the largest margin of victory ever. I vote for Tutman, who gets more votes than expected.

Things go from bad to worse. I smoke too much, drink too much, and repeat an insensitive comment of someone else's to Mary Ann. We fall out. Two of my other friends, Betty Baye of the *Louisville Courier-Journal*, with whom I went to "J" school in 1980 and been tight with ever since, and Audrey Edwards, my editor at *Essence* for years, apparently believe Wickham's version of events, so I stop talking to them, too. Misu gets a cold. Stanley continues to drift around, looking unperturbed.

When I finally escape Miami I feel as if I've been at the four-day-long funeral of someone I never even liked. It is the last NABJ convention I attend.

CHAPTER SEVENTEEN

When I got to the *Post* in 1986, I'd have described myself as a recreational drinker, but by the time I've been there two years, I'd say I am alcoholic, or damn near.

It takes a long time for me to figure this out and admit it to myself. I don't drink at lunch, during the day, before dark. When I do drink, I'm not sloppy or loud, can remember the night before the morning after. But I always know the exact level of liquid relief left in the Stoli bottle, and I always have Stoli, the hard stuff. This is a big change for someone who's mostly been into reefer and an occasional bottle of wine with friends.

The thing that I find so seductive about liquor is that it's legal, and thus subject to quality control. Unlike smoke or dope, you don't have to risk arrest, go into sleazy neighborhoods, deal with a criminal element, or become part of the criminal element to get a drink. You also always get what you pay for. When you twist the cap and break the paper on a bottle of vodka, that's what you get, vodka. It's not like reefer, where you may get what Judyie calls "ghetto reefer," funny-colored grass filled with tiny stones and clumps of dirt that gives you a headache, not a high, when you smoke it. Or coke, where you could find yourself sniffing pure D lactose or quinine. No matter what street, city, or country you cop alcohol in, it always tastes the same, delivers the expected result. Plus, damn near everyone drinks *something*. So, unless you're drooling, drunkenly lascivious, or passed out, no one ever has to know that you've had too much, that you're an alcoholic—not even you.

For me, alcohol is the last drug until no drugs, the final frontier in an odyssey of abusing myself with various and sundry mood- and mind-altering substances that began when I was twelve. By the time I finally quit drinking after three years in D.C., I know life is a bitch. Then I get sober and realize life is a son of a bitch without blurred edges.

I am sitting cross-legged on my bed in the room my sister and I share, watching her unpack her bags. It is late summer of 1966. I am fourteen, my sister is seventeen.

"What was Mexico like?"

"Fantastic. Beautiful. Ellie and I had a ball."

"Doing what? What'd you do?"

My sister Lynn looks at me with a mixture of compassion, pity, and dismissal. "Sis, you wouldn't understand," she says. Then she laughs.

"So, is it true you weren't going to come back?"

She laughs. "Who told you that?"

"No one. I heard Mom and Dad talking about it one night."

"What'd they say?"

"That they hadn't heard from you in weeks, couldn't reach you, and that one of them might have to fly down to Mexico and find you."

"Oh, God, I'm glad they didn't," my sister groans with relief.

"Where were you? What were you doing? Were you really never coming back?"

"I never know if I'm coming back," Lynn says cryptically.

She looks older, smarter, more womanly since she left three months ago, and I don't think it's from studying Spanish at the University of Mexico City, the reason she and her best friend, Ellie Preston, went to Mexico in the first place. Normally pale, with a kind of sallow complexion, Lynn's skin is dark brown and glowing. She wears an embroidered cotton blouse, loose skirt, huaraches, dangling silver earrings. She looks exotic, sensuous, off-beat. The Haight-Ashbury scene is just starting to happen, "hippie" is a new word in America's vocabulary, free love an approaching grinding on the horizon. To me, my sister represents the vanguard of all the change, excitement, freedom that is to come. Why won't she share?

"Tell me about it, tell me." I know I am starting to whine, but my desire to know has overrun voice control.

"Cool out. I brought you something." My sister digs into a gigantic multi-colored woven bag she bought in Mexico, then turns around, clutching a small brown packet. "Little Sis, have you ever smoked marijuana?" she asks, and begins rolling a joint.

"Uh . . . no."

"Wanna try it?"

"Yeah, sure."

"Okay. Open the windows, and just don't get crazy."

I walk over to the windows, yank them up, lean out. I look down eleven floors onto 82nd Street and West End Avenue. There are lots of people on the street, going along with business as usual. I want to scream down at them, "I'm about to smoke marijuana for the first time in my life with my sister who just got back from Mexico a few hours ago and she's going to turn me on. *Me!* Isn't that wonderful?" I feel that Lynn and me, whose relationship often centers around the loathing, idolatry, and casual disdain that frequently characterizes interaction between sisters, are about to make some cosmic breakthrough, smoke the peace pipe, bond. Once we smoke a spliff, my sister will no longer tease me for being chubby, ignore me, have sole control of the ambiance of the room we share. This is the sister I want to be like, want to like me. Once we smoke marijuana together, will Lynn cease terminating what to me are cozy bedtime conversations by saying, "Please don't talk to me when the light is out," then clicking off her night table lamp, turning her back, and going to sleep?

Excited as I am, I'm a little scared too, since I don't know what to expect. Unlike nowadays, drugs hardly conjure up a notion, they are so obscure, both in my world and the larger one. What little sense I do have of them is associated with California, bright clothing, and happy-looking people. It is a long way to the 1980s and crack, brains that look like burnt fried eggs, septum replacement operations, the Betty Ford clinic, and being clean and sober as an option for anyone except squares.

"Okay. Here's the joint." My sister holds a bomb-shaped cigarette, fatter at the center than the ends, in her hand. "Are you sure you've never done this before?"

"Yeah."

"Okay, here's what you do. Inhale as much smoke as you can into your lungs and just hold it there. Don't breathe! When you can't hold it any longer, blow it out the window. Out the window! Not into the room or it'll stink up everything and Mom will come in and bust us."

"Uh . . . Okay."

"Are you ready, Sis?" *Sis!* This could be the start of something big. Lynn's getting downright chummy.

"Ready." Lynn strikes a match and holds it to the joint. The end starts flaming. She casually waves the fire out, puts it in her mouth and inhales. The tip burns fast, crackling. She takes it from her lips and hands it to me. In the tight, squeaky voice that comes from trying to talk without letting any smoke out, Lynn says, "Take as much as you can and hold it in."

Awkwardly, I seize the joint, holding it between thumb and forefinger. Billows of pungent marijuana smoke cloud the immediate area. "Smoke it! Smoke it! You're wasting," my sister wheezes from constricted lungs.

I put the joint in my mouth and inhale. My lungs immediately itch, burn, explode. I cough out a cloud of smoke, can't stop coughing. I'm convulsing so violently I expect one of my lungs to come flying out of my mouth.

"Gimme that." She snatches the joint, sticks her head out the window, exhales a cloud of Acapulco Gold over West End Avenue. I have finally stopped coughing, although I suspect my lungs are permanently damaged. This time I take in less smoke and manage not to cough it back into the room. Instead, I heave internally, sputter but do not expel—dry heaves with smoke.

"Okay, okay, breathe. Blow the smoke out or you'll suffocate."

We stand by the window repeating this action until the joint becomes a roach, which my sister neatly extinguishes and puts in a small wooden box.

"Do you feel anything? Do you feel it?"

"I don't know," I say, plopping down on my bed. "My chest hurts."

"I mean, do you feel high?" she snaps.

"I don't . . . " Then it hits me. I can't finish my sentence because the connection between my brain and lips has been severed. Words simply do not form. Before this bothers me, I notice that my sister is glowing and vibrating slightly. I look around the room and everything is shiny, bright, vivid, trembling. I catch my reflection in the mirror that covers most of the wall of our room. My face looks different, radiant, more alive. I can distinguish first each pore, then every cell, the millions and billions of elements that, together, make up my face. I am mesmerized by my face but then get lost in the air between myself and the mirror. I can see each and every particle that forms the air before me. It comes to me in a flash of brilliance, word and color, that air isn't really see-through, it's a zillion dancing, silvery particles that, when bonded together in the earth's atmosphere, appear visible. Wow.

"Jill! Are you okay? Are you high? Do you feel it?"

I open my mouth to tell my sister what I see and feel. But when I start talking I sound like a 45 record played at 33 RPMs. Like, "Arrrrrrgggggg faaaaaaarrrrrggghhhhh dargggggggghhhhhhh." But it's okay, in fact, it's hilarious. I fall back on my bed laughing hysterically and contemplate the ceiling. Deep.

My sister walks over and peers down at me. "You're stoned," she smiles and shakes her head. "Stoned. Stoned. Stoned," echoes in my brain, a mantra for the next two decades.

"Lynn. Jill." It is my mother's voice calling us. She sounds as if she's on another planet. Maybe she is.

"Are you in your room?" Her voice sounds like Jimi Hendrix on a wah-wah pedal, the aural equivalent of the difference between WAH and wah. She's getting nearer.

"Oh no. Don't let her come in. She's going to know what we did," I try to say to my sister, but like everything else it comes out "Ooooooohhhhhh nooooooaaaaarrrrggggg, daaaarrrrggggghhhhhhh," etcetera. Or maybe my ears just hear it like that, because Lynn says, "Just lie there, be cool, and don't say anything. I'll do the talking," For some reason, I start laughing. "And don't lie there cackling like you're insane!" I stop.

The door to the room opens and there's Mommy, all five foot three of her, a load of clean laundry in her arms. She stands there and surveys the room and the two of us. Twin beds with matching orange spreads, twin night tables, lamps, dressers, desks, even twin windows with flowered cafe curtains on a deep orange background. The door to our bathroom is closed. Her eyes sweep past it, back to my sister and me.

"What are you two doing?"

"Nothing. I'm unpacking and telling Jill about Mexico," Lynn says smoothly.

"Well, we'd all like to hear about your trip," our mother says.

"I know. But I was saving it until dinner, when Dad's home, so I won't have to tell everything twice," my sister says politely yet forcefully. Our mother's gaze swings to me lying on the bed.

"Do you feel all right?"

"She's fine," my sister says hurriedly.

"Why are you lying down in the middle of the afternoon?"

"She's tired." I just lie there in the midst of panic and euphoria, observing their interaction as though it's a movie with subtitles.

"Maybe I'd better feel your forehead." My mother advances toward me, hand outstretched. Lynn moves fluidly between us.

"She's all right, Mom. Don't treat her like such a baby. Lemme finish unpacking and I'll come into the kitchen and talk while you're fixing dinner."

My mother, responsible for four children, a housekeeper, a demanding husband, and last, but not least, herself, leaves the room, back on schedule, doubtless relieved that the disruption of illness has been avoided. My sister rolls her eyes, exhales in relief. I burst out laughing. I don't remember much else besides feeling weirdly fabulous and waking up the next morning with a mouth that feels like it's stuffed with king-sized cotton balls, and the desire to try another joint.

Unfortunately, after the high wore off, so did my hopes for a new intimacy with Lynn. We went right back to our usual rivalries, teasings, competitions. Occasionally we were allies, but only when it was mutually beneficial. The fact that my big sister had initiated me into the world of drugs didn't permanently alter our relationship, although it did start me down the road of experimentation, use, and abuse.

Years later, after I have taken just about every illegal drug you can smoke, drop, swallow, or sniff and then became stone-cold sober, I think about the television ads I used to laugh at, me and my stoned friends. The gist of these early antidrug messages was, don't smoke marijuana, it leads to harder drugs. Back then I found this message ridiculous, just another scare tactic from the people who brought us Vietnam, Watergate, the assassination of Fred Hampton.

Two decades older, sober and with a teenage daughter, I finally admit there's a lot of truth to that statement. But it's not that the evil drugs suck you in; it's that you become a drug vacuum cleaner because the only possible way you figure you can deal with reality is in an altered state. Like the Matt Dillon character says at the end of *Drugstore Cowboy*, the thing about doing drugs is that you always know how you're going to feel based on what you take. The straight life is too unpredictable.

So if you like to get high off reefer, at the very least you're going to be curious about other mood-altering drugs. Likely, you're gonna try them. If you're hardheaded, like I was, like teenagers often are, you're going to keep on trying them until you get off. Even if your nose burns, you vomit, have to watch your face melting into that of a monster before the pretty pictures kick in, or worse.

CHAPTER EIGHTEEN

Everything went wrong three years later, at least partially because of drugs, but I continued to turn to drugs to help me cope, ignore the pain. It took me twenty more years to figure out that alcohol and drugs don't ease the pain, they just repress and compound it.

It is August, 1969. Lynn and I are standing at the bus stop on 56th Street and Sixth Avenue, right in front of the Fred Braun shoe store. My sister has just come from another unsuccessful job interview; I am on my way home from my summer gig as a receptionist at the musicians union, Local 802. New York is hot, funky, and exciting. It is my first summer working full-time, left alone by my mother, who will be on the Vineyard until after Labor Day. It is also the first summer after my father left us.

Word has it that my father is carrying on an affair with a tall, skinny, angular-faced Jewish woman who my mother, Indianapolis princess that she is, calls his "girl," but who is technically his dental hygienist. I don't know about the particulars, just that I've been abandoned. Since I don't see or speak to my father anymore I have no idea what he's doing, not doing, or with whom. Since the break-up, my mother, fueled by pain, rage, and Jack Daniel's, isn't exactly coherent when she talks about him. Or much else, either.

Me, I'm cool. I'm sixteen, bring home $78.00 a week, smoke reefer every day, and have a refillable prescription for dexedrine spansules right here in my pocketbook. My brother Stanley is spending the summer with a friend in Mexico, Ralph is on the Vineyard with Mom, Dad is maybe fucking his hygienist, and my sister and I have an eleven-room apartment, all expenses paid, at our disposal.

My days have taken on a sultry, drug-induced rhythm. Get up, smoke a J, take a shower, drop a dexie, go to work. The only summer hire, I am the youngest person in an office where the median age is fifty, all white women except for our supervisor, Mr. Glover, a black man somewhere between fifty and ninety.

At first I think working for the musician's union is going to be big fun. I have visions of meeting the stars, tickets to concerts, dates with my musical idols, days spent filing in an office where, instead of muzak, Cream, Aretha, and Sly and the Family Stone blare from discreetly placed speakers. The truth is, I work in a cramped, music- and muzak-less office where the dust has been around for so many seasons it's congealed into an impenetrable lacquer of funk, better than Scotchgard if you can get next to the filthy, brown-gray color. I spend 80 percent of my days refiling musician information cards that the four women who work here full-time have pulled and not bothered to replace in order to give me something to do. The other 20 percent of the day I spend running errands.

Occasionally, someone will phone in a request for a specific type of musician, like an oboe player or a five-person polka band. If it's Thursday, Mr. Glover will send me downstairs to the Roseland Ballroom, where unemployed musicians congregate for open call. Jobs are announced on a loudspeaker and whoever's interested writes down the information and scrambles for it. Initially, I thought open-call days would be exciting. They're not. Most of the musicians hanging around are mediocre, has-beens, or addicted to some mood- and talent-altering substance. Although it takes me several decades to admit it, it is at Local 802 that I begin to suspect that drugs which alter one's mood, talent, or personality usually do so for the worse. Musicians with talent are scarce around Local 802. They're either on tour, recording, or out hustling up a gig.

Other than that, most of my other errands are personal ones for Mr. Glover.

"Jill. You busy?"

"Uh, no," I say, rousing myself from that day's reefer fantasy, which involves me and my best friend Judyie floating on a cloud of marijuana smoke, inhaling from an antique hookah and eating gallons of Cool and Creamy chocolate pudding. I'm still a virgin; sex plays a very peripheral role in my fantasies.

"What do you need, Mr. Glover?"

"Could you run over to—" and here he says some word I can't quite make out, but it sounds like "Bozo's" "—and get me something?"

"Sure," I say. Inside I'm going, "Bozo's? Bojo's? Who the hell is Bojo? Maybe it's his dealer or bookie." But I don't really care, just as long as it's outside this silent, boring office.

"What I would like you to purchase for me—" Mr. Glover starts to say, but stops. Once again, his lips are stuck together. He's got that creamy, crusty, yellow stuff all built up in the corners where his lip joints are, and after a while it's like it damn near glues his lips together. Then he has to dredge up some saliva from God knows where and dig out the corners before he can speak again. It also makes it hard to understand what he's saying.

"Yes, sir?" As always, I am eager to do anything that gets me outside onto crowded Eighth Avenue and 52nd Street, pulsating with hordes of white-collar workers, construction crews, peep shows, and perverts. I can smoke a joint and observe, observe, observe while I get whatever Mr. Glover wants from Bozo's, Hodo's, or hey—maybe he's saying Bergdorf's. I know where that is.

"Run on over to Hozo's and get me a container of iced coffee. Light, three sugars."

"Sure, Mr. Glover," I say, getting up. "But, who's Hozo?"

The four women who work in the office, who have been studiously doing nothing, begin to laugh, murmur among themselves.

"What's so funny?"

"What'd she say?"

"She asked what's HoJo's."

"What's HoJo's!"

"I don't know, Mr. Glover, maybe you should just call out for your coffee. She might get lost."

"Yeah. You know, even though it takes up half the block, the prep-school girl might not be able to find it." At this, they collapse into superior, working-class giggles all over again.

Me, I stand there by the door of the small room the five of us work in, getting pissed off. But then Mr. Glover, the brother, comes to my rescue.

"Jill. It is Howard Johnson's. I want you to go across the street to Howard Johnson's and get me my iced coffee," he says slowly, softly, without contractions, enunciating clearly so that I understand him exactly.

"Oh. Okay, all right, Howard Johnson's. HoJo's. I get it," I say, stepping out the door. "It's like a nickname. I thought you said Bergdorf's," I say, trying to save face with a little elitism.

Hustling down the hall, I put my hand deep into my pocketbook, searching for the half joint left over from this morning's hit. In the process of the find-the-joint-in-the-bag archeological dig, the space underneath my nails fills up with bits of paper, shredded tobacco, stray marijuana seeds. Behind me, the voices of my office mates call, "Don't get lost and end up in Bergdorf's, college girl," and "Remember, it's HoJo's, not Bozo's." Then the door to the stairwell slams shut behind me and all I can hear is their laughter.

So, that's pretty much what I do at work. Go to HoJo's for Mr. Glover, file index cards, smoke J's. Around 4:45, I go to the bathroom, take half a dexedrine, and sit in the toilet stall until a few minutes before five, when it's time to leave. It is in the toilet stall at Local 802 on 52nd Street that I perfect smokeless, odorless smoking. This involves lighting a joint, taking a gigantic toke, filling my lungs to capacity, holding it in until I start to see black and red sparkles, that precursor to passing out, and then exhaling. Like hundreds of thousands of potheads, I delude myself into believing that using this technique absorbs most of the smoke and all of the odor de cannabis.

If the dex has punched in and I'm feeling energetic, I walk home up Broadway. Otherwise, I take the subway. Either way, I stop at the supermarket on 79th and buy a package of frozen creamed spinach and some rye bread. Besides Cool and Creamy, dexedrine, and marijuana, that's all I eat the entire summer, rye toast and creamed spinach. I'm determined to be thin when I return to school in the fall.

I spend most of my evenings with Judyie, talking and getting stoned. My sister Lynn, promised a Head Start job that never materializes, spends her days and nights hanging out with handsome, sullen, secretive men, smoking herb and tripping on acid, mescaline, psilocybin, whatever's around. Not working, she has no money. I share my rye bread and creamed spinach with her, but it is not enough. One night a man named Jon arrives with a green plastic garbage bag full of marijuana and Lynn spends the next few days putting it into slender brown envelopes, weighing them on a small scale, and counting the bags over and over again.

After that, the doorbell rings all night. People my sister knows come and go, but just as many of them simply say they know someone she knows who told them she had smoke. The bell rings so often that I stop waking up in the middle of the night and simply incorporate it into my dreams. In the morning when I leave for work, my sister is always sleeping. Sometimes, there is a man with her. They lie side by side, naked, the door to the bedroom casually left open. The elevator man takes to giving me stern, disapproving looks when I ride down on my way to Local 802. At least I think his look has changed, but maybe it's just that I'm hung over.

My father continues to ignore our telephone messages, if his girl ever gives them to him. On the Vineyard, my mother badmouths my father to her friends and alternately attempts to drown herself in either the Atlantic Ocean or another glass of whiskey. She places the obligatory call to us once a week to see how things are going. We always say fine, Lynn's about to get a job, everything's great. Sometimes, after my sister delivers her bullshit line and it's my turn, I am tempted to take the phone into another room and say, "Look, Mom, you've gotta come home, things are really weird, Lynn isn't even really looking for a job, she's got one as a drug dealer, there's people here all the time, lots of men, and things are missing, the Steuben glass owl and some of my money, it just feels like something's about to go very, very, wrong . . . "

But I never do. Because even with the shit, I'm having too good a time, and I know if I bust Lynn I'm busting myself, Judyie too, and anyway, maybe the men aren't as sinister as they seem and I simply misplaced the Steuben and the money, maybe I'm uptight because I'm too high or not high enough . . . So I never say anything to my mother but "Fine, fine, fine," and when I hang up I go smoke a joint, or go to sleep.

It's not until years later that it suddenly hits me that in our family, "fine" means everything but okay. It's just the polite, black bourgeois, Nelson way of saying mind your own or none of your business, or damned if I know, or help. But we're all so busy protecting ourselves and trying to be Numero Uno that when we hear "fine" we hear mind your own or none of your business, and leave it at that. It's like the whole family is playing some weird conservative game of blackjack in which we each stay with the two cards we're initially dealt, take no risks, and bank that someone else's hand is worse. It's like we know we can't deal with not knowing or asking for help—as the gamblers say, "Hit Me!"—so we quit while we're ahead.

Me, I'm so caught up in feelings of love-hate-envy toward my older, thinner, condescending sister, in wanting her to like me, that I trade her my silence for her tolerance. That summer, Lynn occasionally shares joints with me, is supportive of my dexedrine/creamed spinach weight-loss plan, even offers to fix me up on a date with one of her discards. Evenings when the traffic is light we sit and listen to Jimi Hendrix, smoke reefer, snort crushed tabs of psilocybin, and talk, talk, talk. Moments, days, years afterward, I cannot recollect a word we said, only that it was painfully, unutterably profound and intimate. That if I could only remember the words, all that came afterward would somehow have meaning.

"Hey, Lynn. Get up!" I am standing in the foyer of our apartment. It is as big as a room, furnished with delicate marble-topped end tables, spindly chairs covered in orange velvet, a gold love seat. Rugless, this morning the floor is covered with clumps of what looks like green moss. I rub my eyes, squint, bend over. Gingerly, I reach down and touch a clump of the green. Expecting slime, I instead get crisp. Sniffing it, I smell a familiar odor. It's not moss, but it's an herb, all right.

"*Lynn! Get up!* Wait'll you see what your crazy cat did!" I yell over my shoulder, loud enough so my voice exits the foyer, careens into the hall-way, turns left, travels thirty feet to my sister's door, and, I hope, pene-trates. I go into the kitchen, get a glass of water, take my morning dex, put on water for coffee, and sink down at the table in the breakfast nook my mother has papered with orange and yellow flowers. I sit there, staring at nothing, until somewhere deep within my body those spansules begin to expand, explode, race each other through my bloodstream toward my brain. Suddenly, the speed hits home and I'm like a cartoon character hit over the head with some heavy shit. My whole body goes BOY YEUNG! and I'm ready for anything.

"Anyasi? Anyasi? Here, kitty." In her nightgown, on her hands and knees, Lynn crawls around the foyer. She is short, slim, beautifully pro-portioned. The largest thing on her is her afro, which, uncombed, is squashed on either side, forming an inverted V in the middle of her head.

"Well. Aren't you going to help me?" As she crawls she grabs clumps of reefer from the floor, stuffing it into a green plastic garbage bag. I join her on my knees, crawling and calling "Anyasi, Anyasi!" Tiny reefer seeds dig into my plump knees.

"What happened?"

"I guess I didn't close the bag tight last night and she got into the smoke."

"How weird."

"Yeah, maybe she thought it was catnip. I meant to buy her some yesterday but I forgot . . . "

"What is it about cats and catnip?"

"What d'you think? It gets them high."

"Yeah, well, that's logical. Anyasi, Anyasi?"

"Oh, God. I hope she's all right. Where is she?" my sister says. She sounds like she's about to cry. I crawl, call, and stuff faster, more furiously.

There is a skittering, the sound of tiny claws on wood, and Anyasi stumbles out from under the couch in the living room. She is a few months old, tiny, all black except for a triangle of white on her throat, at the jugular.

"Anyasi! There you are!" Lynn screams. "Come here, kitty!" And Anyasi tries, she really does. But her skinny little legs can barely support her bloated, distended stomach. She looks like she's about to burst. Her eyes are like the eyes of the dog in the story in which each room houses a dog more ferocious, with eyes more gigantic, teeth more vicious. Anyasi tries to make it across the room, but collapses after a few feet, falling over on her side.

"Anyasi, I'm sorry," my sister says, scooping her up and trying to cradle her. But Anyasi's legs are stiff, stuck straight out, as if rigor mortis has set in. The kitten's eyes roll back in her head, which lolls over at an impossible angle, like an infant's when you don't support the neck. It looks like it's going to snap. My sister sits on our mother's velvet loveseat in a crumpled shortie nightgown, her Afro pointed heavenward, cradling her reefer-bloated kitten with one arm, clutching a trash bag full of marijuana with the other.

"She looks terrible. Maybe you'd better take her to the vet."

"Yeah. But I don't have any money."

"Take some from my top drawer. You can pay me back when you get a job," I say, even though it is the middle of August and we both know Lynn's not going to get a job, not a legal one.

"Okay. Thanks."

"All right. I've gotta go to work. Are you going to be okay?"

"Yeah. Sure . . . " Lynn says, kind of dreamy, spaced. I think she sounds weirder than usual, but then who wouldn't, her cat's overdosing on marijuana. Maybe it's the speed—maybe I should cut back to a half in the morning.

"Well, call me at work and let me know what happens." I grab my purse, walk to the front door. "Lynn? Lynn? Call me, okay?" She just sits there, holding Anyasi. Doesn't say a word.

She doesn't call, either. I try ringing home a few times during the day, but there's no answer. Plus, it's Thursday at Local 802, open-call day. I'm kept busy running down to Roseland with generic musician request slips and to HoJo's, the Bergdorf's of 52nd Street, for iced coffee. And really, smartass that I think I am, I think everything's going to be okay. I figure the vet will pump Anyasi's stomach, Lynn will sweep up the reefer and put the bag someplace up high, that life will go on as it has been, the two of us living Sly and the Family Stone's "Hot Fun in the Summertime," smoking the pipe and never having to pay the piper. There were no signs, portents, bizarre nuances that day, nothing to hint that the world was about to change forever, irrevocably, not for better but for worse.

"Hey! Lynn, I'm home." The apartment is filled with the golden dusky color of summer twilight. The foyer is swept, empty; only the faint smell of reefer lingers. I walk past the dining room. Glancing in at the long black table, china cabinet, green carpet, I can almost hear my father intoning, "Number One! Not two, but *one!*" Now that he has gone, has left us, does he no longer care what number I am?

I walk down the long hallway past my brothers' empty room, their bathroom, what used to be my parents' bedroom, with its deep purple velvet quilt and pale lavender draperies, now empty. The door to the room Lynn and I share is closed. I knock as I open it.

Our beds are placed foot to foot against a long wall. Twilight just before darkness filters into the narrow room. Lynn's bed fits snugly into the far corner. She sits there now, knees pulled up to her chin, feet tucked nearly underneath her body. Anyasi, still stiff, lies against her toes, eyes open, staring.

"Hi. What're you doing? How come there're no lights on?" Lynn just looks at me, says nothing.

"So, did you go to the vet?" I am taking off my skirt and blouse, putting on shorts and a T-shirt. My sister watches, but does not move, say any-thing.

I shrug. I am used to my sister's silence but have become spoiled over the summer by her new tolerance, the sense of camaraderie we have developed, alone together. I want to ask her what's wrong, if she's mad at me, beg her to talk to me, but cannot risk her mocking my need for her attention. I don't say anything.

"Well . . . I'm going to make some creamed spinach and toast. Want some?

"Well . . . Want the light on?" She sits there with Anyasi, two stiff, silent black balls with just a touch of white.

"Are you okay?" And then, because she doesn't answer, I leave. I'm not sure, but in the good old Nelson tradition, I may well have said "Fine" on my way out the door.

"Hello, Jill. Is Lynnie ready?" Philip Preston, who went all the way through New Lincoln with my sister, stands in the open doorway. It is nine or ten that night. I have eaten dinner and am watching television. I haven't seen my sister again.

"I don't know. I'll go see." When I open the door to our room it is still dark. I turn on the light and Lynn and Anyasi are as they were hours ear-lier, huddled at the end of the bed. My sister's eyes do not blink when the lights go on, she does not move.

"Lynn. Philip's here.

"Lynn, did you hear me? Philip's ready to go. Come on, stop fooling around." I enter the room, walk toward Lynn.

"Hey. Come on. It's not funny anymore," I say. We're too old for play-ing statues, dodge ball, red light-green light, freezing into place to taunt the opposition. I stand above her.

"Lynn!" I reach down, place my hand on her shoulder, shake her. Even though at five foot three and 115 pounds she is probably fifty pounds lighter than me, she does not budge. I think, or imagine, I see her fingers knit closer together, tighten around her knees.

"Lynn! It's not funny!" I yell, pushing her again, harder. She rocks toward the wall, like those dumb inflatable punching toys weighted at the bottom, but sways back to center before impact. Her shoulder is hard and cold, her eyes focused inward, like she is watching her own terrifying movie on a private screen.

I run from the room, down the hallway. "Philip, come here. There's something wrong with Lynn."

The next day Philip drives my still speechless older sister to my mother on Martha's Vineyard. She takes Anyasi, stiff, cold, and dead, along with her, cradling her in a clear plastic bag for the long drive on I-95 North.

After a few weeks of therapy Lynn starts talking. She is never her old self again, but rather someone else. Hints of the old Lynn remain in an occasional grin, cutting of eyes, twinkling of wry humor, but only hints. Mostly there is a trembling woman whose hands shake, who does not like to be touched, who sometimes hears voices. The oldest, number one, whose birth defined for our parents what it meant to be a family, who did the same for each of her siblings, Lynn pulls away from us as she changes until both she, and the whole family, is more memory than reality.

Lynn comes back, sort of, but she is never again the Lynn we thought we knew. A philosophy major, she finishes college, briefly marries, works, is independent. Over time, she redefines her life, with barely a glance at us.

For a long time I feel guilty, convinced that my childhood and adolescent imprecations against my older sister, "Go away," "Drop dead!" and "Leave me alone forever," have been answered by some great cosmic psychological mindfucker. In bed, I lie haunted by the notion that my most evil, reactionary, and irresponsible prayers have been answered, not by Allah the beneficent and merciful, but Yahweh the vindictive and unforgiving. I fear it is my fault that Lynn was rendered speechless, then transformed, that prayers answered with a twist of the cosmic screws are worse than those ignored.

We never, ever sit down as a family and talk about what happened to Lynn. My brothers and I hardly ever mention it except in brief whispers to each other, and never to our parents. In great middle-class tradition, we close ranks around the questions, guilt, pain, grow thick skin over them, not bothering to clean out the dirt and pieces of foreign matter embedded there.

In the lifetime that follows I become familiar with words like catatonic, paranoid, schizophrenic, withdrawal, nervous breakdown, trauma, mental illness, psychotic, neurotic, crazy, drug-induced episode . . . the words, the words are plentiful, the harvest of terms for my sister never ends, it is like an apple tree that bears fruit year-round, all of it bitter. We eat it because she is our sister, the oldest, Number One, and we want to believe that if we understand where she went we can get her back as she was. But we never do. She comes back, but not the same. My sister creates a life largely without us. To this day, we seldom meet and then only on her terms. *We never talk about it.* There is only the pain, loss, bitterness, and yearning that takes life, roots, thrives in the darkness and silence we Nelsons have created together. And we are changed, for better and for worse, forever and ever, amen.

CHAPTER NINETEEN

Thurgood Marshall, Thurgood Marshall, Thurgood Marshall. Thurgood the righteous, Thurgood the revolutionary, Thurgood the race man, general counsel for the NAACP in its heyday, Thurgood the celestial litigator, Thurgood the first African-American solicitor general and Supreme Court justice, Thurgood who sacrificed his health, life, happiness for the greater good, Thurgood the ultimate race man who remained on the nation's highest court because he had to, one of the last dependably liberal voices in an America bounding toward conservatism. Thurgood Marshall the first, numero uno, number one, not two, but One!

That his first name was strange, a name that no one else I knew had, was as it should be. That his last name evoked visions of a dusty western street, swinging saloon door, women with painted faces, men with guns and itchy fingers, raucous, rowdy, dangerous streets that only a Marshall, fastest draw in town, could tame, was even more appropriate.

Thurgood Marshall. Our very own litigious savior, come to breathe life into the law of the land, to make America a better place not only for her colored citizens, but for all the rest of them, too, like it or not. If there was a God in our house he was very much like Thurgood Marshall: educated, erudite, articulate, always number one. Armed not with a gun or a spear but with the word, not of God, but of law. Thurgood the beneficent, the merciful, the lawyer, was our savior in the here and now, not some caucasian Jesus Christ holding out the mere possibility of heaven after a life of hell.

During the late 1950s and 1960s, my mother and the four of us children would gather around the television at night and watch the news from the south. News from places with names like Birmingham, Selma,

Little Rock, Montgomery. Images that hurt to look at, black girls and boys, men and women, people as old as me, my parents, grandparents, tossed along by the frenzied force of water rushing from a firehose, curled into balls, hands protecting heads, as mobs of demented-looking white people beat, kicked, spat on them. A pretty teenaged black girl ordering a sandwich and cup of coffee at some sleepy southern lunch counter and people pouring salt and sugar on her neatly pressed hair instead. Every now and then a glimpse of a rotted body swinging from a tree, eyes popped out, bulging, like those of Amos and Andy, Stepin Fetchit, performers we were forbidden to watch other than on the news. Or a form, covered, unearthed from a swamp, old black women standing to one side, crying, on the other side, white folks grinning. My mother, sitting right there in our living room, her face the same as ever except for the tears that ran silently down her cheeks that she didn't bother to wipe away. Then came the determined, glowing face of Thurgood or King or Wilkins or Carmichael, explaining why the suffering had happened, what redress we had, reassuring us that inevitably, in the end, we would win, promising that the laws of the land could withstand the bitterness of its people. My mother's tears would stop as she listened, her brow again become smooth, she would return from the streets of Selma, Montgomery, Birmingham, return home to the four of us, gathered around the television.

"They are fighting for something very, very important, for all of us," she would say. "Trying to make America really be the great country that it can be. Fighting to end discrimination so that Negroes can have the same chance as everyone else." Her voice was so steady, so calm, so rich with surety, that we would for once be silent, listening, understanding that what she was saying was crucial to who we were, who we would become, and why.

In the 1960s, Gil Scott-Heron had a hit record called "The Revolution Will Not Be Televised." He was wrong. The revolution of the civil rights movement of the Fifties and Sixties, of Thurgood Marshall, Malcolm X, Martin Luther King Jr., the Student Nonviolent Coordinating Committee, the Black Panthers, Fannie Lou Hamer, Chaney, Schwerner, and Goodman, of tens of thousands of other nameless, faceless people who were spat on, beaten, dispossessed, killed, so colored people, Negroes, black people, and African-Americans could have the rights guaranteed us under law: that revolution seeped right through the television screen and under our skin, burrowing first into our flesh, then through our bones, finally into our souls. It became a part of us and changed each of us, forever.

Growing up we were, like many families, more Nelsons than Negroes, number ones, and most of the time we did what we pleased. In my own life, I'd been able to do just about everything I wanted. When segregation denied me access to something, my family didn't necessarily tell me that was the reason. For years, I thought my Uncle Ralph was either mean or didn't like amusement parks because he refused to take me and my siblings to Glen Echo during the summers we spent with my paternal grandmother in Northeast D.C. when we were small. It wasn't until I was a grown woman that I learned it wasn't that Uncle Ralph wouldn't, it was that he couldn't: No Negroes Allowed. By then my consciousness had been raised.

It wasn't just Thurgood Marshall, it was my father and mother who cultivated my belief in the law, in litigation as the last resort when moral persuasion, guilt, and money had failed. My parents viewed the law not as an abstraction, but as a potent weapon. It was the law that was responsible for us living in our first apartment on Riverside Drive, my father being the first black man to have a dental office on Central Park South, and then our moving into the apartment on West End Avenue. Their motto, if they had one, might have been, "If at first you don't succeed, try, try again. Then sue."

In 1951, my parents finally found an apartment at 706 Riverside Drive, after trying every building on Riverside Drive from 155th Street to 72nd Street, all of which refused to rent to Negroes. My father was told by the building's owner, Harlem Congressman Adam Clayton Powell Jr., that the building had enough Negro families—as if the advent of my parents and their two oldest children would tip the balance between home and slum. Ted Poston, a black reporter at the *New York Post*, wrote an article about my father's search for an apartment. Nothing happened until Poston convinced my father to accompany him to see Powell off on a voyage he was taking on the *Queen Elizabeth*. They talked, a phone call was made, and my father got the apartment.

It was a scenario often repeated in my parents' continual search for betterment. As often as not it was the law, or threat of legal action, and not money, status, or education, that in the final analysis enabled them to move forward.

I was twelve in 1964, the summer we moved to West End Avenue. I still remember the excitement, the sense that we were moving not just sixty-seven blocks south, but to another country. This feeling of transformation was supported by the fact that when we moved we left damn near every piece of furniture in the apartment, just walked out and never looked back. My mother spent months meticulously furnishing the new apartment. Laying beautiful rugs, measuring for drapes, searching for luscious fabric, the perfect andirons to flank the living room fireplace.

My father was a successful dentist who practiced downtown and charged the fees to prove it. He did not merely fill cavities or clean teeth, and never molded dentures. His specialty was reconstructive dentistry, rebuilding mouths rather than repairing them. It was, then, only fitting that his family should embark on this new, prosperous life with new *everything*.

Abruptly, after a lifetime in Harlem, we found ourselves a minority. We were the only black faces in our building, besides the maids and the men who ran the elevators and picked up the garbage from outside the service entrance. We had grown up in a community of black supermarkets, dry cleaners, and candy store owners. Now almost all the merchants around us were Jewish, like the kids we went to private school with. Perhaps it would have seemed a more authentic Negro experience if at this juncture I could tell a funny anecdote about eating lox, bagels, knishes for the first time, but it wouldn't be true. We were used to all these foods from a lifetime of being educated with Jews and other white folks, had grown to like them. The summer we moved my mother would send Lynn and me to Zabar's at lunchtime to buy kosher coldcuts and challah bread, which we would slice into thick slabs, spread with Hellmann's mayonnaise, and happily feast upon.

That my father had once again had to threaten legal action in order to obtain our new apartment was simply a fact of life that, as Nelsons, we were used to, accepted, rarely thought about. That our neighbors failed to say good morning to us the first year we lived there scarcely bothered me. I was, above all else, a Nelson: superior, confident, powerful. I could afford, no, I had an *obligation*, to cut everyone else in the world some slack.

"People act that way because they're insecure and if you're secure and understand that there's no reason to get angry with them I understand that most people act badly because of their insecurities something that happened when they were young that messed them up . . . " my mother would explain.

"But what about my insecurities?"

"What insecurities? What do you have to be insecure about? You're a Nelson," she'd say, and of course there was no arguing with that, or with her.

It's not entirely surprising that twenty-five years later I was elected unit chair of the Baltimore-Washington Newspaper Guild unit at the *Washington Post*—the only black, female chair, another first—and that on July 13, 1988 the unit filed a complaint with the D.C. Office of Human Rights charging the *Post* with discrimination based on age, race, sex, and national origin going back to 1877, when the paper was founded. I'd been at the *Post* two years, during which I'd disabused myself of any fantasies about fitting in, let alone being number one.

It wasn't until the Newspaper Guild bulletin published the results of its comparison of salary differences that the African-American women in the newsroom finally stopped either thinking we were *it*, or else commiserating, and actually *did* something. How could we not? According to the Guild report, black female reporters earned an average weekly salary of $791.33, white females $859.37, black males $920.46, and white males $988.68. And these were averages! The truth was that of the seventeen black women in the newsroom, we could identify only two who made $50,000 or more.

Thus began my stint at trying to work with management for change. In late 1986, Marcia Slacum Greene, Dorothy Gilliam, myself, and a few other women had pulled together a black women's caucus at the *Post* to address both individual concerns and the fact that, as a group, we were the lowest-paid reporters in the newsroom. We met every few months to talk about our concerns, strategize, and lend support to the younger women on the staff. We were kind of an encounter group cum subversive cabal, although to tell the truth, after a while the meetings seemed more like emotional gripe sessions than strategic planning.

As is usual among black people, we were split, this time along three lines: those who thought their problems at the job were the result of something being wrong with them, those who believed flaws in the system were responsible for their problems, and those who were just plain intimidated. When it came to actually doing something, it didn't matter that most of us, young or old, editors or reporters, with or without master's degrees, basically had the same problems. We weren't making enough money, getting the plum assignments, being taken seriously. When it came to taking action, what mattered was which of these mindsets we were in. As far as I could tell, the majority of the sisters at the *Post* were intimidated, believed their problems at the *Post* were their fault, or both.

Things were so bad that we dared not even give the caucus a name, simply calling it "The Group" in hushed tones, a la Mary McCarthy. The Guild numbers gave substance to our individual gripes and collective perceptions. So we did what any disgruntled group of employees committed to working within the system would do. In early 1987, we wrote a letter to managing editor Len Downie requesting a meeting.

Downie did what any manager would do. He met with us, listened noncommittally to our concerns, and made no promises. Over the next several months, a few black women were promoted. Jeanne Fox-Alston, Metro's graphics editor, became director of recruiting for the newsroom. Jane Seaberry, a reporter on the Virginia desk, became an editor. As for "The Group"? It faded away from lack of interest, commitment, and nerve.

Every now and then at lunch, Marcia and I would talk about reviving it. Then Marcia would say, "I'm not going to do it. There're other black women at the *Post* besides you and me. Let one of them show interest or initiative, pull a meeting together."

"Yeah, well, I won't hold my breath."

"Think about it, Jill. Besides a few times, the meetings were always at your house or my house. Doesn't that tell you something?"

"Yeah. That we've spent too much money on juice and croissants."

"And that they're not interested. If they were, they'd do something for themselves, not wait for us," Marcia said. She was right. This quiet little black woman from McHerrin, Virginia, knew about doing something. As a girl, Marcia was on the front lines of desegregation; she was bused to integrate a white school, and attacked for her trouble. She was a bona fide freedom rider in yuppie clothing, one of those children on television my mother had cried over. We'd spend the rest of lunch eating apple pie a la mode, alternately talking about either clothes shopping or joining a spa. The former we did regularly; the latter was mostly talk.

A year later, the situation at the *Post* had changed—or hadn't changed—radically enough that I, who had sworn not to run for or join anything when I'd come to Washington, who supported unions whole-heartedly in principle but had never before belonged to one, was running, unopposed, for unit chair.

Don't get me wrong. I ran unopposed not because I was particularly popular, but because the union wasn't. Union membership was merely tolerated by management; union activism was seen as foolhardy, traitorous, downright suicidal, at the newspaper that broke the pressmans union in the 1970s. The *Post* had so denatured its Guild unit that the union ended up giving back profit sharing. Enthusiastically anti-union, management reflected the paternalistic/maternalistic style and mentality of the *Post*'s owners. Katherine Graham's father gave the newspaper to her husband, then she inherited it when he committed suicide; Donnie Graham was content to wait for Mommy to retire to get his hands on the *Post*; Len Downie could reconcile himself to waiting patiently until Ben Bradlee retired; all the Harvard and Yale golden boys were content to plot and labor in the vineyards of the newsroom awaiting anointment. *What was the matter with the rest of us?*

Management viewed the union as a blemish on its facade of being a genteel family-owned newspaper, and treated it accordingly. The rank and file, when they thought about the union at all, viewed it as the final barrier, the last bastion standing between us and institutionalized paternalism, exploitation, racism, sexism, and unemployment. We knew the union was necessary; we just didn't want to get involved.

The perception in the newsroom was that public, vocal involvement in the union was a sure road away from legitimacy, promotion, becoming part of the old boys club at the *Washington Post*. Rumor had it that Tom Sherwood, a white male reporter who covered Mayor Barry for years and eventually left the paper to be a reporter at WRC-TV, was denied ascension onto the national staff because he was a vocal, confrontational, active union member and unit chair.

As a result of this perception that Activism = (Career) Death, most union members had nothing to do with the union beyond having their dues removed from their paycheck every week and sent to the Guild offices. Those who were involved with the union fell into roughly two groups: people in trouble and marginal employees. Come to think of it, maybe that's really only one group.

People in trouble were those against whom management had taken some action that they perceived as (and that very often was) unfair. Denial of promotion, crummy assignments, and not publishing a writer's work were all techniques employed by the *Post* to torture employees they wanted to get rid of but, because of the union contract, they'd have a hard time out-and-out firing. Thanks to the union, it was almost impossible to get canned. As a twenty-year veteran once told me, "For them to fire you, you'd probably have to fuck a duck in the middle of the newsroom at deadline time, and even then," he added with a chuckle somewhere between malicious and smug, "you could probably stay if you agreed to go into treatment."

Instead, management tried to manipulate people into leaving by re-assigning them to obits or one of the rural bureaus, not publishing their work, or simply ignoring them. These people came to the union, the court of last resort, for help.

Then there were the marginal employees, usually people who had been at the paper for a decade or more, realized they weren't going anywhere but would never be fired, had nothing to lose, and were pissed off. Mostly, this group was comprised of heavyset caucasian women over thirty-five who dressed in the anachronistic long skirts of their hippie youth and spent a good deal of time gossiping and complaining. Unlike the caucasian males in this group, who though they were marginal still had penises, and therefore made more money and were treated slightly better than their female counterparts, these women tended to be bitter. They perceived themselves as abused, wronged, and worst of all, trapped. They were mad as hell, but they were gonna take it some more—-not because they thought anything would change, but because they had vested pensions, mortgages, bills, responsibilities. And mostly because they didn't have confidence in themselves, didn't believe there was life after the *Washington Post*.

Where did I fall? I was all of the above, and then some. I was in trouble because I *was* confident, and because I worked on the troubled magazine and was outspoken, critical, and highly opinionated. I was also a tall, moody, African-American female with a strong temper and the mouth to go with it. After my first year at the *Post*, it was clear to me I was never going to fit in. I had nothing, besides a paycheck that got increasingly inadequate as the economy deteriorated, to lose or gain by staying there. So when Guild administrative officer Sandi Polaski, outgoing unit chair Tom Sherwood, and a few others asked me to run for chair of the Guild unit at the *Post*, I figured, why not? At least I could shake the place up while I was there, rock their world. I hadn't planned on rocking my own, too.

CHAPTER TWENTY

"I wouldn't get involved I really wouldn't you've had enough problems with that fool who runs the magazine without becoming the head of the union to boot why you? where are the white folks? I've lived over seventy years and nothing's changed not really in America go for the money like everyone else I wish I had I just think its a bad idea but if that's what you're gonna do I know nothing I can say will change your mind just watch your mouth and your temper . . . "

This is what my mother says when I tell her I have been elected head of the union, or rather the Washington-Baltimore Newspaper Guild unit at the *Washington Post.* She isn't alone. Not one of my friends is particularly enthusiastic about my election, even though as an African-American female head of the Guild unit I am a first, number one, plowing new ground for our people.

"Remember what I told you about keeping a paper trail?" is my friend Allyson's response.

"Yeah. I write everything down now," I assure her.

"Do you keep it at the office?"

"Uh huh."

"Take it home with you. Nothing's safe there anymore," she intones.

I laugh. She sounds so serious.

"I'm not kidding. Those people are dangerous. You can't trust anyone but yourself."

"Yeah, yeah, all right," I say hastily. She is making me nervous and I am eager to change the subject. "So, how's life with your hubby?"

"Jill. Don't forget what I said," Allyson adds, before we launch into a more familiar, more comfortable discussion of love, marriage, and that favorite topic of heterosexual sisters, the Black Man.

That night I stay late at the office and print out copies of all my corre-
spondence to management. It takes quite a while, since I've kept written
records of damn near everything offensive that's happened since my
arrival in 1986. I've also apprised management of awards I've won, sub-
mitted written lists of story ideas, regularly asked for a raise and to be put
on the fast track, which is a nebulous schedule of expectations tied to
monetary rewards reserved for management favorites. At Allyson's
instruction, I've also written memos asking for my written six-month
evaluation for nearly two years, to no avail. Two weeks after my election,
on February 12, 1988, I am finally evaluated. I guess management is creating a paper trail of its own.

On the checklist, I am rated "satisfactory" in every category but organization and flow, where there is an X in the "improvement needed" box.
The written portion of the evaluation is more specific. Under "area where
improvement is needed, if any," Jay Lovinger wrote: "Mutual trust—I
don't think she feels we have her best interests at heart, and she sometimes seems to have her own agenda. The problem is that she may not be
getting all she can in the way of growth from the editing process and we
may not be getting the special things she has to give. There are also racial
and sexual sensitivities—and now, with her union position—management vs. worker sensitivities . . . "

I am stunned, not so much because it is critical of me and my work—
that was to be expected—but because it so blatantly draws a line of
demarcation between management and me. Clearly I am perceived as
troublesome, a sexually, racially sensitive Negress let loose in the newsroom. The expectation that I will become more sensitive now that I head
the Guild isn't surprising; what is surprising is that they wrote it down.

"Dumb move," says Guild administrator Sandi Polaski when I give her
a copy of my evaluation. "It's hard to believe management agreed to this.
Maybe Lovinger doesn't know how the game is played. Now, let's talk for
a few minutes about the complaint."

The notion of filing a class-action suit or complaint against the *Post*
alleging discrimination based on sex or race or age or national origin, or
all of the above, has been floating around the union for years. By 1988, a
confluence of events brought the notion to fruition. First is the fact that
each entity named in the action—women, people of color, older workers,
and a variety of ethnic groups—had tried to get ahead and get over on

their own, and failed. By 1988, it's clear that the EEOC consent decree concerning women has not had the desired effect. Women, particularly black women, remain the lowest-paid group of workers at the *Post*. In 1982, black female reporters were paid 15.8 percent less than white male reporters. By 1986, that figure had risen to 20 percent.

As is typical in the corporate workplace, unity came about as a result of the repeated failure of that American staple, rugged individualism. Second is the fact that the union is in trouble. Management had succeeded in eliminating dues check-off for new hires, which meant that instead of union dues being automatically subtracted from members' weekly paycheck, they had to do it themselves. It seems minor, but $10 or $15 you never see is a lot easier to part with than the same amount in your hand.

Finally, the unit is losing members, as a result of the above-mentioned problems, management's negative attitude, and the insidious influence of eight years under that antilabor prexy, Ronald Reagan. Self-satisfied, smug, clinging to illusions of being professionals, some of us still realize that if we don't do something, we too might go the way of PATCO's air-traffic controllers. It is clear the union needs rejuvenation, action, to take the offensive again. It needs panache, sex appeal, new blood, a facelift. It needs a kamikaze. It needs *me*.

In turn, I need an outlet for my energy, as well as some positive feedback, the ego-feed of leadership. I want to shake things up, be number one, emulate my father, maternal grandfather, and Thurgood Marshall by using the law to force white America to change. I want to serve notice on the *Washington Post* that we are fired up, aren't gonna take no mo', that discrimination must end. That these noble goals also afford me an opportunity to avenge my employer's legacy of abusive treatment of African-American employees like David Hardy, Holly West, Joel Dreyfuss, myself, and others, is as it should be. I never professed to be Christian, altruistic, or nonviolent, and while I respect Martin Luther King Jr.'s ability to turn the other cheek, if I had to throw down it would have been with Thurgood or the gun-toting, no-shit-taking brothers and sisters in the Black Panther Party.

My first order of business is to pump up the volume, and profile, of the union, to get the old standbys off their grim asses and to bring in some new blood. To that end, I propose a celebrity auction, "Bylines for Dollars" in which *Post* employees auction their skills to the highest bidder.

Held in June of 1988, the auction raises $10,000, the largest amount ever raised by the Guild. We not only make money, we build unity. Sportswriter Tony Kornheiser is sold to umpire a baseball game, fashion writer Nina Hyde takes a lucky bidder on a shopping tour. Lunches with columnists Dorothy Gilliam or Bill Raspberry are auctioned off, or you could go with columnist Judy Mann and her pal, Ed Asner, or with political writer and Reaganphile Lou Cannon, or gossip columnist Chuck Conconi, or Paul Taylor. The truly strong of heart bid on a dinner date with Courtland Milloy. We sell a pair of Gary Hart's cowboy boots, filched by reporter Elsa Walsh from fiancee Bob Woodward's closet; a week in Joanne Omang's house in Maine; and Pulitzer Prize returnee Janet Cooke's name plate. And how about a personalized map of your neighborhood by graphic artist Brad Wye? A "talk back to the *Post*" luncheon with two members of the editorial board? Or sailing lessons from Sara Fitzgerald?

There is live entertainment, including Daisy impersonating Oprah Winfrey and *Chicago Tribune* reporter George Curry doing Jesse Jackson, as they had in my play the year before. Financially and spiritually, the auction is a rousing success.

But you know, the trouble with these rousing successes is they usually rile up numerous petty frustrations that'll come back at you, sooner or later. Being a leader often means being the heavy. Having to confront coworkers about phone calls not made, assignments botched, and agreements ignored doesn't win me any popularity contests. In this case the anger comes from some of the over-forty union-standby types who end up angry, mostly with me. They find me opinionated, bossy, moody, and dictatorial, all of which I can be. But the real problem is that they resent new blood, successful new blood, and perhaps especially successful new blood in a black wrapper. I am reminded of the old men who dominate the NAACP, looking down on the younger buppie set and sitting around remembering the good old days as the organization fades into obscurity and irrelevance. Reflecting on the glorious past is safer than planning for the unknown future.

By the time the auction is over, damn near everyone who's been involved in its planning and execution is pissed off, burnt out, and has a few fresh enemies. When happy bidders say, "Are you going to do this next year?" usually followed by "This should be an annual event," their words are often met with glares and snarls.

A month after the auction, we organize a two-day byline strike, asking reporters to withhold their name from stories they've written, to protest having been without a contract for two years. It is almost 100 percent successful. For awhile it seems everything I touch is golden. So it is easy to believe that filing a class-action complaint with the D.C. Office of Human Rights will be equally successful.

The night before the press conference announcing the suit I run into Metro editor Milton Coleman on the subway going home. We chit-chat for a few minutes, and then Milton says, "So. You're really going to file the complaint tomorrow?"

"Yeah, we are."

"I hope you've thought about it."

"People have been thinking about it for a long time, Milton. Now we're going to do something."

"I'm not sure it's the right way to go," Milton says, shaking his head.

"Why not?"

"A lot of careers could be hurt in the process . . . " But before I can ask him what he means, really get into it, we are at my stop.

I think a lot about this conversation in the next few years. I think Milton was trying to warn me about the wrath of management, but I didn't get it. I thought he was simply trying to intimidate me. I didn't hear between the words. Even if I had, I don't think I would have backed off the complaint, although I would have watched my back, and my ass, more closely. But that night I was like a junkie on a binge; my drug was power. I didn't want to hear anything that messed with my chasing the dragon, getting my hit.

The next morning, myself, Sandi Polaski, and several Guild members and officials hold a press conference at the National Press Club building announcing the complaint. It is low-key, nonconfrontational, cool. I walk back to work in the heat feeling proud of myself, excited, relieved that now the Office of Human Rights, with its attorneys, investigators, and other staff members will take over. It is out of my hands. I suspect that Harriet Tubman and Thurgood Marshall would be moderately proud of me. I have done the right thing, stood up for what I believe. I am looking forward to a trip to Long Island to visit Arthur Swan, my third-grade teacher, about whom I am writing a magazine story, and then on to the Vineyard for a week.

Walking up 15th Street I find myself humming the theme from the old Wyatt Earp show. But unlike Marshall Earp, my guns aren't cocked, my head doesn't swivel as I walk, I'm not watching my back for trouble, and I haven't deputized any allies. Don't ask me why. I am a child of the civil rights movement, and I've also seen enough westerns in my time to know that the Marshall has to be ever vigilant. So why am I surprised when, a week later, the bad guys ambush me, guns blazing?

CHAPTER TWENTY-ONE

Mostly I try to forget the Ex-Husband, to whom I was married for fifteen unhappy months in the early 1980s. Having broken most of the black bourgeois rules—having a daughter at twenty without benefit of marriage, making it through college and graduate school as a single parent, and then building a successful career—at thirty I temporarily regressed, deciding to go straight and have it all, and I married a plump, economically solvent wannabee.

There was only one incisive thing the Ex-Husband ever said that I can remember. This utterance occurred one August day on Martha's Vineyard after we'd parked and swam in Ice House Pond, which is located on private property, and returned to the car to find that it wouldn't start because someone had taken the distributor cap. "Someone" turned out to be the white man who owned the land and pond, who eventually emerged from the surrounding woods like some character from *Deliverance*, gave us a stern lecture on the rights of property owners, and returned the distributor cap. That's when my husband said, "You know, there's nothing worse than being wrong around white folks."

Not that there's anything inherently horrible about making a mistake, but when you're a Negro in America it's usually not just you who's making the mistake, it's y'all, the race, black folks in toto. One individual's fuck-up becomes yet another piece of evidence that affirmative action equals incompetence, that people of African descent somehow just don't fit in, that America cannot rely on spooks to do the right thing, no matter what Ossie Davis and Spike Lee say.

Nowhere is this more true than in corporate America, where black folks were ignored and unwanted until we used the law (and the specter of the lawless in the guise of rioters in the 1960s and black nationalists in the 1970s) to jimmy open the doors a crack so a few of us could squeeze in. Once inside, with our good jobs, professional profiles, and tennis racquets, most of us still could not be trusted. We were, after all, black first, members of the corporate family second. Anything less than perfect behavior was construed as proof that as people of African descent we just never would fit in, didn't have the intellectual equipment to ever fully integrate into the corporate culture, were basically subversive, and thus should be viewed with suspicion.

One reason black folks in corporations usually seem so uptight is because we're so aware of all the above. We spend a great deal of time trying to be perfect, to never make mistakes around white folks, because when we do we suspect those mistakes go into an amorphous White Folks Sin Bank Against The Negro. We fear that, once discovered, our little *faux pas* is stored in the same bank with the really scary sins—also imaginary—of Angela Davis, Alton Maddox, and Malcolm and Martin, before they were killed and transformed into harmless T-shirt icons.

On July 26, 1988, thirteen days after the union files the discrimination complaint against the *Post*, I am scheduled to go to Long Island to interview my third-grade teacher, Arthur Swan, for a story about segregation as a function of growing up. Mr. Swan was a mentor to me at New Lincoln. Like most of my mentors through secondary school, he is a white man. Graduation from high school seems to have been some cutoff point: in the twenty years since, I have found my contact with white folks to be more and more superficial, my mentors fewer and farther between. After being reunited with Mr. Swan at a funeral, we get to talking. I abruptly remember how much he meant to me, how long it's been since I knew anyone like him.

In Mr. Swan's third-grade glass we studied Native Americans and pioneers. For nine months we lived as they did: the boys wore beaded loin clothes, the girls beaded dresses, all of us wore headbands. We cooked and ate the foods the Plains Indians ate, including buffalo meat we ordered special and which the cafeteria staff cooked. We had our lessons in tepees. As pioneers, we sewed smocks and bonnets, built a life-size log cabin in our classroom, studied the "Little House" books of Laura Ingalls Wilder. We wrote and performed two plays, one about the settlers and another about the Indians. Me, I was always partial to the Indians. I starred as Raging One, a Pawnee woman who avenges her daughter after her tongue is cut out. My big lines were, "What have you done to my daughter?" and, once I found out, "Now I will do worse to you than you have done to her!"

Seeing Mr. Swan, a thin, sandy-haired man with a mischievous smile and blue eyes that actually twinkle, starts me remembering a time when people were defined by who they were, rather than race, gender, or politics. It makes me wonder how and when that all changed, and why. It doesn't take long for me to decide the subject would make a good magazine story. For the first time in months I find myself not only excited about a story, but confident Lovinger will be, too. It has all the elements he loves: childhood, sentiment, angst, reconciliation.

When I return to work from the funeral I sell Lovinger on the story, then travel to Mr. Swan's house on Long Island to do half the interview. When I get back, Jay and I talk about the trip. We are both excited, and both believe that looking at my relationship with Arthur Swan, at how and why it changed and yet endures, is a way to talk about race and racism that will be both interesting and educational.

I'm revved. It's late July, I haven't been to the Vineyard all year, and I'm burnt out with regular work, union work, and moving work: a few weeks earlier I had bought a house. I had planned to drive my own car, but the previous weekend I'd been in an accident on the 14th Street bridge, and the Volvo is out of commission for three weeks. I've decided to rent a station wagon so I can take a tree to Arthur and Bob, his significant other, who are both avid gardeners, spend a few days interviewing Arthur, then drive on to Woods Hole, drop off the car, and take the ferry to the Vineyard.

I've reserved the car, but when I look for Steve Petranek, the magazine's managing editor, to sign the travel voucher, he's nowhere to be found. Neither are any of the other editors, who are all in a meeting. Hyped about picking up the car, the tree, and getting out of D.C. later that evening, I initial the travel voucher with Petranek's initials, "S.P.," even though he usually signs "SSP," and hand it in at the travel office so they can finalize arrangements.

Then I go to lunch and start feeling guilty. Or more accurately, paranoid. The Ex-Husband's words about being wrong around white folks echo in my ear. So do Allyson's about creating a paper trail. It occurs to me that Petranek might be pissed that I signed his initials. Even though the trip was approved and he knew I was going, I have breached form seriously by initialing it for him. I am *wrong*.

So after lunch I fill out another travel voucher and take it into Petranek's office to be signed, which he does, no problem. Then I say, "Listen, there's something else I want to talk to you about . . . I put in another voucher earlier and—" but before I can finish, correct the error, beg forgiveness, he whips out the first voucher and says, "I want to talk to you about this! You're in big trouble."

He then accuses me of forgery and trying to defraud the Washington Post Company. I want to laugh, because the suggestion is so ridiculous— but then it's also insulting, which isn't very funny. I didn't try to imitate his handwriting or duplicate his signature, the trip was already approved, I came in to confess . . . what's the big deal? Anyway, what's to defraud? I figure I'm actually saving the *Post* money by driving to Long Island instead of flying. As far as I'm concerned, what I did is a minor breach of etiquette, not a felony. I've always gotten along fairly well with Petranek, but when I look at him it's clear those days are over. Something about the expression on his slightly harried, cherubic face suddenly reminds me of Tom Wilkinson, the North Wall's dirty-water carrier, even though they look nothing alike. Suddenly I understand that this isn't about me and Steve; it's about the unit chair who less than two weeks earlier filed a major discrimination complaint. Uh oh.

I explain that I wasn't trying to defraud the company, then offer to pay the rental fee for the three hours I'll be using the car between Long Island and the Vineyard. I confess to the crime of impatience, apologize. He chews me out moderately. I get up to leave, the legit voucher in hand, ready to get on the road. At the door I say something like, "Sorry again, Steve." Then he says, "I don't think you should leave yet. This won't end here, because other people know."

Oh shit.

CHAPTER TWENTY-TWO

"Jill? Pat O'Shea. Leonard would like to see you. As soon as possible." When summoned to the office of the managing editor by his red-headed sentinel, ASAP translates immediately.

I place the telephone receiver back in its cradle and take a deep breath. I've already been grilled by Tom Wilkinson and had hoped the matter was settled. I sit there, staring at the bulletin board in front of me. Misu's smiling face, Winnie Mandela's serene one, Harriet Tubman's frowning, serious visage all stare back. Above them, my white-on-black *Washington Post*-issue name plate screams "Jill Nelson!" Next to it is a white-on-green metal plate, a memorial to segregation given me by Thulani, that states simply, "Colored Women." It is Thursday, July 28, 1988, and the shit is about to hit the fan.

"Hi. I'm here to see Leonard."

"Go right in," Pat of the red hair says. But before I can get my two feet over the threshold, Downie greets me, gestures toward the open door across the hall.

"Let's go into Ben's office."

Great.

"Have a seat." I sit in the chair directly opposite Bradlee's desk. Downie sits to the side, slightly behind me. I should not construe this as back-up.

"We're very concerned about this," Bradlee says, waving his hand over a sheet of paper on his desk.

"Well, I know. I made a mistake."

"I can't believe something like this happened. Behavior like this is not acceptable at the *Washington Post*."

"I know. I'm sorry."

"We cannot tolerate forgery at the *Washington Post*."

"I wouldn't describe it as forgery. I wasn't trying to trick anyone."

"Has this sort of thing happened before? Any place else?"

"What sort of thing?"

"Forgery," Bradlee says. I want to laugh. I have a fleeting fantasy of throwing myself on his desk and dramatically confessing to a lifetime of petty forgery, evenings spent filling legal pads with ever more accurate facsimiles of the signatures of the rich and famous. Then I look in his face and realize he is dead serious, and really pissed.

"No. I wouldn't describe it as forgery, either." After all, I didn't try to duplicate anyone's signature. Petranek signs his initials "SSP", I wrote "S.P." Besides, forgery implies illegality, secretiveness, a desire not to be discovered. My desire was simply to get out of Dodge, go interview Mr. Swan, and go on to the Vineyard and vacation. While I didn't think my colleagues would mourn my absence, I was fairly sure they'd notice it. It wasn't like slave days, me trying to steal away to Jesus in the form of a rent-a-car while Massa thought I was at church services. Or was it?

Bradlee sits there, his ruddy face hanging in folds, giving me what I guess is supposed to be a penetrating stare. I remember newsroom stories in which going into Bradlee's office is the earthly equivalent of heaven or hell. For me, it's politics, pure bullshit, plain and simple. He sits there giving me this theatrically intense scrutiny about a bullshit travel voucher, whereas I'm convinced we both know the real deal is the discrimination complaint and any resemblance I might possibly have to his nemesis, Janet Cooke.

"We're extremely disturbed by this. We've looked into this, we've looked at the record. We've decided that your punishment will be suspension, without pay, for one week."

"Are you kidding?"

"No."

"I made a bad decision, but the punishment doesn't seem to fit the crime." I explain to Bradlee what happened, how I subsequently went to Petranek, fessed up, and he signed another travel voucher. I explained once again, as I already had to both Lovinger, Petranek, and Wilkinson, that I was renting a station wagon in order to take my third-grade teacher, an avid gardener, the gift of a cherry tree: that I planned to spend three or four days interviewing him, then drive three hours to Woods Hole, where

I would drop off the car and go on to the Vineyard and vacation. I repeated my offer to pay for the time I'd be using the car for personal reasons.

Bradlee just looks disgusted. Now I know what Petranek meant when he told me, "This won't end here, because other people know." I tell him, "The story was approved. I'm supposed to leave tomorrow."

"Forget the story. I don't want it in my magazine. It gives me a bad feeling."

The remainder of the discussion is logistical. My suspension is to begin at the end of the day, but I ask Downie to postpone it until August 1 so I can finish the story I'm working on.

"I don't want this to happen again," Bradlee says as I am leaving.

"It won't." I walk back to the magazine along the same route I first took on the day I was hired over two years ago, a piece of not-so-fresh meat, definitely on a hook. More and more my nominal boss, Jay Lovinger, is conspicuously absent these days, just fading away. As the magazine continues to lose money, he loses power. Rumor has it that Bradlee and Downie now control the story and assignment list, that Jay has been stripped of all power except titular. By the new year he will have "resigned," floated away on his fat golden parachute. Two of the four writers he brought from New York have already left the *Post*.

I keep remembering that afternoon with the Ex-Husband after swimming at Ice House Pond. Sitting in the woods, the pine needles poking into my thighs, wondering how we'd get out of there without the car's distributor cap, not looking forward to the several-mile trek to town for help. Then that guy coming out of the woods, holding the cap high up in his hand as he chided us recalcitrant darkies.

I feel like that today. Like most black folks who ever wanted to amount to anything, I've known my whole life that it wasn't about being as good as white folks, it was about being better. I knew that when it came to spooks, there were no short cuts, no bending of the rules, no forgiveness. Even though I know the *Post* is overreacting, being vindictive, punishing me for crimes other than the one at hand, I know that the real, ultimate crime is mine. It is the sin of being less than perfect, of making a mistake, of not watching my back: of being wrong around white folks.

It is axiomatic in the black community that when politicians are caught with their hands in the till, or civil rights leaders shot in the butt exiting motel rooms with white women, or entertainers sent to prison after being busted with drugs, someone will inevitably say, "What was the matter with that fool? Did he think he could act like the white folks and get away with it?" Then we will all laugh, shake our heads at the absurdity of the very notion that we might be judged by the same standards as white Americans. Being black is like being kosher—we answer to a higher authority. Except in our case it's not God, it's the dictates of American racism.

Frankly, I'm also insulted by management's attitude, their contention that I have a rip-off mentality, somehow trying to defraud the *Washington Post*. Of what? It's no thrill for me to drive a station wagon 340 miles from D.C. to Long Island, and my requesting a car with a tape deck, something mentioned by management with great suspicion, seems like a sensible request from any sane music lover. But they're acting like I'm some crazed Negress about to embark on a *Post*-financed joyride in a disco-blaring rented station wagon. It doesn't seem to matter to the bosses that I'll be working for all but the few hours it takes me to drive from Mr. Swan's to the Vineyard. In fact, I get the feeling that my winding up at Mommy's summer home on Martha's Vineyard adds the ultimate insult to injury. As my friend Daisy says, "They're mad because you're a Vineyard girl, that's what this is about."

I disagree with Daisy there—this is mostly about me biting the hand that feeds me in the form of a discrimination complaint. The Guild unit files a grievance protesting my suspension, and digs up instances of a famous reporter "losing" a rental car in a public garage for six weeks and being verbally reprimanded, a cub reporter making up a quote and being scolded over breakfast by Bradlee, a national reporter suspended for a week for plagiarizing. Our contention that the punishment hardly fits the alleged crime falls on deaf ears.

Before July 28, I might have been busy singing "Oh you can't stop me/I'm sticking to the union," but after my suspension it is pretty clear that the rank and file aren't sticking with me. Overall, my fellow union members, already disgruntled by my style of leadership and the successes during my tenure, appear to view my crime and punishment as sufficient grounds for abandonment.

My suspension and its immediate aftermath is the pinnacle of horror for me at the *Washington Post*, the moment when Jill Nelson, the snowball, starts rolling down toward hell. It is the moment I fully recognize the viciousness of management, the hopelessness of my tenure there, the despair of any resolution I might have to succeed. In our own middle-class, corporate, all-American way, the *Post* and I are as far apart as the Palestinians and Israelis. War has been declared. Without someone's defeat, reconciliation is impossible.

There is no consolation in the knowledge that I am the first black woman ever suspended for a week without pay for alleged forgery. Being number one doesn't mean squat when you've earned it by being wrong.

I spend the week of my suspension at home in D.C., writing and editing a cover story for the magazine via messenger and telephone. Each day I put in a full day's work. I do not receive my weekly paycheck of $1,043. Can we talk about volunteer slavery?

CHAPTER TWENTY-THREE

I sit on the deck of the ferry *Islander* as it moves through the Atlantic Ocean toward Martha's Vineyard. The sky is gray, overcast, bulbous with plump rain clouds, but as we pull away from the terminal in Woods Hole, my spirits lighten. It is a familiar feeling after a lifetime of summers spent on the Vineyard. Sitting in a deck chair on the prow of the ship, I face toward my mother's house in Oak Bluffs, home, and let the wind sandblast away the frown, the tension, the animosity. The windy ferry ride removes the outer layer of bad vibes and city funk. Days spent swimming in the cold ocean slowly, methodically wear down the deeper psychic grime. Always, after time spent on the Vineyard, I am purged, rejuvenated.

The ferry nears Oak Bluffs harbor. I stand, lean over the rail, peer forward for a view of the house. And there it is, taking up the whole corner on the end of Ocean Park, our great big house with porches on every side and two bubbles in the roof of the attic. Across the street in the middle of the park is the green and white gazebo where the island band holds concerts every summer Sunday. I can see the outline of the glassed-in porch overlooking the ocean, with its antique wicker swings covered in a neo-African print, the great pots flanking either side of the porch overflowing with the blood-red geraniums my mother plants each year. Leil's Perch we call it, after my mother, and tease her that when she dies we'll have her stuffed and seated for all eternity on the swing by the ocean side, shades on, glass of Jack Daniel's in hand. She does not think this is a bad idea.

If there is a down home for me, it is up north on Martha's Vineyard, not Virginia or North Carolina or Alabama. The porches we swing in are not bordered by the red clay of Georgia but the beige sand of New England, and a traditional welcoming dinner isn't Smithfield ham and corn bread, but boiled lobsters with new potatoes and corn on the cob.

There is no Ku Klux Klan, no crackers, no southern gentry to contend with, but formal, reserved Islanders with their own distinct sense of land, justice, community, humor.

For a few years in my early twenties, I stopped going to the Vineyard in the summer, convinced that it was not an authentic Negro experience, that the beauty of gingerbread cottages, the red cliffs of Gay Head, the ocean right outside my doorstep, the Nelsons' own private self-cleaning pool, was not sufficiently down and dirty to qualify as a valid entry in the collective racial experience.

I yearned for southern roads out of Toni Morrison novels, juke joints, squint-eyed, mean-looking white folks in trucks with gun racks mounted over the back window. I coveted some segregated experience I'd read about in a novel or newspaper, or seen on television; I wanted to swim in a muddy pond with slime on the bottom and leeches on top, ached for hard times, mean times, bad times. It took me a few years to accept that the Vineyard, what I had, was my authentic Negro experience, and to be thankful for it. This awakening came as the result of a few summers spent sweltering in Manhattan as much as from any great spiritual catharsis. Necessity may be the mother of invention, but when it's ninety-eight degrees and funky in the Big Apple, it can also be the death of pretension.

It is here, on the Vineyard, that I have a sense of community, of belonging, of poignant familiarity. Not in the apartment buildings in New York in which I grew up, but right here in Oak Bluffs, where the same people that sat on porches when I was ten still sit there when I am thirty-six. Where the man at the little post office and I get grayer and grayer each year, together, and laugh about it when I open Box 1895 each spring. Where I know every street, every beach, most faces, and they know mine. If they do not know me, they know where I come from. Sometimes, it is simply that I am A'Lelia's daughter, Stanley's girl, Misu's mother, one of the Nelsons, part of the authentic Negro experience in Oak Bluffs, on Martha's Vineyard, made up of Bostonians, New Yorkers, people from every place else.

I come here for surcease, relief, to recharge. I sleep in the great house that my parents bought before they were divorced, a house big enough that all the Nelson egos and craziness can peacefully coexist. I swim, eat, read. Mostly, the social scene on the Vineyard passes me by. When I go out at night it is to walk the beach, or infrequently to a movie. The

Vineyard of *Ebony* magazine articles and the *nouveau riche* Negroes who either cannot swim or won't because they don't want to mess up their hair, who spend their time playing tennis, sipping cocktails, and gossiping, is seen but unknown. I come here not to network but to rework. The people I see, mostly on the beach or visiting my mother's house, are old friends, not colleagues or acquaintances. As I get older I come to understand that there is comfort, safety, affirmation simply in knowing someone for thirty years, a lifetime. You don't even have to like them.

It is August of 1988. My mother's house is full of people. My brother Ralph, his significant other Susana, and Max, my only nephew, are here from California. So is Helen, my mother's sixty-year friend from Philly, my brother Stanley, various others.

In the Nelson tradition, I don't tell anyone in my family about my suspension. I just act as if it hadn't happened and everything is okay. I spend most of my days in the ocean, diving deep, swimming far out into the waves, submersing myself in some dimly remembered ritual of purification. When I'm not swimming, I lay on the beach and bake, convinced that I am exchanging the sun for the stress, that one replaces the other. By the time evening comes, the exhaustion of my body has spread conveniently to my mind. I escape into early, dreamless sleep. On those days when exhaustion does not come quickly enough, I help it along with Stoli gimlets or champagne.

"Jill. Your mother told me you were here. How's the *Washington Post?*"

I am lying on the local beach, fondly called the Inkwell. It is after five o'clock and deserted except for the diehards. I open my eyes, push up on one elbow. John Lloyd and his wife, Ada, friends of my mother's, sit near me.

"Hey, how are you? Everything's fine," I say.

"You know, I read a lot about Ben Bradlee and what's her name, Graham, but what are they really like?" asks John. He is one of those avid newspaper readers who is smart and cynical enough to know that the real news often doesn't make the paper. Like most people, he can dig a little gossip about the rich and famous.

"Well, I don't really know . . . "

He laughs. "Come on. Don't really know? You work there."

I want to say, yeah, but just barely, but of course I don't. I grew up summers here, on the Vineyard, with people who've seen me through many stages. Mostly, they're proud and happy I'm working at the *Post*. After all, it's not just me, Jill Nelson, who's working at the *Washington Post*, it's all of Negrodom. It'd be the same, only negative, if I was a mass murderer; we'd all see my having machine-gunned my boss and a few coworkers as somehow reflecting negatively on each and every one of us. Sometimes it's really hard to know who I am under the burden of this collective identity. Cynically, I suspect that people see me as a "real" writer only now that some caucasians have legitimized me.

So instead I say, "Really. I don't think I've ever spoken to Katherine Graham." John looks disappointed. His wife Ada perks up. "Well, maybe I've said good morning to her in the elevator a few times, but we don't hang out together." They laugh, but it's the truth. I've seen Katherine Graham's photograph more than I've seen her. And most of what I've seen of her is her back. I can tell you this on good authority: she wears some beautiful, expensive clothes. I know this by the way her zippers are hand-stitched, the buttons just so.

"So, what's Bradlee like?"

"Very macho, and with a filthy mouth." Everyone laughs.

"I bet he is. I just bet he is!" says Pauline Flippen, the mother of a good friend of mine, a longtime activist in New Rochelle, and a woman who does not bite her tongue. Heavy and with bad knees, she comes to the beach every day her legs will carry her, patiently swims laps, then sits until the sun begin to go down and her husband, Wilton, comes and picks her up. Like me, it is only in the water that she is buoyant.

"I bet he can be a son of a bitch. Because the media, the media," she says in a trilling voice, like she's singing opera, "is so goddamn corrupt I don't know what to say about it. Am I right? Am I right?" This time, the trill segues into a rich, round sound somewhere between a laugh, a cackle, and a croon.

I want to say, "Damn straight you're right! Going to work there was the dumbest move I ever made, I can't believe I thought it'd be okay, that I could actually do some good work. I feel like my writing's getting worse since I got there, not better. I just came off a week's suspension for which I got just about no support from my colleagues and I only have four more days until I have to go back. Oh God!" But I'm afraid if I do I'll start crying. Plus, as much as I am filled with dread and foreboding, I feel a greater sense of obligation to their expectations, never mind my own.

"Yeah, you're right." I sit up. "I think I'll go in the water." I get up and walk toward the waves, force myself into the icy water, swim out, out, out until my arms get tired. I turn over and float on my back, eyes open, look up at the deep blue sky. A gull circles overhead. I try to think about nothing. That makes me think even more intensely about my suspension, my job, my future, my unhappiness, my-my-my-my-my, as Grandma Nelson would say, shaking her head, when she surveyed something hopeless.

After a while I glance back toward land. I can see the folks sitting on the beach, my mother's house on the street above us, watching. I don't start slowly swimming in until I see John, Ada, Pauline, and the last of the stragglers packing up their umbrellas and beach chairs.

CHAPTER TWENTY-FOUR

"So. My understanding is that you're no longer on the staff of the magazine. But that doesn't appear to be your understanding. Is it?" the woman sitting across the table from me says, or rather screeches. This is a person whose normal conversational tone is a combination of fingernails on blackboard and the mating call of a cat in August.

It is January, 1989, and I am having a very late lunch date with Mary Hadar, the assistant managing editor of the Style section and the only female assistant managing editor at the *Post*. Now that Lovinger has been disappeared, it is Hadar—rather than the magazine's new editor—who has been given managerial responsibility for the magazine. We are at Twigs, a yuppified, pseudodramatic yet nondescript restaurant on 16th Street, right around the corner from the paper. The only other time I can remember eating here is with Tom Wilkinson several days after I became chair of the Newspaper Guild unit. After lunch with Hadar, I am convinced that eating at Twigs with a manager is the corporate equivalent of the kiss of death.

"No. That's not my understanding," I say. "Why don't you tell me why it's yours?"

Hadar smiles vacantly, butters a piece of roll. "Well, haven't you talked to Milton? My understanding is that he really wants you on Metro and you'll be moving over there in a few weeks. Milton has talked to you about this, hasn't he?"

"Yes. We've talked about it. But I didn't think anything was settled," I say. What I really want to say is, "Shit, motherfucker. I can't believe this crapola. Now that you all have gotten rid of Lovinger and most of the people he hired, it's time to get rid of me, too. Throwing out the baby with the bath water. Now, ain't that nothin'. Why me? I mean, what did I do?"

But of course, I don't. Instead I say, "Well, I'd really like to stay on at the magazine. I mean, that's what I came here to do. I'm a magazine writer. I've never worked on a daily in my life."

Hadar stares at me, batting her eyes like she has sand under her contact lenses. A few crumbs of bread rest on her prominent bosom.

"My understanding is that you haven't been happy on the magazine, and that Len and Milton felt you'd be happier in Metro," she says. I bet, the newspaper equivalent of Coon Town, where Negroes are happier among their own (you see, it's not segregation, they *like* it that way).

Lunch lasts for about an hour, during which Hadar does a good deal of her aural equivalent of talking, but I can't remember much of what is said. What I do remember is that early on it became clear to me that Hadar, like Wilkinson, is simply a messenger girl, carrying water for the real powers-that-be from their offices on the north wall. My moving to Metro is a *fait accompli*; the only power I have is to iron out the details. The notion of working on the daily side of the newspaper means only one thing to me, chasing fire engines, something I know damn well I'm too old and too obstinate to do. Avoiding this fate is worth trying to cop a last plea. When the coffee comes, I pull out a cigarette and say, "I think there were real problems between me and Jay Lovinger, especially after the first issue, but there are a lot of stories I'd still like to do for the magazine."

"Oh, you smoke. I've quit. But may I have a cigarette?" Hadar says. I give her one. "Please don't tell anyone," she says conspiratorially.

"Okay. Of course not," I say, even though I cannot imagine this woman who's in the process of fucking me thinking I'd keep a goddamn secret of hers if I thought revealing it would do me any good. This lunch is about taking my job away from me, not nicotine bonding.

"Tell me about your story ideas. What kinds of things do you think the magazine should be writing about now that Bob Thompson's the new editor?"

I almost guffaw a big cloud of smoke into her face. I've just essentially been corporately, genteelly, non-legal-actionably fired over a lousy lunch, and now I'm supposed to give this woman my ideas? But I don't cackle insanely. I have been at the *Washington Post* for nearly three years, long enough to project the coloration, if not of a team player, then at least not of a downright seditious Negro. Almost, but not quite.

I pop in my third-level idea cassette, the one where I index story ideas that are kind of good, half-baked, full of unrealized potential, and that I haven't been able to sell as freelance pieces. She actually seems interested in some of them, although it's hard to tell what with my being so distracted by her constantly blinking eyes and scratchy voice. What seems like interest could just be wishful thinking, not that it matters. The deed is done. I am destined to become a Metro reporter if I want to stay on the corporate tit. Ironically, Milton Coleman comes to my rescue, providing the only harbor left for me at the *Post*.

That weekend I drive to New York for a date. Really. It has come to this. Two-hundred and forty-one miles for a date with a man I haven't laid eyes on since my bon voyage party at Earl Caldwell's three years earlier. But I am glad to get out of D.C., relieved to be anticipating something besides the next axe falling. I figure if nothing else, I'll get a good dinner in exchange for 500 miles worth of Volvo depreciation.

I'd like more. I'm lonely, bored, and horny. The last time I had sex it was with a man whose thighs were smaller than my arms, who jumped out of bed and started playing with a yo-yo soon after he came. I can't even remember the last time I had good sex with a man. Or conversation. Or companionship.

I'm ready to get into something. So a few Saturdays earlier when my phone rang and a slightly lyrical man's voice said, "Jill Nelson? It's Michael. Michael, from the shoe store."

I said, "Oh, hi. How are you?" And then got into a fairly long conversation, even though I had been on my way to the supermarket and couldn't remember much about him, except that he was fine and that I would have given it up to him after Caldwell's except he was with someone.

"So. Do you ever get to New York?"

"Sure. A lot."

"I know," he laughs. "I've seen your daughter on Broadway a few times."

"Oh. I think she mentioned she'd seen you."

"Did you get my letters from Europe?"

Now it's all coming back to me. As I was moving to D.C., he was about to go to Europe to find fame and fortune as a model. I have a vague recollection of receiving sporadic communiques from him, but I never really focused on them, or on him. But hearing his voice makes me focus. Right. *Right*. The brother is fiiiiinnnnnne!

"Well, when will you be in New York again?"

"I'm not sure. Maybe in a few weeks."

"Well, why don't you call me? I'd like to take you to dinner." "Okay. I'll let you know when I'll be there," I say, playing it cool. The minute I get off the telephone I grab my calendar and start figuring out how soon I can take him up on his offer without seeming overeager, desperate, or trampish.

It's just my luck that the weekend I'm supposed to see him there's a blizzard and I can't drive for three days, which is how long it takes the dedicated employees of the D.C. Department of Public Works to show up on my street with a snow plow. But then, maybe it is lucky, since by the time I do make it to the Big Apple a few weeks later, it's just after my Hadar luncheon and I'm about as much in need of some R&R as a mortal can get.

As far as men are concerned, Washington is the black woman's equivalent of T.S. Eliot's wasteland. To begin with, women outnumber men, although exact figures are hard to come by—not because they don't exist, but because their release would result in a mass psychotic episode among the sisters.

But let's take the few men there are. Then subtract those who are alcoholics or drug abusers. Then those who are overtly gay and, more insidious, those who are covertly gay. Next take away those who are unemployed. Then those who are married, although it often takes some effort to discern this, since both wedding rings and honesty are in short supply among the men here in the nation's capital.

What you're left with is a tiny number of men who are, in the most broad and generous sense of the word, available. Once you subtract from this number those who are bourgeois social climbers, liars, egomaniacs, moochers, self-important, stupid, impotent, sexually perverse, or just plain boring, there's damn near no one left.

Those who remain are usually trouble. The men I meet are crazy, and not even in an interesting way. I've seen shit like a date spending a third of dinner in the bathroom, coming back to the table rubbing his nose, and trying to play it off like he wasn't in there snorting coke—not because he cares what I think, but because he's too cheap to share. Or another one spending all evening telling me about the work he does and then suggesting what an interesting article—in the *Washington Post*, of course—the story of his life would be. Or the guy with the yo-yo.

With their Italian leather briefcases, faux Armani suits, pencil-thin moustaches, and smooth talk, the men in D.C. are mirror images both of each other and their corporate masters. Women, when we exist, do so as accoutrements, trophies, meal tickets, or feminine rungs in the ladder of success.

Since coming to D.C. I've had two tawdry affairs, and one pseudorelationship with a man who works at the *Post*. He was relatively bright, looked all right, and was nice to me. Plus, he smoked reefer, a big deal in Washington. For a few months we went to the movies and to bed. In bed, if I kept my eyes squeezed shut, I wouldn't have the weird out-of-body episodes that have become a barometer of the meaningless relationships I've had in my thirties. Like, I'm lying there on my back doing the nasty, and when I look up at the ceiling, I am there too, fully dressed and smoking a cigarette, commenting disdainfully on the proceedings.

Ceiling Jill: "Ooohhhh, roll those hips. Now do the fingernail trick on his back."

Bed Jill: "Go away."

Ceiling Jill: "How can I? We're here. Moan like it's really good to you. You know men love that."

Bed Jill: "Shut up and mind your own business."

Ceiling Jill: "I am, I am. Why don't you say something now, like, 'Oh, Daddy, you know it's good to me.' Men just love to be called Daddy. It makes them feel so masterful."

Bed Jill: "Fuck off!"

Ceiling Jill: "Hey, I'm trying to get off, although it won't be easy with this dork."

Bed Jill: "Leave me alone. Please."

Ceiling Jill: "God knows I'd like to. Why don't you freak him out and do some Kegel exercises while he's thrusting?"

"Come on!" I scream at my alter ego. I make the mistake of screaming out loud. Hearing me, my partner obeys, thrusts hard and fast, then collapses on my breasts and murmurs some generic post-orgasm line like, "Was it good for you too, baby?" On the ceiling, my alter ego exhales a cloud of smoke and smiles silently.

Right before I start dating the man from the *Post*, who I affectionately call the King, and then later, more appropriately, the Con, Misu—who is now fifteen and filled with the offhand viciousness of adolescence—tells me, "Mom, get a life." This is in response to my suggestion that we spend the weekend together, touring local slave plantations. Hey, it sounded like fun to me.

"Sorry, Mom. Me and my friends are going to the mall."

"The mall? You can go to the mall anytime. Let's go check out the plantations."

"I don't think so . . . "

"Don't you want to see the slave shanties, the shackles, the land our ancestors slaved on, died for?"

"Yeah sure. I guess so. But not this weekend. I want to hang out with my friends."

"Look. We can drive around Virginia, then stay in a hotel, order chocolate shakes and cheeseburgers from room service, even watch one of the pay movies." I resort to bribery.

"That'd be nice, Mom. But how about another weekend? This weekend, the mall's where it's at."

"The mall? The mall? How disgusting. Are you becoming a D.C. airhead, only interested in lurking around some tacky shopping center, ogling boys and giggling?" I am nearly screaming. I know I'm losing it, turning into every teenager's version of the parent from hell, but I can't control myself. "What about history, culture, the sacrifices of our ancestors? I mean, where would we be if Harriet Tubman hung out at the mall instead of freeing her people?"

That's when Misu turns, looks me dead in the eye, and in a voice so dry it could wither a cactus says, "Mom, get a life."

So I did what any lonely, depressed, professionally unrewarded woman in her mid-thirties would do. I got a man, hoping he would give me a life, that I wouldn't have to work for one of my very own.

That only lasts a few months. I knew the Con and I weren't long for the world of coupledom when I visited his house in a predominantly white suburb and he showed me his fairly extensive gun collection. Just as disturbing was a photograph over his bed, about four feet long, of white women's asses. I'm not surprised when one night he comes late to pick me up for the movies, looking stricken. I ask, "Is something the matter?"

"Yes. I have something to tell you. Something horrible happened tonight as I was leaving work."

"What?" I ask, sitting down on the couch near, but not next to him, already establishing distance, somehow knowing what he was going to say.

"Milton Coleman called me into his office and told me that a white woman I work with has accused me of sexual harassment."

You know, it was like I knew exactly what he was going to say, like the whole time I'd been going out with him I'd just been waiting for this axe to fall. I had made him swear he wouldn't tell anyone we were dating, so it wouldn't fall on me, too. Being an S.B.W. (Strong Black Woman), I didn't dump him right then and there, even though, to tell you the truth, I think he probably did harass her, simply from thinking she was a friend. He probably thought hey, people are people, it's okay to tell dirty jokes and sexual tales to women just because they sit across the desk from you every day and they're civil to you. After all, many harassers never realize they're being offensive—they're just joking, trying to be friendly.

Not being a Stupid Black Woman, I squashed the Con's suggestion that we "go public." As far as I could tell, his reasoning was that public association with Guild-chair, pro-black me would make the charge of sexually harassing a white woman laughable, thus helping his case. But I nixed any P.D.A. As Leon Dash, a wonderfully principled brother on the investigative staff, said after helping the Con strategize his way out of getting canned, "I'm willing to help the brother, but where there's smoke, there's fire." I stood by the Con until the paper's investigation was completed. He wasn't fired, but he was admonished by Bradlee, "Don't shit where you work."

Years ago, my friend Allyson, who I met as an undergrad at City College of New York when we were both single mothers struggling to raise ourselves and our young daughters, told me a wonderful thing: "There are three kinds of people in the world, friends, colleagues, and acquaintances, and it's important to know the difference. Because when you treat colleagues or acquaintances like friends, you make a big mistake. If you go out for drinks after work with someone from the job, it's still work. You don't say or do anything you wouldn't in the office. Because if you do, it'll come back to haunt you. That's for sure."

This is a piece of very good advice I've used for years. I now proceed to apply it to the whole subject of office romances. Too bad King Con didn't have a friend like Allyson.

CHAPTER TWENTY-FIVE

"I mean I've never seen him like this he's emaciated he looks like he's starving to death and he smells I've never smelled him before but he stinks I don't know what I'm going to do he's gone for a week or more at a time and then comes home closes himself up in that room and does nothing but sleep or eat he won't talk to me I think he's on that crack . . . " my mother says.

"Huh?" I say, shaken out of my romantic reverie.

We are sitting in her living room in New York. It is a Saturday in late January, the morning after my first date with Michael. I would much rather fantasize on the date, the man, the sexual vibes, than listen to my mother, but she's persistent.

"I don't know what to do but we've got to do something I'm afraid your brother's going to kill himself this time I really am he won't say anything and then just when he's beginning to look better he's gone again sneaks out the door and I won't see him for another two weeks," she says, her voice cracking.

"Okay. I'll try to talk to him. Is he here?"

"I think he's asleep in the back room."

I walk down the apartment's short hallway to the back room, the room Misu and I lived in for over a year before we moved to Washington, the room where my brother Stanley now stays, sometimes. The door is closed. I knock.

"Stanley? Hey, Stan. It's me. Can I come in? Let's talk. What's up? I haven't seen you in months." I continue to tap on the door. My knuckles make an empty, abandoned sound against the wood. My mother stands at the bend in the hallway, watching me.

"Okay, well, I'm coming in. Hope you're decent," I say, weakly attempting a joke. Then I turn the doorknob, open the door. The room, with twin beds, is in twilight, even though it is a bright, brittle, winter's day. One wall is all glass, windows and a door leading out to a small terrace, but no light comes in. The windows are closed, the curtains pulled tight, pinned in place.

Nearly every surface is covered with clothing, blankets, books, papers. Sweaters, shirts, pants, and socks drape over chairs, spill out of drawers, mound on the rug, paper the floor. What little air there is smells thick and sour. The sweat of impurity, of street reefer, of dope and crack, permeates the room. It is the stench of the rush of the high, of instant cold sweats, of scratching, scratching, scratching, of yellow crud oozing out of the pores on your face because your body's so full of bad cut that the pimples pop spontaneously.

Both beds are lumpy, piled high with the debris of my brother's addiction. I cannot tell if he is there, buried somewhere beneath the pain and drugs and funk. "Stanley?"

"Hey, Jill." The voice is thin, gravelly, muffled from under the blankets, far away.

"What's up?"

"Nothing. I'm just sleepy. I'll see you later."

"Let's talk, okay?"

"Yeah. Sure. Later."

"Well . . . " I can feel my mother's worry behind me. "Are you all right?"

"Yeah. I just need to get some sleep. Close the door on the way out." He pulls further under the covers.

I am dissed, dismissed, don't know what else to say or do. This is my older brother, my Gemini twin, my protector since we were kids. I love him, do not want to violate him. But I am angry at his addiction, at the pain he causes himself and all the rest of us. For one of the few times in my life I do not know what to do, so I just stand in the doorway, clutching the doorknob.

"Come on," my mother whispers. "Let him sleep. You can talk to him later."

As I back out, pull the door closed, something round and silver across the room catches my eye—a film can. It lies with several others in the one corner of the room that remains sacrosanct. It is neatly piled with video cassettes, film cans, lighting equipment, the paraphernalia of my brother's life, not his death.

My mother and I go into the living room. I sip my vodka on the rocks and page through one of the dozens of magazines neatly arranged on the coffee table as my mother talks about my brother's addiction.

"He looks terrible I've never seen him look this bad it's like he's trying to kill himself I don't know what the shit to do," she says.

"Kick him out. Tell him he's got to go into a program and if he doesn't, throw him out," I say. "Want me to do it for you?" I offer, always the dutiful daughter.

"No . . ."

"Well, what are you going to do? You can't live here with him, trapped and worried all the time. You have to do something."

"I know that," she snaps. "I'd just like to get some professional advice."

"I'll call Beny Primm," I offer, getting up. Primm is a doctor and expert on drug addiction. He is also a Vineyard person, which means we can depend on his being discreet. As my mother always told us as children, "Discretion is the better part of valor."

I go into the other room and dial Beny's number. I sit there on the side of my mother's big bed listening to his telephone ring. Her television is on with the sound off. A white couple jerks by, hand dancing, like they used to on "American Bandstand", our favorite show way back when in the late Fifties, early Sixties, when no one was dying, crazy, or in therapy, when we were still a family.

One of the few things the four of us children could agree on was the importance of watching "American Bandstand" every weekday at four o'clock. We'd crowd into the living room a few minutes before four, pushing and shoving to get the best viewing seat. Usually Stanley, one year older than me, would turn the television on. Then he'd pretend to switch the channel to cartoons or a western while Lynn and I howled angrily, suffering the pains of pre-teen withdrawal.

Stanley was, of course, just as enamored of "American Bandstand" as we were. After a few moments of this ritualistic torture, the ancient black-and-white television would crackle to life and the music to the wordless "American Bandstand" theme would come on. We'd all grunt along.

"Welcome to 'American Bandstand!' " the host, Dick Clark, would say, shouting to be heard above the music and the sounds of happy teenagers.

In the background, a few dozen couples, all white, would be doing the stroll or the bop. "Today, we're going to rate the records and our guest stars will be Joey Dee and the Starlighters, singing their hit song, 'The Peppermint Twist!' Don't go away, we'll be right back!"

We loved commercial breaks. My brother Stanley jumped up from his chair, ran and stood in front of the television. His elbows held stiffly at his sides, brow furrowed with concentration, he started to do the twist.

"Move!" Lynn screamed. "I can't see!" This made Stanley twist even harder, faster, his frown turning into a smile. Ahhh, the joys of successful teasing.

"Move, you idiot," Lynn wailed, getting up from the couch and advancing toward him. "You are so infantile," she said, her voice full of pity. Words were always one of my sisters best weapons. It was hard to argue or play the dozens with her, because she'd call you some word you didn't know the meaning of and win by default. But Stanley was, in my mother's words, "hardheaded." My sister's anger only made him twist more frantically, his face contorted into a twelve-year-old's version of lasciviousness. Lynn advanced toward him, climbing on top of the coffee table that separated them, overturning a bowl of walnuts left over from Christmas in the process.

I watched my sister and brother. I was afraid to laugh at Stanley, whose exaggerated rendition of the twist really was pretty funny, his hands flying stiffly and his ass poked out. I was afraid for one reason only: I shared a room with Lynn. One does not cross her roommate, especially if she is an older sister. I learned this lesson the hard way. Once I spent a week in silence because my sister refused to talk to me. Another time she insisted on telling me scary stories every night when we got into bed. I was afraid to go to sleep for weeks, lying awake listening to her contented snores as my eyes checked the curtains and the dust ruffle around our dressing table for goblins, and examining our shelves to see if any of our dolls had come alive and were moving in on me.

It wasn't easy not to laugh—Stanley was funny. If I had an ally in the family, he was it. Maybe it was because we were the same sign, Gemini, born a year and six days apart. As the years passed we came to look so much alike we often passed ourselves off as twins. Perhaps it had something to do with being middle children, sandwiched in between an older sister and younger brother, able to become lost in our parents' eyes because somehow it was assumed that because we were in the middle we'd be okay.

"You kids! Stop fighting!" my mother yelled from the kitchen. Sometimes, even when we were quiet, she'd call out for us to "quiet down," like she was just checking, keeping all the bases covered, anticipating and heading off the inevitable fights that come from having four damn near stair-step children.

But Stanley was hardheaded, remember? Lynn's anger and Mom's admonishment only made him twist harder. Ralphie, the youngest, then seven, simply sat on the couch, watching. He did that a lot, like he couldn't believe the level of teasing and bullshit the three of us engaged in. His eyes darted from Stanley to Lynn like he was watching a ping-pong game about to transcend the table.

Me, I tried to hold it in. But then I did what I usually did, which was burst out laughing. Hiding my feelings has never been my strong suit. Immediately the focus shifted. "You're gonna get it later," Lynn yelled at me, turning and giving me one of her patented evil looks. "Wait until we go to bed."

"Hey, Jill. Look at this," Stanley called out. Without a break in the rhythm, he twisted his body around to face me. Still moving his arms rapidly from left to right, right to left, he begins swinging them in circular patterns, drawing small obelisks in the air, faster and faster. Then, he jumped! Contorting his 100-pound body, using the force of his weight as impetus, he rose a foot, maybe eighteen inches into the air, still twisting frenetically, did a 360-degree turn, and hit the ground twisting. His face was intent, bent into something between a grin and a grimace.

"Yeah! Yeah! Yeah!" I shouted. Who could help it? He had done the impossible, a 360-degree jump and turn while still twisting, without losing the beat. Was there any doubt he was "American Bandstand" material? Would that Dick Clark, back from a commercial break and introducing a record to be rated—"I give it an eighty. I like the beat and it's good to dance to"—could have seen him. Instant stardom.

Lynn was not impressed. "You idiot, you idiot, I hate you!" she screamed. "Shut up!"

Ralphie and me, laughing pretty hard now, tried to stifle it. The party was over; Lynn's wrath was not something to be courted. Consequences, though sometimes swift, were just as often painful and protracted. My sister was the most patient of us all.

Abruptly, the swinging door between the kitchen and the living room rocked open. My mother stood there, her hands covered with flour, an apron tied around her waist. "What's going on in here? What are you four fighting about this time?"

Me, Lynn, Stanley, and Ralph exchanged brief glances, in that instant taking a vow of silence. We knew that our mother's authority was absolute, her punishment swift. The television will go off, we will be sent to our rooms to do homework. We look at her innocently.

"What's all the fussin' about?"

"Nothing. We're just playing around," said Stanley.

My mother looked at us skeptically. "I hope so. Remember what Granddaddy Nelson always says, 'Act nice everybody.'" She turned back to the kitchen from whence she came. We turned our faces toward Dick Clark's on the tube. Joey Dee and the Starlighters sang "The Peppermint Twist."

I don't know what makes me think about the four of us watching "American Bandstand" twenty-five years later while I'm waiting for Beny Primm to answer the telephone and tell me how to save my older brother.

It has something to do with remembering how funny and smart and full of life he was once, back then, by way of trying to wash away the smell of death and despair that surrounds him now, lying there, just a few feet away.

"Hello. This is Beny Primm."

"Beny? Hi. It's Jill Nelson. Stanley's sister. From the Vineyard. Listen, I'm really worried about him and need your help . . ."

I spend the next two weeks in Washington falling in love with Michael long-distance and marshalling the forces of the Nelson family to intervene in my brother's addiction. In between romantic, getting-to-know-you telephone calls with Michael, I talk to my brother Ralph, who agrees to fly from Berkeley to New York the following weekend so that we can confront Stanley about what his addiction's doing, not only to him, but to the rest of us. My father, Popi New Age, is into his latest guru, an ex-lawyer named Arnold Patent, and declines to become involved, even though Beny Primm tells us it's best if all family members are present when we do the intervention with Stanley. Lynn, of course, is out of the picture; we know she won't participate.

"I love Stanley, unconditionally. Just the way he is," my father responds when I tell him the plan. "He's exactly where he wants to be. He is doing the only thing he can do . . . "

"Are you kidding? You think the only thing he can do is be a crack fiend and die?"

"Jill. Jill. He is exactly where he wants to be. He may well have come onto this earth to take himself out in this way," my father says. His voice is in what I call his guru mode: monotone, thick, orally catatonic. Condescending. Nonjudgmental my ass.

"Are you serious? So, you're not going to do anything. You're not going to come to the meeting?" I am almost screaming.

"No. I think not. But I love and support my son, unconditionally . . . "

"Have you seen him lately? He looks half dead. If we don't do something, he's going to die."

"Jill. He is exactly where he wants to be. There's no place else he could be."

"Well, if we don't do something, he'll be dead. Dead."

"Maybe that's what he came here for."

"Okay. Fine." I slam down the receiver.

You know, it may be fine for him, but I'll be goddamned if I'm going to let my big brother, my ally, my numero uno since Lynn went away and left us, kill himself without my trying to stop him. I know him. I've been there. Initially, doing drugs may be about getting high, but sooner than later it's simply about deadening the pain that comes from living real life on its own terms. At that moment, I think my brother Stanley is more likely to die than to live. I realize this intervention is as much about soothing my conscience so I won't feel guilty at the funeral as it is about having any positive effect.

My brother Ralph arrives from California with a bad cold and fever. I drive from D.C. through the rain. When I get to New York, Ralph is lying on the living room couch, swaddled in blankets. Stanley is barricaded in the back room, asleep. My mother is in the kitchen, cooking and afraid of what is about to happen. But she is *here*.

Even though we have agreed that Stanley must begin treatment immediately, or we are going to move him out of her apartment and change the locks, my mother is equivocating. Having already lost Lynn, she is terrified at the thought of losing another child. She wants to modify the program, settle for promises of good behavior: not because she believes it will work, but because she thinks nothing else will.

After hours of waiting, small-talking in hushed voices, Ralph goes into Stanley's room and gets him up. At first Stanley tries to play the crisis off, comes into the living room making jokes, greeting me and Ralph like it's a family reunion, a holiday and not a meltdown. But he's emaciated, his skin is gray and cracked, he looks like an elephant starving on the Serengeti Plain, slowly making his way to the burial ground to die.

Even so, nobody says much, or not much I can remember. But for once our silence isn't full of denial, fear, commitment to keeping those race secrets, never letting anyone know that maybe we're not the perfect Negroes, the ones most likely to be chosen to integrate this, be the first that, the ones whose lives are so neatly, perfectly repressed that we can withstand the scrutiny of the media, the crackers, and each other.

Years later, when he has been clean for three years and is on a perennial diet, his weight no longer controlled by drug abuse, I ask Stanley what he remembers about that weekend. It is not words he recalls, but feeling. "I remember lying in bed sick. I heard somebody outside and it was Ralph and thinking, 'I guess I'm pretty bad,' and then when you showed up, I thought 'The shit is bad'. In a weird way, I felt good. I think I wanted somebody to stop me from getting high. I don't remember exactly what was said, but I was glad you all were there, because before, in a way, when nobody said anything, it was like, 'Stanley's okay.'"

I remember that it was Ralph—not Mom, who's afraid of completely losing her son, even though he's already damn near lost, or me, the confrontational, "dramatic" one—who finally says, "Look. You have to do something, Stan. You're dying. You've got to make a choice: either go into drug treatment or we're going to pack your stuff and move it out of Leil's apartment. I love you, man, I don't want to watch you die."

I add, "You can go into treatment here or come to Washington with me and get into a program there," and Stanley says, "I'll go to Washington, if that's okay."

Even though we are all full grown, in our thirties, that weekend in Leil's apartment it's like we're kids again, it's been that long since we've been together under one roof in the wintertime. We are learning not just how to talk but to communicate, not only with words but with our feelings. Much later, Ralph, who slept in the room with Stanley, describes what happened between them, lying side by side at night, as "unspoken rebonding."

Monday night, after Michael, Stanley, and I drive Ralph to the airport, we pack the car for the trip to D.C. I lean against it, hug my new, still-unconsummated boyfriend, who presses his pelvis into mine and whispers, "You're doing a good thing," in between long kisses, and then he suddenly pulls away, saying, "Look at Stanley." I see my brother on the passenger's side of the car, pantomiming a slow, exaggerated bop away from the Volvo, us, salvation. "Stanley!" I yell, frightened. He stops, turns, opens the car door. His thin, gray, emaciated face is smiling, mischievous, teasing, just like that little twister's twenty-five years ago.

CHAPTER TWENTY-SIX

"I thought you were spending the night at Rashiki's?"

"I was. But she decided to go to the movies with Malcolm at the last minute," Misu says.

"Why don't you go with them? I'll give you the money."

"Mom. They're going on a date. You know, alone," Misu says.

"Well, what about my date?"

"What's the difference? I'll stay in my room. Anyway, Stanley's here, too."

Wearing a stained apron, I stand in the kitchen of my house in Washington, my belly pressed lightly against the stove, feeling the warmth enter my body as I talk to my sixteen-year-old daughter. Around me food abounds. A Dutch oven of blackeyed peas bubbles on one burner, brown rice simmers on another, a bowl of carrot and raisin salad sits on a counter. In the oven, a pan of eggplant parmesan cooks slowly. A bowl of sliced apples sits on the drainboard marinating in sugar and cinnamon, waiting to be wrapped in pie crust.

This is not my usual mode of cooking. It is not Christmas, Thanksgiving, Martin Luther King Jr.'s birthday. It is the weekend of consummation. Michael is arriving on the late train. I've cooked enough food both to seduce him and to nourish him for the weekend.

I blink my eyes, but the face of my lovely daughter standing in front of me is still there when I open them. I think about clicking my Reeboks together three times and whispering "Home alone, home alone, home alone," but don't. Instead I say, "Well, what about spending the night at someone else's house? Janice? Kim? Abena? Someone?"

"Sorry, Mom. Everyone's either busy or I don't like them. What's the big deal? I won't ruin your Cosmo Girl weekend."

I want to yell, "Yes you will. Just by being here. Even if I don't see you or Stanley. Look, you're the one who told me to get a life, and now that I have one you're mooching in on it. All I wanted was one damn weekend alone, but was that too much to ask? Yes! I told you and Stanley weeks ago to find something else to do when Michael came, everyone said okay, but here we are at the last minute and both of you are home with Mommy . . . "

Instead I say, "Yeah, all right. Are you at least going out tonight?"

"Uh huh, to the movies. I'll be back late."

"Good," I snap.

"Mommy, Mommy, why you buggin'?" Misu sings.

"I'm not buggin'!"

"God, Mom, a little hyped aren't you?" Misu says smugly. In the instant it takes me to turn from the stove and on her, she's disappeared up the stairs.

"That food smells good, Jill. When are we eating?" Stanley comes into the kitchen laughing, wearing socks, walking his slue-footed walk. Still thin, he is no longer gray. He has been living with us for a month, going to Narcotics Anonymous meetings two or three times a day.

"We're not. I'm cooking this food for Michael," I say, and viciously punch stuffing into the cavity of a chicken.

"I guess Love Man eats a lot," Stanley teases.

"Don't call him Love Man."

"That's what he is, isn't he?"

Well, no, but that's what I'd like him to be after a month of what Misu calls phone sex, late-night conversations held after the rates go down when we're sleepy, in bed, or both, talking about feelings, feelings, feelings, because it's so safe doing so when the other person can't see or touch you. Hanging up the phone and snuggling under the covers feeling damp and throbbing, nipples tight and aching to be sucked, considering masturbation but deciding against it. I opt instead for the exquisite torture of caressing every part of him with my mind while my body represses itself. Anyway, masturbation has never been my thing. It is too singular, too lonely, there is no one to talk to afterward. For me, who grew up in so much silence, the talking is as good as the doing, sometimes better.

But after a month of unrequited passion, I'm ready. But *alone*—without my brother in the room next door or my daughter across the hall.

Of course, the best-laid plans get fucked up. Is it Misu's fault Rashiki's got a date? And what could I say to Stanley when he came to me and said, "Look. Is it all right if I stay here this weekend? I don't feel comfortable going to New York yet, I don't want to relapse . . . " It's not that I don't love them both madly, but it's not easy to relax into unbridled passion with your big brother and little daughter on either flank.

Michael, of course, is his usual easygoing self when I call him up ranting. "They won't leave, they won't get out. They're going to be here all weekend," I wail.

He laughs. "Are they going to sleep in the bed with us?" Over time, I will come to understand that responding with a question to what he sees as unreasonable anger or demands is part of his persona. But right then, even after hours of phone sex, I don't know him well enough to say, "Of course they're not going to sleep with us but they're going to be there. Here. In the house. We'll have to whisper, put on robes when we go to the bathroom or get something to eat. I'll have to bite the pillow when I come. I don't know about you, maybe you're one of those strong silent types . . . "

"What time does your train get in?" I ask instead.

A little after ten. I finish cooking, Misu goes to the movies. I call Deborah, a woman who became a close friend during my union crisis, herself a former union activist who was part of a successful suit against Amtrak some years ago, a truly trustworthy person. She comes and takes Stanley to Takoma Station, a local jazz club. I change into a skirt that shows off my legs and a pair of short boots, Puss n' Boots I am, I am, and go to the train station. Typically, he's on C.P.T. (colored people's time) and damn near the last one off the train. He comes sauntering out the door from the track, looking finer than I remember, taller, blacker, teeth whiter than in my imagination, flanked by two short white girls looking up at him adoringly.

Before I can question or get pissed, he smiles me a smile full of happiness, eagerness, and lust; that smile crosses the fifty feet between us and wraps itself around me so tight I shiver. The girls see the smile, follow it to me, smiling back, the big black woman, full grown, standing there waiting for her man, and they just peel off, disappear, now you see them, now you don't.

"Are you hungry?"

"Not for food."

"Want something to drink?"

"Maybe some juice."

"How was the trip?"

"Long."

"What'd you want to do this weekend?"

"Get to know you."

"Ha ha ha," nervous-like.

I've shown him my house and we're sitting on the couch in the living room, next to each other but not touching, both of us wanting to but not knowing if the other does. It's the slow dance of sex, redux, redux, but it's simultaneously a war: her and him waltzing, circling one another, dipping, feinting, the old cha cha cha, sparring partners we are, both knowing that when the first blow lands, the first touch touches, it'll be lust that explodes.

"Do you think it would be all right if we went upstairs now?" he says finally, bravely.

Then the door of my bedroom closes and he tackles me, throws his long, lithe body over mine. I am waterfalling backward onto my bed but not afraid of drowning, his arm is wrapped firmly around my waist, cushioning my descent. Once down his weight on top of me feels good.

Even with our clothes on I can feel his body heat, his temperature always a few degrees hotter than anyone else, his face close above me, teeth and eyes so white, white, white, tongue bright pink, uncoated, his smell the faint smell of sweat and goodness rolled into one, and that black skin that absorbs and refracts light and color glowing above me.

This time there is no ceiling Jill, no running commentary, no squeezed-shut eyes, after a time no words at all. He takes off my clothes and slides down my stomach. Holding my legs open he stares between them and I cannot believe my ears when he says, "You have a beautiful pussy, look at all those colors," but then he says it again and again in between licking and kissing and sucking.

He is a young man, but he's not in a hurry. He moves slowly over the terrain of my body, inspecting, caressing my hips, stomach, thighs, nipples. I watch him. He is smiling, a happy man getting to know my country but already speaking my language. Then he finally enters me, slow and hot. I burst into tears.

"Are you all right?" he asks, stops, looks down at me.

"I'm fine," I say, laughing and crying together.

"Don't cry," he says. "I love you." I wrap my legs tighter around his waist and hold on for dear life.

Later, we sit up in bed eating cold food and laughing. It is as if we are not only new lovers but also old friends who haven't seen each other in a few lifetimes and are playing catch-up. We spend most of the weekend in the bedroom, but the funny thing is, we're talking as much as making love, a lot of the time doing both at once. And laughing. I have finally found a man who can hear me laugh in bed and not lose his erection.

For the first time in years I'm not consumed with thoughts of the *Washington Post* or my family, worrying about Misu, dreading Monday, watching my back, fearing success as much as failure, being number one. My various traps do not seem so inescapable with Michael because he is so young, smart, unformed, and free. He is trying to figure out what he wants to do with his life, trying to build a business as a personal trainer. He has little money but offers emotional and spiritual support and understanding in abundance. He is not the ideal bourgie professional man who makes more money than I do, drives an expensive car, has a gold card, and is emotionally unavailable, just as I am not the trophy girl-friend/wife. He is not the Ex-Husband or any of the other men in my life.

Michael loves me without artifice. Not because I am a latter-day Harriet Tubman, or a Vineyard girl, or have nice legs, "good" hair, a good job with white folks, one-fourth inheritance of a house in Oak Bluffs. Without all that, he still likes me. I begin to see that "all that" is weighing me down.

Meanwhile, I am still chair of the Guild unit at the *Post*, although not much is happening as we wait for the investigation of the complaint to commence. After I returned from my week's suspension I put out a bulletin about what had happened, but malicious rumors crop up about faulty expense vouchers for other stories I've done. I'm not writing much, publishing much, saying much. Generally, I'm in limbo. Being with Michael makes me realize that things can go either way, they don't have to go down.

One weekend in New York, Michael asks me if I find him attractive. "Of course. Why?" I laugh, sipping my drink.

"Because it seems like you don't approach me until you've had two glasses of wine," he says.

"You think so?" I hold my wine glass, try to think straight.

"I just thought maybe you have to have blurred edges to be with me," he says softly.

A few days later, on March 9, 1989, back in D.C., Stanley sits in the living room, lacing his shoes to go to his third N.A. meeting of the day. Several yards away, in the shadow behind the kitchen door, I gulp down a shot of Remy, not wanting to drink in front of someone who's in recovery. My brother does not lecture or proselytize, but gulping drinks behind closed doors in my own home while my brother fights for sobriety in the next room makes me wonder why I have to drink at all. I pour the rest of the bottle down the drain. I have not had a drink since.

CHAPTER TWENTY-SEVEN

I am sitting in the *Post* cafeteria with assistant city editor Phillip Dixon when he drops the bombshell on me. It is May, 1990.

"I wanted to be the first to let you know," he says with what could be a smile or a smirk, "Milton and Mary Jo want you on the Barry trial."

"Are you kidding?"

"Nope."

"I don't want to do it." After more than four years at the *Post*, both on the magazine and the Metro desk, I have learned that working on the current "big story" may mean a chance to go A1; but it also means having not only your own editor, but also Milton Coleman, Len Downie, Ben Bradlee, and untold others looking over your journalistic shoulder. By now I know it's not worth it. Life at the *Post* has taught me that when you are black and female, always look a gift horse in the mouth—then gallop away from it as fast as humanly possible.

I've already had my flirtation with covering Barry. On Saturday, January 20, a few days after Barry's arrest, Dixon called me at home around ten at night.

"Jill, I need help."

"So why are you calling me?" We laughed.

"Seriously, the mayor's supposed to make a statement tomorrow morning and have a meeting with his advisors beforehand. I need someone to relieve Reuben outside the mayor's house in Southeast and stay there until whatever happens, happens."

"What time?"

He hesitated. "Six A.M."

"Are you kidding?"

"No. Look, you know I wouldn't call you if there was anyone else . . . "

"Okay, okay, what's in it for me?" We cut a deal for me to be paid one overtime day plus one day off with pay.

"I'll be there."

"Don't be late. Poor Reuben will be out there all night."

"I'm on my way to bed." I hung up.

The next morning I arrived at the mayor's house a few minutes past six. Reuben Casteneda, the newly hired night police reporter, looked tired, miserable, and cold. A Chicano from L.A., east coast nights must have been killing him. When he left, I stood across the street from Barry's darkened house, shooting the shit with Gary Cameron, the photographer. Around eight, Deneen Brown arrived, a young sister and a wonderful writer on the Virginia desk. Rumor had it that Jesse Jackson would be attending Barry's pre-statement powwow, and she'd been assigned to follow Jackson. The three of us ran our mouths, fidgeted to keep warm, and kept a sharp eye on the door of Barry Manor to see who went in or out.

Even though it was cold and wet, it was kinda fun out there. Dozens of media people lurked across the road from the Mayor's house. When someone approached, a pack of journalists lurched across the street, shouting questions and getting no answers. I liked it that two black women had been assigned to a "big story." This could have been a momentous day for me, Deneen, the *Post*, America. Somewhere, maybe, Martin Luther King Jr. was smiling.

Then Saundra Sapperstein Torry, a legal affairs reporter at the *Post*, showed up, and the dream was deferred. She looked like a yuppie version of the Wicked Witch of the West: skinny, pasty white, her hair jet black. She announced to Deneen that she was dismissed. Deneen stood her ground, gently insisting that she would stay and also work on the Jackson story. Sapperstein scurried off, called city editor Mary Jo Meisner, and *tattled*. As if Jesse Jackson anytime, but especially on the day the recently busted mayor of Washington makes his first public statement, wasn't big enough for both of them. Deneen went off to find a phone and call the office.

Just before nine, Rob Melton, who covered the mayor, arrived along with fellow reporters Michael Yorke and Steve Twomey. Late once again, I finally got it. Deneen and I were the Negro stand-ins. But when the real action started, this was a job for . . . White People!

They actually came up to me and asked me what had been going on, as if I was their early morning understudy, sent out to cover for them so they could catch a few more Z's. The early bird—a crow—catches the worm and then stands around holding it in her mouth until the late bird snatches it away? Maybe that's the part I had been cast, but I wasn't having any. I told them forget it, I didn't work for them, get their own damn news. Then I called Dixon at home, woke him up, and yelled at him for both of us. He sounded embarrassed, apologetic, chumped. Editor or not, it looked like he too had been a stand-in for the . . . White People!

So by May, I've had my fill of the Barry case already. I suspect covering the trial won't be any better. Am I being paranoid? Then again, in the 1960s, H. Rap Brown of the Student Non-Violent Coordinating Committee said, "Any black man who isn't paranoid is crazy." I kept a copy of that quote tacked on my wall for years. Now I'm asked to suspend disbelief one more time.

"Awwww, Jill. Come on. Why not?" Dixon asks. His voice is teasing, affectionate. Not only is he the only black editor on the Metro desk, he is my friend.

"I really don't think I'm the right person to cover the day-to-day of a trial—I don't think I have the patience. Can you imagine me sitting in a courtroom listening to testimony all day? I'd go berserk. Why not get Marcia Slacum Greene or someone else who's done that type of reporting and—" Before I can finish, Dixon interrupts.

"Slow down. They want you to be the lead feature writer, not the legal reporter, to do react pieces that play off what goes on at the trial. You won't have to be in the courtroom every day."

"Who's going to do the daily stories?"

"Other reporters. It'll be a team effort."

"What other reporters?" I ask suspiciously.

"Tracy Thompson, Michael Yorke, Bart Gellman for Metro. Occasionally a columnist or someone from Style might come for a day."

"Oh." I sit there across from Dixon, sipping herbal tea, and it all comes clear. The White People are going to have complete responsibility for the daily interpretation of the trial of Marion Barry, the black mayor of the nation's capital, on ten counts of cocaine possession, three counts of perjury, and one count of conspiracy to possess cocaine. The only black person involved in the coverage will be me, the colored writer writing "color" pieces. This assignment is a must to avoid.

"Phillip, I really don't want to do it."

"Why? It'll be fun," he says, laughing sarcastically. Easy for him to say, he'll be away all summer at Northwestern University's Management Training Center attending a "multicultural management program."

"You won't even be here. Who's going to edit me?"

"Well, Mary Jo is in charge of the coverage, but the editors will probably be Mintz and Pianin. Pianin will mostly be doing the political/legal stuff, so you'll probably be working with Mintz."

Like Dixon, John Mintz is an assistant city editor. I don't know him well, have never worked with him, but think he's a pretty all-right guy. My reasons for feeling this way are frighteningly simple: he's Jewish, which, since I come from New York, makes him a little more of a known quantity; his wife died several years ago from cancer, so he knows tragedy and personal loss; and the day I came back to work from my week's suspension, Mintz, on his way out to lunch, greeted me warmly and said, "Welcome back."

While I've never worked with Eric Pianin either, I'm not eager to. The reporters I am friendly with who are edited by Pianin characterize him as obsessed with office politics. Unlike Mintz, who has left me with three favorable impressions, Pianin has left only one. Walking by his desk I notice that he has the front page of the February 20 paper prominently displayed. The banner headline reads, "South Africa Frees Mandela After 27 Years." Underneath is a picture of Nelson and Winnie, fists clenched. I have the same page on the bulletin board above my desk. But is it enough to make us soulmates? Can I deal with him editing my copy merely because of our shared Mandela-itis, a popular affliction in the winter of 1990?

As for city editor Mary Jo Meisner, no problem. I am confident that she will be too busy playing politics, watching her back, and trying her best—within the bounds of journalistic objectivity, of course—to "get Barry," to worry about this little colored girl's color stories. Meisner is over six feet tall, thin, angular, and hyper. Helen Asenath Moody, a black woman who runs a business as a personal shopper and is incredibly astute at reading people based on their clothes and body language, met Meisner once and summed her up thus: "She's like a white man. You know how you'll be driving up Connecticut Avenue during rush hour and two white boys in Armani suits and leather briefcases will be standing on the corner, and without looking at the light they'll just step off the curb and start crossing the street, because they know they won't get run over? That's Meisner."

I ask Dixon, "Do I have to do it?"

"I think you should."

"Why?"

"It's a great assignment, it might be fun and it'll show that you can do that type of reporting," he says.

"It's a horrible assignment. It means I'll be stuck in D.C. all summer and won't be able to go to the Vineyard or New York to see my boyfriend," I whine. "Sitting around listening to Marion Barry all day and then coming back here to fight with these caucasians about the story won't be fun. Plus, who cares if I can do that type of reporting? I came here to be the weird feature writer."

Dixon laughs. "It'll be good. It'll show them you're a team player," he says.

"You really think I should do it?"

"I don't think you should refuse. You're the only black person on the team."

"Can't they get someone else? What about Patrice Gaines Carter, Marcia, someone?" I pause, searching for names of other African-American reporters.

"Patrice will just be getting back from her fellowship at Michigan, Marcia will be leaving for her Neiman Fellowship. Baby, it's you," Phillip says with a chuckle, quoting the words from an old song by the Shirelles.

During these grim months at the *Washington Post*, Phillip Dixon is the only thing standing between me and metamorphosis into a bitter paper pusher, a basket case, or the first newsroom mass murderer. A wiry, compact man who the *Post* hired away from the *Los Angeles Times* in 1989, Dixon and I first met when I took him to lunch at Ben's Chili Bowl on U Street several months before he moved to D.C. I was curious about the brother from another coast who would soon be editing me.

I chose Ben's for several reasons. One, the chili dogs are smokin'. Two, I am a big fan of Virginia Ali, a native of Virginia who, with her Trinidadian husband, Ben, owns the Chili Bowl. Three, I figure there's no better way to find out whether he's down than to take him to a soul food restaurant in de ghetto. Dixon did all right over lunch. But he won my heart when, as we were leaving, a man approached us selling two hot five-foot ficus trees. Not only did we cop, splitting the cost, but Dixon bargained the man down. A brother after my own heart.

Over the time we work together I come to know him as a man with a sharp sense of humor, as a superb conceptual and line editor, and as someone with enough ambivalence and angst about the newspaper business and his place in it to make me both like and respect him. But make no mistake—this is a man who's movin' on up, ambivalent or not.

Dixon is also black, which in my world started him out with a couple thousand bonus points. Of course, appearances can be deceiving. Even though, by virtue of race, Dixon started out in the plus column, it's fairly easy in the Jill System to lose that initial advantage, whatever color you are on the outside. Dixon stayed in the plus column and we did some good work together, not because he's black, but because he's smart, he listens, and when he puts his hands on a story he does so to make it better, not rewrite it in his own image.

This is a radical departure in style from my previous editor, Marc Fisher, who left to become Bonn bureau chief. From the minute I joined the Metro staff in February, 1989, Fisher was on my ass. Even though I'd negotiated a deal with Milton Coleman where I'd be primarily writing feature stories, the ones that take several days, Fisher was hellbent on "teaching" me how to turn out dailies.

Fisher was younger than me, shorter than me, and a team player. I suspect that to him I was a tall, arrogant, loudmouthed Negress, and he appointed himself the one who would cut me down to size. To that end, he obsessed relentlessly on where I was and what I was doing, tattled to Milton or Mary Jo when he didn't know my exact location, and got angry when I went to my desk in the morning instead of automatically punching in with him. When he got my copy, he didn't just edit it, he rewrote it, then sent it back to me moments before deadline with instructions that I give it a read-through to make sure it was all right. By that time a story might have been all right, but I wouldn't have written it.

Not unlike a few of the other editors and reporters at the *Post*, Marc Fisher appeared to be driven by two things: his own personal agenda for advancement within the institution, and adherence to the institution's requirements for success. As far as I could tell, nothing else seemed to matter to him.

When I arrived at the Metro desk in February, 1989, it had already been announced that Fisher was on his way to the foreign staff in a few months, so I tried not to let him bother me. It wasn't easy. He seemed to feel that he was the great literate father and I was the childlike native he'd come to teach journalism. He didn't seem to notice that I was thirty-seven, that I had been in this business longer than he had, that I was already good at what I did, and that I worked best when guided gently, as opposed to bullwhipped. Even though I had a plateful of feature stories in the works already approved by Milton or Mary Jo, he delighted in sending me out on some scarcely newsworthy daily assignments. Did he dream these up just to fuck with me?

On March 21, 1989, the *Post* published an A1 story by Tom Sherwood and Eric Pianin headlined, "Local Board of Trade Rebukes D.C. on Crime; Members Worried About Negative Image." The story was a report on a meeting of the board of directors of the Greater Washington Board of Trade at which several business leaders suggested that the high rate of homicide and drug-related arrests were injuring the District's economy and quality of life. The group adopted a resolution stating that D.C. "is perceived to be suffering from inefficiency and inconsistency of government." Buried in the middle of the twenty-nine-inch story was this sentence: "Yesterday, an official of George Washington University told the Board of Trade that parents of students had expressed concern about student safety at the West End campus."

A few days later, Fisher asked me to read the story, then go visit George Washington and other area campuses, interview students and administrators, and write a story about fear of D.C. in academia. He was really pumped. I wasn't, but the weather was nice, so what the hell. For a few days I prowled the local campuses: G.W., Howard University, Catholic University, Mount Vernon, Georgetown, talking to students. I didn't find one frightened student. Cautious, yes, but not frightened. No one was thinking of transferring to a university in safer, drug-free Wyoming, either, although a young woman from Colorado attending George Washington said that since national press reports appeared describing D.C. as the nation's "homicide capital," her mother had taken to telling her to "be real careful" at the close of telephone conversations.

According to the administrators I talked to, applications for the following year showed no decline. Were members of the incoming freshman year balking at the thought of learning and living in the "homicide capital"? No one knew. Most institutions hadn't even sent out their acceptance letters yet. I reported this back to Fisher; he instructed me to go out and dig harder. I dug harder.

"Marc, I really don't think there's a story," I said after a few days.

"Yes, there is. You have to dig deeper."

"I've talked to dozens of kids on campuses all over the city. None of them thinks it's an issue."

"Are they aware of the problems with crime and drugs?" he asked incredulously, as if only a moron could be aware and not petrified.

"Yeah, they are. A few of the college students I talked to said that while they weren't worried about their own personal safety, hearing about the drug and crime problems had made them more sensitive to what confronts young black kids, particularly males, who live in high-crime areas," I said. "Maybe that's the story, something about the geography of crime. Maybe I should go talk to public high school students and then contrast their perceptions with students at private colleges."

"No. I still think there's a story there," he said petulantly.

"Where?" If he was going to be petulant, I'd be sarcastic.

"Have you talked to the parents?"

"What parents?"

"The parents of the students you interviewed."

"No. For what?"

"Maybe the kids aren't being honest with you. Maybe their parents are worried and want them to transfer and they're not saying so."

"I doubt it, but maybe they are. But the story isn't about their parents, it's about them," I reminded him. He was looking away distractedly. Or was that his visionary gaze?

"I want you to call their parents and ask them."

"Ask them what?"

"If the news reports on D.C. have affected them."

This directive was so unbelievable, so ridiculous, so downright stupid, that I just stared at him for a few seconds.

"Are you kidding?"

"No."

"Come on, that's absurd," I said. "You want me to call up someone's mother in Colorado and say what? 'Hello, I'm a reporter for the

Washington Post and I'm just calling to find out if you're worried because Suzie is at school in the nation's homicide capital.' Are you kidding? Even if she wasn't worried, she would be after my phone call. I won't do it."

"What? You can't just refuse to do what an editor wants," he said with disbelief.

"I won't do it, Marc. It's creating news, creating an issue. It offends my sense of journalistic integrity. More important, it offends my sense of personal integrity." I wanted to say, "So there!" and stick out my tongue, but I didn't.

Fisher went ballistic. "You can't do this! You can't do this! A reporter can't just refuse to do an assignment!" He was so mad he sputtered, got red in the face, and trembled, the human equivalent of a core meltdown.

"I won't do it," I said calmly.

"I'm going to take this up with Milton and Mary Jo." His voice sounded like a little kid's yelling, "I'm gonna tell." I didn't say anything, just sat there and watched him stomp away.

Tell he did. A few days later I was summoned to a meeting with Fisher, Milton, and Mary Jo. We sat in Milton's fishbowl office with its four glass walls, a set piece on display for the rest of the newsroom. Milton and Mary Jo looked from one of us to the other as Fisher and I verbally bounced around each other, almost but not quite colliding.

Mary Jo, when she was around me and Milton, two African-Americans, nervously tried to be conciliatory, sensitive, and played both ends against the middle. Fisher was less short and condescending than usual. Milton sat impassively, listening, interrupting occasionally to ask for a clarification or more information. The upshot of the powwow was that I would track down the unnamed "official of George Washington University," talk to him, and report back to Fisher. Then we would decide if there was a story or not. A compromise.

Since Tom Sherwood had left the *Post* for more profitable—and ideally, more hospitable—climes at WRC-TV, Channel Four, I talked to Eric Pianin, his co-author, about where he got the quote. "I think it came from Bill Regardie," he said.

Black Alert! Bill Regardie, a member of the Board of Trade, owned *Regardie's* magazine, which he used primarily as a vehicle to celebrate himself, collect advertising revenue, and attack Mayor Barry. As far as I was concerned, Regardie was possessed when it came to Barry, and definitely not a man to be trusted when not double-sourced. "Did you call the guy at George Washington?" I asked Pianin. The answer was no.

Next I called Bill Regardie and refreshed his memory on the story. He told me that the name of the George Washington official who was at the Board of Trade meeting was Vice President and Treasurer Charles Diehl.

I called up Diehl, explained who I was, what I was doing, read him the sentence in Pianin and Sherwood's article that started this debacle. Before I finished reading he interrupted, "I didn't say that."

"Pardon me?" I said. "Was their someone else at the Board of Trade meeting from George Washington besides you?"

"No. And I didn't say that," he said. "I don't know where the reporter got that from, but it was not from me."

"Really." Old unstunnable me was stunned. I could feel sweet waves of smug self-satisfaction rising up inside me.

"I remember that article. At the time, I thought to write a letter to Ben Bradlee about the misquote, but never got around to it."

"So, you didn't say it?"

"No, I didn't."

I thanked him, hung up, and went looking for Fisher. When I found him I told him what I'd been doing, leading slowly up to the punchline: Diehl never said it. The quote that initiated Fisher's obsession with a nonexistent story was itself nonexistent. Just as Diehl did on the telephone with me, I had to tell Fisher several times, "He didn't say it. He didn't say it." I concluded, "He didn't say it, Bill Regardie just said he did. And no one double-sourced it." Love that journalist lingo.

Fisher looked surprised, then angry, then uptight. I could almost hear his small mind working, scrambling to protect himself, Sherwood and Pianin, and most importantly, the ultra-sourced, super-sleuth reputation of *Washington Post* reporters. We were still playing ping-pong, but suddenly he didn't have a paddle. Would I follow his lead and rat him out? Should he tell on Pianin and Sherwood first, to save his own ass? Would he get in trouble? Would this incident infringe on his Bonn Vie?

He looked at me like he was waiting for me to tell him what I was going to do, so he could figure out what he should do. But I'm not a tattle-tale; I wasn't going to do anything. I'd made my point: I have news judgment, I'm a good reporter, and I'm too smart for you to fuck with me. I didn't care what he or his cronies did as long as they left me alone.

"Like I said, Marc, there's no story," I said.

"Right," he said.

"See you later," I said, and walked away. For once he didn't ask me where I was going, what I was doing, or when I'd be back.

I finally acquiesce to Dixon's reasoning and agree to cover the Barry trial. I'm afraid that if I don't, no black person will have a piece of it. This would be a real tragedy, since even before Barry was arrested most of my colleagues were convinced he was guilty of *something*.

The morning after Barry's arrest on the night of January 18, at a hotel across the street from the *Post*, the newsroom was damn near giddy. Many of my colleagues walked around grinning at one another, clotted in small groups whispering and smirking. When Negroes passed by, they would grow silent, voices lowered. Still, snatches of self-congratulatory conversations bombarded me that day. "We did it!" one colleague exulted. "Now we'll finally get rid of Barry," someone else squealed. "Now we can take the city back," another voice creamed. For the first time during my tenure, a feeling of self-satisfied contentment pervaded the newsroom. White Boys, 1, Black Boys, 0. Crackgate, the Watergate for the nineties.

In the months since Barry's January arrest, many of my caucasian colleagues have already indicted, tried, and convicted him. The trial is a mere formality. The only question in their minds seems to be what punishment is heinous enough for this powerful, arrogant, crack-smokin' Negro. An apology, conviction, jail, community service, public humiliation, destruction of his career, loss of wife Effie and son Christopher— none of these likely possibilities, singularly or in conjunction, will satiate my rapacious coworkers. Lynching would not satisfy them, though a public stoning might, provided each and every one of them got a chance to pelt the mayor personally for what he's done to "their city." The fact that many of them live in Maryland or Virginia does not give them pause.

I agree to become the spook who sits in court because I am afraid my colleagues' vindictive attitude toward Barry will overwhelm the larger issues: that the United States attorney's office systematically went after Marion Barry for years; that under threat of jail and loss of her children, they coerced one of his old lovers, Rashida Moore, into luring him to the Vista Hotel, where she turned him on to crack furnished by the U.S. Attorney; that after the arrest the government then threatened, blackmailed, and strong-armed Barry friends and associates into testifying against him; that while Marion Barry undoubtedly is a crack-smokin', fornicatin', sleazeball, the U.S. government—and not only in this instance—is just as bad, if not much, much worse.

I also say I'll do it because I trust Dixon. Or at least, I don't believe he's trying to fuck me. And the truth is, what he said about being a "team player" kind of got to me. In the years I've been here I've tried a number of strategies, but never that one, so I'm willing to give it a chance. Not that I think it'll work, but as my mother always said, "If at first you don't succeed try try again always finish whatever you start follow-through is crucial life will always have another challenge for you and it's important to overcome after all nothing beats a failure but a try and you've got to keep on trying remember the story of the little red engine I think I can I think I can and so he did . . . "

But this little engine is tired. It's not that I don't think I can—it's that I don't *want* to. When I came to the *Post* I said I would come to get my daughter through high school and into college. There have been times in the past year when I doubted that would ever happen. Like me, Misu is indifferent to school. My recurring nightmare during her senior year was that she wouldn't pass all her courses, wouldn't graduate, would drop out and go to work as a countergirl at a fast-food chain. In my nightmares, the terrors are specific. My daughter would be unable to get a job at an A-level franchise like McDonald's or Burger King. No, she would end up slinging greasy burgers at a C-level joint like Arby's, living at home and spending her off-hours hanging out with similar low-achievers.

It was just a nightmare. Misu pulls through. In a few weeks she graduates from Wilson Senior High School. She has been accepted at Hampton University, which she will attend in the fall. I have done what I came here to do. What's next?

Being a Gemini, there are always at least two voices in my head. Being me, there are often many more. Right now, two dominate. One comes to me when I am gardening, reading fiction, with my lover. Its tones are friendly, familiar, slightly loud in order to be heard over the funk or R&B blaring in the background: "You've accomplished what you came here for. As soon as Misu graduates, get the hell out of Dodge. You already spend half your time in New York visiting Michael, so why not just move back there? You hate your job, don't have many real friends, what's keeping you? With Misu gone there'll be no need to maintain that big old house. You did your bit. She lived out the Cosby fantasy, now she's going to college to live in 'A Different World.' It's time for you to do something for yourself. Remember, life is a one-shot deal. Go on, girl!"

Then there is the other voice, cool, patient, eminently practical. It speaks in thoughtful, measured, quiet tones. There is no music in the background: "How are you going to pay for Misu's college without a job? It's only four more years, what's the big deal? You're making almost sixty thousand dollars, you don't work all that hard, and you'll never get fired or be laid off. If you stay another year your pension will be vested. You're getting over. You're spoiled and think you're a star, that's your problem. Everybody has to work a job, why should you be special? You got a house, a Volvo—the good life. You better learn to compartmentalize like everyone else. That man's too young for you anyway."

On the subject of covering the trial the voices are, as always, discordant. "F the trial, being a team player, the moolah, all the rest of it. Let's split!" says one.

"Don't do anything precipitous," says the other. "The trial could be your big break, your final chance to prove to the *Post* that you're a good reporter, committed, a member of the family. Hang in there."

In the end, I decide to cover the trial and make no momentous decisions until it's over, probably sometime in August. Misu goes off to Hampton in late August, Barry will be out of limbo, I'll be able to think clearly. Maybe covering the trial will be a good thing, like Dixon said. Once again, hope springs eternal.

CHAPTER TWENTY-EIGHT

I am lying on a beach in the Caribbean, peacefully tanning and thinking about asking one of the many fine brothers with dreadlocks lolling about to fetch me a rum punch—without the rum, of course. I push up on one elbow, squinting in the relentless white sun, and open my eyes to look for a suitable minion. But suddenly I'm not on the beach anymore, I'm floating in a vivid blue sea, although this sea ain't wet. As far as I can tell, everything's blue, I am blue, or maybe just kinda blue. It's all pretty groovy except there's something cold and rough poking into my back. I look down.

Shit. I'm not blue, I'm screwed. I'm not floating either, I'm skewered by the point of the Washington Monument, D.C.'s big old white stone phallic symbol on the mall, the city's highest structure under law. As my friend Judyie says. "We fuck the world, how appropriate." Am I number one yet?

"Aiiiyeeee!" I scream when I look down and realize how far up I am. Below me, a circle of American flags hang limply, lifelessly, like people's hair in Washington humidity. Hundreds of miniature figures circle the monument, looking upward. The point presses against my back, piercing my flesh. Can penetration be far behind?

"Help!" I holler down toward the mass of people, my saviors. I promise myself that after they get me down I will never make fun of the cameras, polyester clothing, too-tight shorts hiked up in the crotch, and funny accents of *turistas.*

The sun is damn near frying me to a crisp and I think my back is bleeding. I need help. I briefly contemplate praying but, agnostic that I am, the only prayer I can remember is the one that begins, "Now I lay me down to sleep." I hear voices rising up from down below, but they take a while to reach me. I can't make out the words. I assume they're instructions.

"What? What should I do? I can't hear you. Louder!" I bellow.

"Jump! Jump! Jump! Jump!" the crowd answers.

I don't know if I can fly, but it's better than staying where I am and getting fucked to death, so I jump. Instead of crashing downward, I drift languidly toward earth through that kinda blue, as if every one of my pores has sprouted teeny wings fluttering in unison, keeping me effortlessly afloat. I close my eyes and enjoy the trip.

But before I reach earth someone grabs my shoulder and yells, "So, Jill, Jill. I thought you was gonna put me in the paper today." Simultaneously I open my eyes, touch ground, and look into the face of Florence Smith, one of the regular spectators at the Barry trial, leaning over me and saying, "Oh, I'm sorry, I didn't know you were sleepin'. So, what happened to that article, anyways?"

Then it comes to me. This is not the Caribbean, it's D.C. in July, day who-the-hell-cares-what-number of the Marion Barry trial, and I've fallen asleep on a slab of allegedly ornamental granite outside the Federal Courthouse on Constitution Avenue.

I sit up quickly, rubbing sleep out of my eyes and surreptitiously looking around to see if any of my colleagues have busted my sleeping move. Barry Beach, the area in front of the courthouse where the daily dozens of newspaper, television, and radio people covering the trial hang out while waiting for something to happen, is as crowded as usual, but no one seems to be glancing my way. In fact, everyone's just waiting around. While the print, television, and radio reporters tend to stand, twitching, their heads jerking from side to side at the slightest sound, the scantiest hint of someone, anyone, to interview, the television cameramen (there are no women, so I'm not being sexist) have this whole trial game down. Years of covering trials, stalking the infamous, have taught them that, 99 percent of the time, nothing happens. When it does, the piranha-like feeding frenzy of the other journalists at the scent of blood tips them off in plenty of time to get the requisite thirty seconds of film.

They come equipped with lawn chairs, collapsible chaise longues, umbrellas, suntan lotion, portable televisions, and well-stocked coolers. Dressed in shorts, T-shirts, sleeveless tank tops, shades, and sneakers, this subsect of journalists eschews dressing for success. Why bother? It's too damn hot. Besides, they're television cameramen, they're already successful. With fat base salaries and—on a beat like the Barry trial—lots of overtime, they're making as much or more than most of the "serious" journalists scurrying around in suits and stockings. They are no longer hungry, curious, or ambitious. They've reached the top and intend to relax and enjoy it. While the rest of us roam restlessly, looking for a scoop, a source, an angle, something to get us on television, radio, in the newspaper, they could not care less if Barry ever leaves the courthouse. Their worries are grassroots, fundamental, earthy rather than esoteric. "It'll be a bitch if it rains," someone says on an overcast afternoon. His compadres look at the sky, squint, and nod agreement.

It would be good to say that I spend my time ferreting out news like my colleagues. And it would be hip to confess that I wear hot pants and a halter every day, carry a lawn chair along with my reporter's notebook, and bond with the fellas on Barry Beach. Neither is true. The truth is that when I'm not in the courtroom—which isn't much, since the permanent passes went to the white folks—I spend my time watching manifestations of in-group hostility between the pro- and anti-Barry factions of the black trial hangers-on, eating exotic flavors of frozen low-fat yogurt purchased in the courthouse cafeteria with obsessive regularity, and trying to stay awake. I expend a decent amount of energy pretending not to be a reporter in order to avoid the attentions of the several dozen trial groupies. To little effect. Each morning they greet me by name, comment on my time of arrival, occasionally even comment on my attire. When I am late, they fill me in on what's gone on: what time the first spectator arrived to stand in line for one of the nineteen seats allotted to citizens (the media gets forty); who acted out and was thrown off the line by the court officers; whether the mayor or his ice-queen wife, Effi, has been spotted yet.

Each day the *Post* sends down some news aides to stand in the spectators line on behalf of me and the four other reporters who regularly cover the trial. That this clearly circumvents the taxpayers' right to know by taking up the meager number of seats allotted them by U.S. District Judge Thomas Penfield Jackson seems to bother no one. After all, the public has a right to know . . . whatever we tell them. So much for journalistic—or personal—ethics.

The news aides are young people in their early twenties, graduates of mediocre to excellent colleges, who want so desperately to be reporters that they have signed on to do scutwork at the *Washington Post* at $8.00 an hour for the chance at a chance at a chance. Many freelance for the *Post*, hoping to be offered a permanent position. Few are. Most get wise after a year or so, put their experience at the *Post* on their resume, and go to work at a small paper in the boondocks.

The aides work hard for their money at the Barry trial. On days when some much-ballyhooed testimony is scheduled, like the screening of the videotape of Barry smoking crack at the Vista Hotel, or like when Rashida Moore, dubious Delilah to Barry's sex-addicted Samson, takes the witness stand, news aides are at the courthouse and on line before the street lights go out and the sun comes up. They just stand there with the taxpayers waiting for me or Bart Gellman or Elsa Walsh or Tracy Thompson or some other "real reporter" from the *Post* to show up and take their place, which is really *my* place—I just don't have to work for it.

The line is on the third floor of the courthouse. Appropriately, the public stands against the left wall, the press against the right. Up front, next to a metal detector, stand several court officers. Around nine or a little after, they begin ushering first the nineteen chosen of the masses, then the members of the fourth estate, into the courtroom. Before entry, they confiscate all newspapers. Is this really done to protect the sequestered jurors, or to torture the spectators by affording no surcease from the tedious boredom of the trial? Let's face it, this is real life, not "L.A. Law" or "Divorce Court," and Thomas Penfield Jackson is a far cry from the entertaining Judge Wapner.

The two assistant U.S. attorneys prosecuting the case against Barry, Judith Retchin and Richard Roberts, are themselves studies in boredom. Retchin is small, blonde, with a tight pinched face and undistinguished clothes. Her delivery is clipped, smug, and dull. If you're looking for the repressed passion of Susan Dey, forget it. Retchin's style is much more on the order of "I know I'm as good as any man and I'm gonna prove it by acting like one."

Roberts is tall, thin, black, and needs a haircut. His suits aren't Armani or deconstructed Willi Smith, but nondescript. Robert's delivery is methodical, detailed. Sometimes too detailed, like in slooooowwww. Occasionally, while he's speaking, I find myself yearning for Retchin.

The only player who has a chance of a guest appearance on "L.A. Law" is R. Kenneth Mundy, Barry's principal defense attorney. Pecan-colored, of medium height, with a fringe of hair and a penchant for rakish hats with colorful bands, Mundy brings life to an otherwise comatose proceeding. His cross-examinations and objections—usually overruled—are swift, incisive, often witty. He plays to the jury, the press, and the spectators shamelessly, making sharp asides and subtle jokes. Where the government ploddingly presents its case inch by boring inch, Mundy dazzles, throws up a handful of twinkling questions, then races around like a kid, snatching up answers.

As for Judge Thomas Penfield Jackson, he is Porky Pig forty years after Looney Tunes, fat, gray, and grouchy. He sits on the bench looking alternately angry, bored, or like he wants to suck his teeth, the former and the latter usually when Mundy is cross-examining a witness or presenting evidence. Before ascending to the bench, Jackson's law firm defended CREEP (the Committee to Re-Elect the President, those famous people who, at Nixon's behest, brought us Watergate) when it was sued by the Democratic National Committee and Common Cause. Both cases ended in settlement. In 1974, one of the firm's partners was indicted for conspiracy stemming from his work with CREEP. He was acquitted. In 1982 Jackson became the first Reagan appointee to U.S. District Court in D.C.

Jackson seems to me to have tried and convicted Barry before the trial even starts. He communicates this to jurors, spectators, and press alike via his pinched nostrils, rolling eyes, and snappish responses to Mundy's occasionally eloquent, witty, and astute legal arguments.

Mostly, I don't hear much that's eloquent, witty, or astute from anyone. It seems like half the time I'm in court is spent listening to the judge's white-noise machine as the attorneys huddle before the bench. Another 40 percent is taken up listening to one of the prosecution's dozens of witnesses testify for several hours in order to place Barry at a specific location, at a specific time, doing something slimy or illegal. Once this is done, the courtroom comes alive for the few seconds it takes Retchin or Roberts to stride over to a large, grid-like chart of dates and locations spanning several years and fill in another brick in the mayor's crack-rock road to hell.

I sit there, sucking TicTacs, trying to stay awake and not squirm on the hard oak bench, an admonishable offense in District Court if the bailiff hears the wood groan. I listen to the testimony casually, since by now it's long been made clear to me that I will have zero input in how it is cast and interpreted in the next day's paper. The cynical but grudgingly optimistic thrill of that day in May when Dixon told me I was wanted on the trial beat has disappeared, gone to that hopeful hell to which all my optimism goes, sooner rather than later, during my tenure at the *Washington Post*.

Early on, like when I realized I wouldn't have a regular courtroom pass and that I'd be working with not two, but four white folks, it became clear to me that my role at the trial was primarily as beard. "Extra! Extra! Spook Who Sat by the Door Promoted; Becomes Spook Who Sits in the Courtroom!" Read all about it, if you can ever find a story under my byline.

The trial begins on June 4; the verdict is rendered on August 10. In nearly two months I write six stories, two of them with other writers. This is nothing new, but it teaches me a crucial lesson: hope doesn't spring eternal. By the time the trial is over, mine has damn near dried up.

CHAPTER TWENTY-NINE

"Hey, Jilldo. How's it going?"

"It's going," I say sullenly.

"Are you coming to New York this weekend?"

"I don't think so."

"Why? Is court in session on Saturday now?" Michael asks. There is more than a touch of bitterness in his voice.

"No. But I'm exhausted, in a bad mood, and have to do a weekend story," I snarl. I'm pretty bitter myself.

"Oh. I see," he says. But I know this man. What he means is, "I don't see why you have to work during the weekend, why didn't you just tell them no, maybe it's because you don't want to see me as much as I want to see you. This whole trial separation is pushing my insecurity buttons like mad, and plus, I miss you."

"Do you?" I ask suspiciously. I can't help it, even though I know we're about to get into an argument without winners.

"Do I what?"

"See."

Michael scat-sings the melody to "Do You See What I See" in response. He's got a song for every occasion. A few days after our first date he called me up, played Tuck and Patti's "Mad, Mad Me" over the telephone, and sang along. I never sing, except in the silent closet of my mind. Is it any wonder I am the lover of a man who not only sings *aloud*, but appears to know the lyric to every hip song recorded between 1955 and the present? How is this possible when he was born in 1963, the year Kennedy was assassinated? It's magic.

But I'm not into songs, puns, or metaphors just now.

"Michael . . . "

"Look, I gotta boogie. I've got a session," says my personal trainer boyfriend.

"I'll call you tonight, okay?"

"Sure. For our regular sad, why-aren't-we-together-on-the-weekend, long-distance-relationships-suck conversation," he says.

"Look, you knew I lived in Washington when you called me up a year and a half ago," I remind him.

"That's true," he says perkily, "But I didn't think I'd fall in love with you. I just liked your ass. Later."

I sit in the cramped, empty *Washington Post* office on the fifth floor of district court, staring out the window, feeling sorry for myself, cradling a dead telephone. In the early days of our relationship we used to talk on the phone every day, but that's died down recently. I like to think this is because we know each other better, have less need to use the telephone for reassurance, have matured. Inside, though, I know it's largely the result of our both having monthly phone bills well over $200, and becoming fed up with telephonus interruptus.

Of course there's that other voice in me that whispers, "It's not maturity, it's wear and tear, the distance thing is hell. I mean, do you really think a young, fine man like that is wasting his time being monogamous, with you 200 miles away? Get real and get out there. It's just a fling, and it's been flung."

Certainly the trial from hell isn't helping. Before, I just disliked my job; now I hate it. I cannot adjust to being party to a de facto conspiracy on the part of U.S. Attorney Jay Stephens, the *Washington Post*, and various and sundry others to "get" Marion Barry. My integrity, my sense of who I am and what the values are that shape and define my life, is receding fast. I have taken to reading to myself the definition of integrity in *Webster's Ninth*: "1: an unimpaired condition; soundness; 2: firm adherence to a code of esp. moral or artistic values; incorruptibility 3: the quality or state of being complete or undivided: completeness."

I know Michael loves like Duke Ellington, madly, but I think he's getting tired of my angst about my job. For over a year he's been saying, "You're a writer, you carry your work with you. Fuck the *Washington Post* and come to New York and be a writer with me." But I don't do it. Lately I don't do anything but complain. He always listens to my ranting about insults from editors, butchered copy, what a bunch of creeps I work with and for, and he tries to be supportive. But we both know what the bottom line is. Once, after I dry-heave long-distance about a particularly heinous rewrite, he says, "You know what you're like? You're like a wonderful seamstress who's hired herself out to a sweat shop in Taiwan." Unlike integrity, I don't have to write this down or look it up to remember it.

So here I am, thirty-eight years old, making nearly $60,000 at a job I loathe, living far away from a man I love, waiting for the end of the trial from hell and my darling daughter, Princess Misu, to abandon me forever to go to college.

In anticipation of more loss and misery, I have already begun withdrawing emotionally from just about everything. In the summer of 1990 I take to not answering the phone. I simply let it ring, ring, ring, ring or unplug it altogether. I can face neither good news, bad news, or questions of any kind, especially "How are you?" I figure most people don't really want to know; they just want me to say "fine," so they can tell me, usually in painful detail, how they are. The few who are sincerely interested in what's happening with me, like Daisy, Thulani, Allyson, and Lynn, I don't want to tell. I mean, these are the real homegirls, black bourgeoisie style. Individually or collectively they've been through my one marriage, a few miscellaneous shack-ups, dozens of break-ups, and my various fat girl/fly girl/Vineyard girl/black nationalist sistuh/career girl stages. They've endured my I'm-going-to-kill-Misu-she's-making-me-crazy stages, my Princess-Misu-is-a-goddess-and-I'm-going-to-give-her-the-master-bedroom stages, my I'm-a-great/shitty-writer phases, my three therapy phases, my therapistless phases, my I-love/hate-my-family-phases, my, my, my, my . . . enough already.

I love each and every one of these sisters too much to ask them to accompany me on this latest, meanest trip. It's the real thing, babeee, this ain't no self-indulgent bullshit, not this time. We're talking mythological proportions here, the phoenix plunging into the pyre, Leda fighting off the rape of the swan, *Chicago Tribune* columnist Leonita McClain killing herself at the heart-breaking age of thirty-two, even though she'd "made it." Serious shit. I don't even know how to begin to articulate what I'm feeling. For the first time in my life as a writer, I cannot distinguish between myself and words. Like, am I angry or am I anger itself? Do I feel loss or am I lost? Am I mad or am I having a nervous breakdown?

I don't answer the telephone, or say much the few times I do, because, literally, I can't. Still, always a race woman, even in the midst of this collapse, I save my scant clarity and scraps of energy for work. I apply it to the few stories I manage to squeeze out, but mostly to my arguments with editors about our coverage of both the trial and the African-American community's response to it. If I don't bear witness, weird as it is, who will?

If "impact" is the buzz word at the *Post*, as in "impact" stories are the ones that make the front page, I don't have much impact before or during the trial. In my seventeen months on the Metro staff, I go A1 four times: first with a story on a Maryland family of three who turned their lives around when they began attending meetings of Narcotics Anonymous; second with the lead story in a seven-part monstrosity on regular people battling drugs and crime, which was so heavily rewritten that I wanted my name taken off it until Milton convinced me otherwise; next came a heavy investigative piece in March 1990 headlined "Area Leapfrogs Over Spring With an 89-Degree 'Winter' Day" (D.C. is big on aberrant weather); and finally, on June 29, with a Barry case piece, "City Transfixed By Arrest Scenes."

This last story is what my Metro colleague Carlos Sanchez calls "Triple A," or "Ask Any Asshole." In response to the screening at the trial and on television of the infamous Vista videotape of Barry allegedly smoking crack, me and six other reporters fan out across the metropolitan region to query citizens on their response to the tape. This story is cowritten with Mary Ann French, who is now working at the *Post*, but who I can't imagine lasting much longer than I do.

Mostly during the trial I write stories that either don't get in the paper, become a graph in someone else's story, or languish in the white hole of intype until time—or intype overload—erases their relevance.

My days are predictable: go to the courthouse and go into the courtroom if I have a pass (which means that no one else more important than me wants to go). Spend the day wandering around looking for a feature piece, a scene story, an odd angle. Go back to the office, talk to my editor, Mintz, and occasionally sit in with the rest of the trial team when they meet to cast the next day's story.

Unless something truly interesting has occurred in court and I'm worried about the potential for real distortion of the event on my colleagues' part, I try to avoid these meetings. When I do attend them I'm far from a team player—more like a sullen, disgruntled Mau-Mau who everyone listens to but doesn't hear, before proceeding to do what they planned anyway.

I may justify this dynamic by being hinkty and calling it "bearing witness," but what I'm actually doing is covering the *Post*'s collective ass. If the community erupts with charges of racism, my corporate overlords can point their fingers at me and retort, "How are we racist? Jill Nelson was on the trial team and everyone knows she's pro-black, outspoken, and sensitive to racial issues. She was there."

I try to be "there" as little as possible, which isn't very difficult in Washington; to adapt Gertrude Stein, "There's no there there." But on the day Linda Creque Williams testifies for the prosecution, I make sure I'm inside the courtroom. Williams is another in a stream of women who testify that they did drugs/had sex with Marion Barry, sometime, somehow, somewhere. *Why?* Overweight, greasy, usually dripping with sweat, Barry speaks English like it's his second language. Are times really this tough, even in Chocolate City?

After a few weeks of listening to fairly detailed testimony from Barry's paramours, understanding dawns. Marion Barry is not only an alleged drug addict and alcoholic, his jones of origin is sex. Most of the women who testify against him are disgruntled losers in Barry's version of "Dialing for Dollars"—call it "Balling for Bucks," in which minimally qualified and marginally attractive women stalk the man, armed with aspirations, resumes, and, one hopes, condoms. Whether the women are procured by convicted felon, drug dealer, and Barry enabler Charles Lewis, or they are approached by Barry himself, as Rashida Moore was after she posed for the cover of *Essence* in 1976, or they pursue him on their own initiative, almost to a woman they're looking for a J-O-B—and they are willing to take off their drawers to get it.

A few weeks of testimony against Barry from these black women leaves me sickened. Just as, in my own mind, I try to give black people a little extra credit, I try to give black women double that. But not these women: willing victims in their thirties, forties, and fifties, it is as if they are latter-day Rip Van Winkles who slept through the feminist, civil rights, and self-actualization movements. Then along comes Linda Creque Williams.

Thin, plain, tackily dressed, Williams is a friend of Charles Lewis from St. Thomas who, one night while Barry and Lewis were visiting that island, came to their hotel resume in hand. According to Williams, Barry was swilling liquor and kept disappearing into the bathroom and then acting weird when he emerged. He also made sexually suggestive remarks and gestures. While Williams didn't respond, she didn't leave, either, but sat tight, drinking. At some point, she and Lewis smoked crack. Eventually Lewis left the room, and, according to Williams, Barry forced himself on her. The government retires triumphantly: add rape to Barry's myriad sins.

Dapper Mundy brings out in his cross that no physical force was used in Barry's alleged forcing, nor any verbal threats. Most significantly, Williams admitted she never cried out for help, even though, as she testified, Charles Lewis was "right outside the door."

But the damage has been done. Outside the courtroom, print reporters rush back to the office, television folks fight for a scenic location from which to do their stand-up, radio folks scramble for the telephones. I overhear my colleagues talking excitedly, hear the word rape, and head for base camp.

The newsroom, always tense between five and six-thirty—deadline time—is positively vibrating with news of Williams' testimony. The trial team sits in a circle, excitedly discussing the day's events. Mary Jo Meisner, wearing one of her signature minidresses, is damn near salivating as Michael Yorke, Tracy Thompson, and Bart Gellman recap the testimony. Elsa Walsh is also there.

"Tell me about it, tell me about it," Meisner squeals. Everybody talks at once, but she gets the idea.

"So, was it rape?" she says eagerly. "Can we go with that? What do you think?"

"Well, it sounded like rape. But she didn't use the word," says the ever-cautious Yorke.

"She did say he forced himself on her, and isn't that rape?" a woman asks.

"Well, can we go with rape?" Meisner asks again.

"We probably could," says someone hesitantly.

I can see the banner headline, "Woman Testifies Barry Raped Her; Made Suspicious Trips to the Bathroom."

"I don't think so," says someone, I think Bart Gellman, who mainly writes about the legal issues raised by the trial. He is a thoughtful, careful reporter, to my mind the most objective on the team, and that includes me.

"Definitely not," I weigh in. "She went there, sat around drinking with Lewis and Barry, didn't leave when he made advances, and now says it's rape? That's ridiculous. He dogged her and she gave it up." I look around at the group; their faces are blank. Maybe I lost them on "dogged."

"I mean, black men do it all the time, and I'm sure white men do, too," I turn imploringly toward Tracy and Elsa, who look at me blankly. Am I speaking in tongues, or Swahili, buried deep in my molecular memory? "You go out to dinner, get drunk, and when the guy takes you home he won't leave. He just hangs around begging for some play until you finally give it up, just so he'll shut up and go home. That's not rape, that's being dogged."

I'm standing up now, raising my voice to make my point, because I'm so afraid we'll go with "rape" tomorrow and I'll feel compelled to quit immediately. My colleagues look either preoccupied, uncomfortable, or bored, I'm not sure which. They drift rapidly away: is it from me, or toward deadline?

I go to my desk and sit there, feeling sick, humiliated, angry, disgusted with myself and everyone else. The next day the headline reads, "Woman Says Barry Forced Her Into Sex; Mayor Calls Testimony 'Not Believable.'" No use of the "R" word. Now, that's spin control.

CHAPTER THIRTY

By the week of August 6, the Barry trial is slouching toward an end. The jury has been deliberating for three or four days and the verdict is expected at any moment. I plan to wait for the verdict, write a round-up story, and go to Martha's Vineyard. I've already put in for vacation time starting August 11, so I'm chanting for a judgment day no later than the tenth. Like Michael, my family has been bugging me all summer about when I'm coming up there. Me, I've just been bugging.

"Honey you've got to get up here can't you take a few days off the weather is absolutely gorgeous one of the nicest summers ever and you should see your nephew Max that little sucker has really grown everyone asks about you when you're coming you know the summer's almost over and I'm not going to live forever I know it's a long drive maybe you can fly . . . " my mother says during her bimonthly phone call.

"I know, I know. I'm trying my best to get there. I told the jury to hurry up." I change the subject to something really important, like the current temperature of the Atlantic and what friends of mine she's encountered on the Inkwell.

That topic exhausted, my mother always asks, "So, how are you?"

"All right."

"Really?"

"Yeah. As well as can be expected," I say cryptically. Inside a voice is screaming, "Ask me more, Mommy, ask me again!"

But she doesn't. Instead she says, "Well, hope to see you soon."

"Me too."

"Bye."

"Bye."

We leave it, as we usually do, at that. My relationship with my mother is so larded with unspoken memories, resentments, competitions, and anger, that the radius within which we can talk politely is severely proscribed. In a way I am my mother's only surviving daughter, and for that she is both relieved and enraged—at herself, at me, perhaps most of all at Lynn, who deserted her altogether a decade ago.

It is easier to say that Lynn started going off at eighteen or nineteen because it was the Sixties and she took too much acid, or because she was egged on by Dom, her pot-smoking shrink, who wore velvet robes and slippers that curled up at the toe, or because one of her many boyfriends made her crazy. That's easier for my mother than thinking that maybe it was a result of something she did, or something my father didn't do, or something about the whole family dynamic that made Lynn as we knew her disappear that day Anyasi overdosed on the reefer. It's easier, too, than the possibility that what happened was inevitable, in the stars or cards, that all of us were powerless to stop it. Instead, she clings to the belief that Lynn would still be with us in the way we want her to, if only, if only, if only . . . *what*?

For most of the time we were growing up, I hated my older sister because I wanted to be like her, which also meant being like my mother: short, petite, cute, popular yet essentially aloof. I was the outsider among the women in our house: tall, overweight, awkward, given to raging tempers. Always, always, I wanted my sister's approval; seldom did I get it. At eleven or twelve, smack dab in the middle of my first serious crush, I asked my sister, then sixteen, if I could borrow her pink mohair sweater, the perfect plumage/armor for actually talking to the object of my affections. "Are you kidding? You're too fat. You'll stretch the sleeves," she said. Twenty-five years later, I still judge the way clothes look on me by the sleeves: are they too tight? too baggy? just right? Do they leave room for movement without danger of fabric disfigurement?

Stretch the sleeves, stretch the sleeves, stretch the sleeves. This was my own personal litany of sartorial disaster. No matter that mohair gives, that my arms were not really so fat, that my sister was being mean, not truthful. For years, in moments of rampant insecurity I ritualistically peruse old photographs of myself—images of a big girl, a plump girl, but not a *fat* girl—to reassure myself that I'm not, never was, as bad as I think. Once, in Lord and Taylor, I almost buy an ugly pink mohair sweater I don't want in some spontaneous reversion to adolescence—just to have it, to show my sister that I have it, and that the sleeves fit perfectly. I am standing in the cash register line clutching the sweater when I realize I'm twenty years too late; both the fat girl I was and the sister Lynn was are long gone, and mohair is too retro for me. I don't hear the "stretch the sleeve" litany after that.

My mother and I seldom communicate about my sister. She simply stands between us. As a family, of course, we never discuss what happened to Lynn. It is like this horrible tragedy that no one gives voice to, so in silence it grows larger than all our lives, subtly pervades all that we do and are.

My older brother Stanley, myself, and Ralph, the youngest, each experiment with being smoke-dope-coke junkies, but Stanley is the one who for twenty years chooses drugs, along with documentary filmmaking, as his avocation. Tall, thin, bespectacled Ralph chooses music as his means of escape and expression, hunching over his guitar in soundproof rooms playing haunting riffs, drifting away, just like the notes. To save his life, he finally packs his clothes around his guitar in its case and moves to Berkeley.

My father, he withdraws, goes spiritual. He quits dentistry and treks first to Switzerland, then back to Martha's Vineyard (where he buys another house for himself, alone) in search of enlightenment. Or is it just that he wants to get away from us, from the pain, the guilt, the feeling?

I try to be the dutiful daughter, the successful one, the one my mother can depend on, the functional one. Against both the spoken and the assumed expectations of my bourgeois upbringing, I decide to have a baby at twenty to create a family to replace the one I used to have. The birth of Princess Misu grounds me, gives me a reason to go only so crazy and no further, a reason to enshrine my demons in the edifice of middle-class success. I turn my rages inward.

I go to Columbia Journalism School at twenty-eight and write my thesis, "The Dope Kids of 115th Street," sitting cross-legged on the floor in front of my typewriter late at night, sniffing drugs. I seek out men who are mentally, physically, or emotionally inaccessible, place them on the pedestal Daddy vacated when I was fifteen, and then snap, "I told you so" when, like Humpty Dumpty, they have a great fall. I search for the authentic Negro experience in other people, in various drugs, in sexual obsession, in being a race woman. I avoid finding it, or not finding it, in myself.

I am a dealer, not a player. Like Chauncey Gardiner, I don't mind being there as long as I don't have to participate; I like to watch. I can deal with all manner of black folks, white folks, other folks, just not myself and my family. Part of my becoming a journalist has to do with getting in other people's shit before they even think to get in mine. It is both a power and a powerlessness trip, a way of defending my crazinesses and doing myself and others some good at the same time.

I deal, and most of all I keep my mouth shut and *don't talk about what happened to Lynn.* And to the rest of us. Years later, Michael angrily calls me an "escape artist." Reflexively, I deny it, but it bothers me. Doesn't he realize I'm trying to escape from being an escape artist, change my emotional job description mid-life? Won't he be my emotional rescuer?

I generally stay within the lines when I talk to my mother, who holds us together with her love and will. When I drank and used drugs the lines would get blurred, or I'd get brave and step on the line accidentally-on-purpose, raging and screaming at my mother. We would go for each other's verbal jugular, but were either scared enough or smart enough to never quite reach it. To her credit, my mother, a Jack Daniel's drinker, would be sorry in the morning. I never was.

Now, I am just tired of the lines, the silence, the circles of bullshit. I want out of my closets.

CHAPTER THIRTY-ONE

With the jury deliberating, I spend more time back at the *Post*, waiting. Like my grandmother used to say, idle time is the devil's work, so while I'm waiting I get caught up in the gossip, paranoia, rumors, and office politics that permeate the newsroom.

Since I've been through my change-the-system-from-within phase, African-American Women's Caucus phase, Newspaper Guild activist phase, disgruntled Negro phase, and am now rapidly winding up my team player phase, I really don't give a shit about most of what goes on, as long as it doesn't overtly affect me. Then I hear rumors—quickly substantiated—of the great, big, day-after-the-verdict, definitely-A1, zillions-of-reporters-scattered-throughout-the-metropolitan-region, Ask-Any-Asshole story being planned. Who's going to write it? Perhaps the lead feature writer on the Barry trial? But no. Surely I jest. It'll be the great white hope, Steve Twomey, an okay guy and a good writer, but, in the context of the competitive *Post*, my nemesis. When it comes to choosing between a white male with a unique eye who's good, and a black woman who's the same, there's no contest.

I plan to spend the day of the verdict at Faces, a bar on Georgia Avenue frequented by city officials, Barry cronies, politically connected members of the black bourgeoisie, and sugar daddies. I have suggested, fought for, and pitched to the editors a scene piece on what this particularly relevant segment of the African-American community thinks of the verdict. This trial, like everything else in Washington, is marbled by race, by black folks' fears that white folks are trying to steal the city back from them and white folks' fears that, once in complete control, the Negroes will run amok. As usual, no one seems to want to come right out and deal with race, specifically regarding its role in the Barry case. Faces is a black bar, one that spans the classes, the perfect location to get black folks' responses to a trial that has more to do with race, power, and the future than it does with the law.

Now I hear that after months of my being held hostage to the trial, the courtroom, and the heat, Twomey is being given the "big story." I have been at the *Post* long enough to know that there is only one "big story," which makes mine a "little story."

I'm not surprised. I should have figured this out weeks ago when the editors agreed to my angle. By then hope may have reached damn near rock bottom, but I guess it hadn't dried up yet. I go see John Mintz, my editor and ally throughout my Barry trial tribulations, and go ballistic. "I don't believe this bullshit. It is so typical. I bust my ass all summer and then you all give Twomey the lead story. This shit is so insulting. He gets the big piece that goes A1 and I get to write a sidebar about what the natives think. I mean, I told Dixon I didn't want to do the trial from the beginning, but he convinced me I should be a team player. Well, a lot of good it did me. I mean really, John, I am so sick of this shit . . . " John sits in front of his terminal, looking stunned.

"Wait a minute. Slow down. What are you talking about?" he asks.

"Steve Twomey getting the main verdict story, that's what!" I snap.

"I don't know anything about that."

I believe him. "Well, that's the word around the newsroom, and I'm sure it's true. After all, he's the great white hope, so why am I surprised," I say bitterly.

"I'm surprised, and if it's true, I'd be pissed, too," says John. "I'll find out what's going on and let you know."

A few hours later, Meisner comes over to my desk, sits down chummily, and tells me that if I want to do the Triple A I can, although she loves my Faces idea and thinks it will get great play. I tell her I don't know what I want to do anymore, but will let her know, which isn't really true. I know I want out, out, outta here!

That night I call Dixon at Northwestern, where he's in management training camp and possibly reverting to sophomoric behavior. He is also so glad to be away from the *Post* that I suspect he has a hard time giving a shit, although he musters a decent rendition of concern.

"I think you should do the Faces story," he says after I bombard him with my high-strung version of the verdict scenario.

"Why? Do you really think the *Washington Post* is going to give it any play?"

"Why not? It's a good story."

"So are most of my stories, and it usually doesn't help."

"I think this is different. You've been on the trial all along, and Milton likes your story." I guess he's been keeping in touch with Coleman, apparently.

"Really?"

"Yeah. He thinks it's a great idea."

"I don't know . . . "

"Do you really want to spend all night in the newsroom, taking feeds from a dozen reporters and trying to weave them into a coherent story with ten editors looking over your shoulder?" asks Dixon. I pause, visualizing what he's just said. It looks and feels very much like Jill Nelson's personal vision of hell.

"No . . . but, I don't want to get fucked on my story."

"I don't think you will. Milton really likes the idea."

"So, you think I should do it?"

"Yeah. I think you should use that Nelson Voice to write yourself onto the front page." Dixon knows I love to hear about that "Nelson Voice," crying out in what Louis Farrakhan calls the "wilderness of North America." We talk a few minutes longer, and by the time I hang up I am flattered, pacified, seduced. I decide to stick with Faces, let Twomey do the big, bad Triple A, and write myself onto A1 with that Nelson Voice. I forget that besides me, Dixon, Mintz, deputy Metro editor Fred Barbash, and a few others, most people at the *Post* couldn't care less if they ever heard that "Nelson Voice" again.

Friday, August 10, is the eighth day of jury deliberations. The vibe in the newsroom is like the calm at a surprise party moments before the guest of honor arrives and everyone jumps out, laughing and yelling, "Surprise! Surprise!" All around me there are some 'bout-to-be-happy white folks.

Most of the black reporters and staffers have that stricken look on their faces that kids get when they're about to be spanked but the first blow hasn't landed yet; call it "anticipation anxiety." It would be nice if we could think that a guilty verdict would be just about Barry and his various crimes and misdemeanors, but even the most assimilated and apolitical among us aren't that dumb. Just as we black journalists have paid for Janet Cooke's pathology in terms of increased skepticism and scrutiny from our corporate masters, we know a guilty verdict will likewise taint all black politicians, public figures, and somehow (though less directly than the Cooke fiasco) us colored members of the fourth estate.

The televisions suspended from the ceiling of the newsroom remain on all day. Periodically, small clumps of reporters gather beneath them, look up anxiously, hopefully. Me and the other members of the team prepare to cover our stations—in my case, a bar stool at Faces.

Just before six, the verdict comes down. For the first time in my tenure here, the newsroom is almost absolutely silent. Barry is guilty on one count of cocaine possession, not guilty on another, and the jury is hung on the remaining twelve counts, including the government's *piece de resistance*, the videotaped sting of Barry at the Vista Hotel. He might as well have been acquitted. There is an abrupt, massive, basically racial role reversal in the newsroom. Now, it is the black folks who look like they're about to smile, the caucasians who look stricken.

I grab a notebook and hurry toward the elevator. On the way out I pass Ellsworth Davis, a photographer. He is in his sixties, a Washington native, a walking encyclopedia of D.C. lore that has nothing to do with government or monuments. I love to work with him. As he walks by, he holds his index finger up high. "It just takes one," he says, and laughs a great big belly laugh.

"Amazing, huh?" I say as I rush past Keith Harriston, D.C. education reporter.

"Yeah." He grins.

"I'm happy."

"So am I."

Luckily, I get into a taxi driven by an African-American native of D.C. The all-news station on the radio is blaring coverage of the verdict and recaps of the trial. He is so happy he can barely drive. "I'm happy about it, I swear I am," he says. "Ain't no doubt about it, the mayor was wrong, but the government was worse. They been after Barry for years, and then to use that poor woman to entrap him, coerce him, it's just wrong. I'm glad he got off, he needs to get on out of office and go somewhere quiet and get his life together."

When I arrive at Faces it is filling up. All eyes are on the big-screen television in the corner, where U.S. Attorney Jay Stephens is making a statement. The patrons boo, hiss, and finish Stephens' sentences for him, in terms sarcastic, scatological, or just plain obscene. The mood in the bar is smug, celebratory, the way Daniel's favorite watering hole probably was after he escaped from the lion's den. I drink club soda, interview folks, have dinner, and call the office regularly. Around 10:30, they tell me to come in and start writing—for the Style section. I hate Style, but what the hell. I figure my piece will earn a guaranteed front page of the section with no argument.

When I finish, I call Dixon at Northwestern and read him my story. When I'm finished he's silent. "Well, whaddaya think?" I ask.

"There's that Nelson Voice," he says, in a tone that makes me know he's grinning that Dixon Grin. "It's a really good story."

The next day my story runs deep in the Style section, page four, buried in the corner usually reserved for notification of the seasonal rereleases of Disney films like *Dumbo*, *Sleeping Beauty*, and *Snow White*. When I find it, while standing in the middle of the Safeway on Piney Branch Road, I burst into tears.

The headline reads, "After the Verdict, Food for Thought."

It is the last note heard from the Nelson Voice as a staff writer at the *Washington Post*.

CHAPTER THIRTY-TWO

When I finally let go, I do so very quietly, methodically, without screaming or yelling or stamping my feet. I flip out neatly.

Some people who "go crazy" simply get tired, disgusted with life and with themselves, and decide to let go. It's a psychological version of Zen submission, except instead of entering an ashram or going to meditate in the Himalayas, they retreat inside themselves.

It's not that I cannot cope. I simply no longer want to. The notion of ever setting foot inside the *Washington Post* again is overpoweringly dismal. Not because I care about the paper, people, politics, or anything else the *Post* represents, but because I *don't* care. That's what's bothering me, me who runs on passion and commitment.

Briefly, I contemplate high drama: confrontation, tearing of hair, a semi-public suicide attempt. But I've tried all that before. Even though I wasn't sure what response I was looking for, I knew I hadn't gotten it.

One Monday night when I was a chubby twelve-year-old, I gulped a handful of diet pills in the tiny maid's room off the kitchen, which I had moved into to escape the tortures inflicted by my older sister. Then I lay down on my bed and waited for my mother or one of my brothers to come past the door on some casual errand. I rolled the words around and around in my mouth, waiting to greet them. "I took pills and I'm committing suicide," I would say. That would be enough. They would come to my rescue, save me, make everything all right.

No one came. Finally I began to feel nauseated and dragged myself into the kitchen, where my mother stood, smoking a cigarette, stirring a pot on the stove.

"I took pills and I'm committing suicide," I said to her back.

"What pills? The ones the doctor gave you for your diet?" my mother asked, without turning.

"Yes. I'm gonna die."

My mother didn't respond. "Stanley," she called my brother, still not looking at me.

From the living room my brother yelled, "Whaddya want? I'm watching the football game!"

"I need you to go to the store for me at halftime, okay?"

"What for?" my brother moaned.

"Your sister has an upset stomach. I need some Ipecac so she can vomit," my mother said.

"What's the matter?" my brother laughed, "Fatso ate too many Twinkies?"

"Leave your sister alone."

"Okay. Halftime's in about twenty minutes," my brother responded, turning up the volume. Much later, I found out the pills were a harmless placebo.

Twenty-five years later I go crazy softly, silently, without expectation. When I used to scream or yell or stomp my feet, my family simply laughed or shook their heads and said, "Stop being so dramatic," until even I couldn't distinguish between acting and feeling, or if it mattered.

By this time I was tired of rescuing other people, and past thinking anyone would come to rescue me. I was tired of thinking and wanting. I just wanted to lie still and alone. I waited until my daughter was away at college because I didn't want to take her along with my craziness. Because then I would have had to think about her, worry about her, and she about me.

Stoically, on August 26 I drive down to Virginia and leave Misu for her first year at Hampton University, mouthing cool words about this being a commencement, not an ending. Part of me wants to hold on, not leave her, but the other, stronger part just wants to get out of there and let go.

I spend a day and a final night with her. Together we unpack her trunks and hang posters, both of us trying not to get sentimental. I think she feels that if she starts crying she'll embarrass herself and me, reveal that underneath the grown-up breasts, long legs, and elaborate hairstyles she is still my little girl, Princess Misu, afraid of our separation. She knows college isn't the same as Brownie Camp, when she could call me up in the middle of the night when the rain, bugs, and great outdoors got to her, confident that I'd come to her rescue.

I don't cry for a lot of reasons, but mostly because I am pretty sure that once I start I won't be able to stop. I'd never be able to drive the three hours home. I'd have to stay in my daughter's dorm room, blubbering. When she was eleven she'd asked me, "When you come to school, can you look like the other mothers?" I wasn't sure then or now what the other mothers look like, but I don't think they're weeping uncontrollably in the dormitories.

So we both hold back for different reasons, until the very end, at the car. I hug and kiss her, then take my watch off, still warm from my wrist, and give it to her.

"Thanks," she says, hugging me, "Is this so I'll always be on time to class?" She is kind of smiling, but with big old tears poised on the rims of her eyes.

"I guess so," I say, turning away so she won't see the tears rolling down my cheeks. Maybe she sees them anyway, or senses them, because she hugs me again then, fiercely, and says, "I love you, Mom, don't worry. We'll see each other a lot."

"I know, I know," I mutter. "It's just that . . . " I leave it hanging right there, because the important thing is to let my daughter go without crying or clinging or making her feel like she owes me something, which she doesn't; she's given me so much already.

I pinch in the tears, hug her one last time, get in the car. "Have a wonderful year and think of me when you look at your watch," I say.

"I think of you all the time," my daughter cries. I want to jump out of the car, throw my arms around her, and cling to her so as not to be swept away, but I don't. By then I am already shrinking back, growing brittle and dry. I am afraid that, in hugging me, my daughter will feel how small I really am, and will want to stay with me, protect me, just when her own real life is commencing. I stay in the car, waving as I pull away, and watch her teary, beautiful face in the rearview mirror until I turn a corner and she's gone. On the drive home I listen to the same Phoebe Snow tape over and over, loud, perfect music for letting go.

When I get home I pay all the bills in advance, writing the mailing dates on the corner of the envelopes where the stamps go. Then I water my twenty-four houseplants, mow the grass, and go to bed.

In the morning I start to get up and then remember that, after seventeen years, there is no reason to. Lying in bed, my body feels like one of those things the Egyptians buried mummies in, a sarcophagus. I can feel the outline of what was supposed to be me, the five-foot-eight and 150 pounds of who I looked like but wasn't.

Who I really am is something much smaller somewhere way deep inside all that flesh and bone, something that's shrinking away. The real me, if that's what it was, was a tiny toy soldier. I had nothing to do with the big, strong body lying there in bed.

The telephone rings and rings until the sound of it annoys me and I turn off the bell. After that there is silence except for the sound of the wind as it rustles the lace curtains at the bedroom window, me lying there watching them in slow motion and thinking about nothing.

I don't feel much of anything except when I look at the close-up photograph of my daughter's face, or the snapshot of me and Michael, grinning, stuck under a corner of the mirror. Looking at these, I feel as if I'm submerging myself in hot waves of caring so intense they burn. I want to scream, but I don't. I'm not sure if the scream would be real or if it would just be little old me, acting dramatic again.

Instead, I take one or two or three or however many of the little pink Xanax pills a doctor prescribed for me months before. I swallow however many are required either to not care or to fall asleep, whichever comes first.

After a few days I don't have to take the pills anymore. I just lie there in my container of a body, the incredible shrinking woman, watching my life projected on my mind like a movie. My life doesn't flash past; it just kind of drones, not exactly boring but not compelling either, like I am ten feet under water, holding my breath effortlessly and looking up, watching it go by.

I lie there, cool and not dramatic, and watch the movies of my life, for once not wanting to change a thing, not wondering or caring what would happen at the end.

CHAPTER THIRTY-THREE

"I really can't take it anymore. Well, I could take it, but I won't."

"What is it that you can't take?"

"My job. I feel like it's a daily assault on my integrity, my sense of self, who I am. Every day I have to justify myself, my ideas, the people I write about, to a bunch of people who don't care—a bunch of white folks who assume they're superior solely on the basis of their skin color.

"At work I'm treated like a great, big, intimidating Negress, so I spend half my time trying to make myself nonthreatening, even though I'm not *really* threatening, so the caucasians can deal with me—even though it's not *really* me they feel threatened by, it's their *image* of me. I mean, actually, I'm a really nice person, a softie. I wear my feelings on my sleeve. Is that so wrong? I feel like a criminal every day I go to work because I love myself and I love African-American people. I really feel if I don't get away I'll go berserk, get a machine gun, go into the office, and go off."

"Where do you work?" she asks.

"I'm a journalist at the *Washington Post*." I say. What I want to say is. "Lady, are you listening, isn't it obvious? I work at the number-two newspaper in the country, you're a shrink, can't you identify a high-class, corporate-Negro breakdown?" But I don't. Instead I surreptitiously check out the framed diplomas on the wall, making sure she's accredited. It is August 30, 1990.

"You've told me about them. How do *you* feel?"

For one of the few times in my life, I am speechless. We sit there in silence, me looking down, Dr. Rankin looking at me. I wonder if she can hear all of the different voices in my head screaming for dominance. I try to keep my expression neutral so she won't have an inkling of what's going on inside me.

Months later, I see a picture of myself taken around that time. My hair is grayer than ever, too long, shapeless, matted in pseudo-dreadlocks that stick out from my head every which way. I look like an African-American Medusa. I am convinced that if this picture were a videotape, my hair would be squirming. Of course Rankin knew what was going on in my head; a woman's hair is the mirror of her soul.

How do I FEEEEELLLLLLLLL? I open my mouth, but no words come. There is something wet on my face. Is it raining in here? Then I realize I'm crying. Sobbing, actually, big, sloppy toddler tears. "I feel awful, like I'm disappearing, don't know who I am anymore, for the first time in my life, I'm losing myself, how can that happen? I'm all I have . . . "

I leave Dr. Rankin's office with a prescription for Elavil, two more appointments for that week, and a note to Milton Coleman stating that "because of her condition she should be away from work for a period of four weeks." I get a month off—the exact amount of my accumulated sick leave.

The only thing I know about Elavil is that it's what junkies used to sell to other junkies on Eighth Avenue as a cheap substitute for heroin. I rush to People's Drugstore and fill the prescription. Am I hallucinating, or paranoid, or does the pharmacist give me a disdainful look?

The Elavil takes me into a new level of nothingness where I don't even feel the need to worry about what I'm feeling, since I feel so little. Maybe I'm getting better, because I turn on the telephone and call my friend Deborah, a.k.a. Chocolate. But maybe I'm not, since I start crying as soon as she asks me how I am, and then hang up.

Chocolate rushes over, takes one look at me—on heavy tranqs and resplendent in a dirty pink chenille bathrobe—and moves in. It's okay having her there. She goes to work, she doesn't talk unless I want to talk, she cooks regular, delicious meals, and she reminds me to take my medicine.

One day I call Michael. I guess I sound spaced, because he asks who's with me and then immediately asks to speak to Chocolate, and then he shows up himself a day and a half later. The last time I saw him had been a few weeks earlier. We'd had a big argument about doing the laundry—me doing his—and he split abruptly. A lot has transpired since then, so it's real weird seeing him again, because we're not together, I'm not together, nothing is.

Chocolate moves back out, and Michael moves into the guest room, a skinny, unadorned space my mother calls "The Nunnery," and takes care of me in a new way. We don't sleep together, or talk about deep subjects, or laugh and tease like we used to. We don't even argue. I don't cook shepherd's pies or bake chickens or produce bowls of nachos dripping with cheese. The earth mother is gone. Michael doesn't make a lot of phone calls to New York, worry about his business, or rush around making male-type repairs on the house. No more macho man. I sleep a great deal, and Michael, who I didn't know could cook, makes pretty good meals. We spend a lot of silent time together, reading, watching movies, or not doing anything at all.

When we do talk, it is usually Michael talking gently to me about getting well.

"I know you're feeling bad, baby," he says one day. "But I know you can get through this. I know Jill's in there someplace. I want her back. But you have to want her back, too."

I lie in bed and watch the lace curtains blowin' in the wind.

"I don't know what will happen with us. It seems that everything is changing, it won't be the same again. I don't know if we'll be lovers again, but if not, that's okay. I'm here for you, I love you. I'll always be your friend. I just want you to get better. I'll stay as long as you need me."

Sometimes he talks to me about the Elavil, what it makes me feel like. "It makes me not feel at all," I say. We talk desultorily about the whole notion of drug therapy. "I think maybe drugs serve a purpose in crisis, but not as a regular thing. Not that I'm a doctor or trying to tell you what to do, but if you're taking mood-altering drugs, is that really you? How long does your doctor think you'll be on pills?"

Then he asks me if I have to go to the bathroom, something he's taken to inquiring about periodically since, along with my emotions, the Elavil deadens my bladder sensitivity. Now that he's asked, I realize I do. My muscles and mind are so relaxed he half-carries me there.

Later he drives me to my appointment with Dr. Rankin. I tell her I want to go to the Vineyard, the most familiar place in my world, and figure things out. She suggests I stay and continue seeing her twice a week. We compromise; I'll go to the Vineyard and stay in touch by phone. When I leave she gives me a prescription for something called Ludiomil.

When we get back to the house, Chocolate comes to visit. Michael goes into the kitchen to make tuna salad with mustard sandwiches. Elavil'd, I lie on the loveseat, floating. Deborah comes and kneels beside me. "Jill," she says, "while you're lucid you need to think about giving someone your power of attorney so your bills and stuff will be taken care of until you get better."

For the first time in weeks, I hear something loud and clear. "While you're lucid, while you're lucid, while you're lucid." Suddenly I'm hearing everything like its been digitally remastered and is playing on CD: Michael's fork separating clumps of tuna in the kitchen, the bugs nattering outside the window behind me, my heart beating. The unintelligible din created by the voices in my head fighting each other to be heard abruptly stops. Briefly, there is absolute silence.

Then one authoritative voice says, "Lucid? Lucid! Girl, you'd better get up, take a shower, and get your shit together. You know you've been in this nervous-breakdown lane too long when they start trying to catch you during your brief moments of lucidity and get your power of attorney. Arise, and get yourself to Martha's Vineyard. Take your lucidity and power of attorney with you."

Two days later I am sitting on the porch of my mother's house in Oak Bluffs. It is the second week in September and the rest of my family is packing up to leave. I will remain here alone except for Marvin Jones, family friend, eclectic chef, sort of caretaker, good guy.

When I arrive, my mother looks at me hard. Then, old undemonstrative Leil hugs me long and close.

"How are you?"

"Okay, I guess."

"Well, you don't look okay. How are you really?" my mother asks.

"I think I had a nervous breakdown and I think I'm going to quit my job," I say.

"Good. The *Washington Post* never did treat you right. You did well as a freelancer and you'll do fine again. You know I support you whatever you do." I just stare at her. Is this my mother talking?

"You know, I'm not going to ever be the person I was," I warn. "I have to take care of myself, not worry so much about everyone else."

My mother looks at me. "You can be anyone you want," she says. "I love you." And then, damned if she doesn't hug me again.

I spend almost three weeks on the Vineyard. Marvin and I go swimming nearly every day, even though the water and air are getting colder by the hour. I eat tons of food. Marvin cooks lobster and new potatoes, smoked bluefish, eggs and home fries, macaroni and cheese, fat pitas stuffed with vegetables and fish. I read mysteries and sleep a great deal. I hesitantly finish a story for *Essence* and mail it off. Even though they ask me to rewrite it later, it reminds me how much I love to write.

Once, my brother Ralph calls.

"What's up?" he asks. "You sound horrible."

"Nothing."

"Still fooling around with that silly job?" he asks.

"Yeah," I say

"Get rid of it," he says. "You'll survive. I mean, can you really see yourself ending up huddled in a doorway in the snow?"

I spend a lot of time thinking about the shit in my life that got me to this point. Mostly, it's heavy old stuff, big and little, that's going to take time and lots of energy to work through. But the one big, rotten, relatively new pile of shit in my life is my job at the *Washington Post*, and I can get rid of that in one broad stroke, if I have the nerve.

I keep the Ludiomil with me at all times. They are white, oval, large-sized pills that make a lot of noise bouncing around in my bag, reminding me they are there for me. I never take them.

At night, Marvin and I rent videos and eat whatever weird snack I've coaxed him into whipping up. One night we forget to pick up a movie and sit on the couch in the den, me flipping through the channels with the remote control. Everywhere I stop, there's trouble: cops chasing someone, people gathered around a deathbed, women angsting about their biological clocks, George Bush bullying and posturing about Saddam Hussein, a woman crying, a man yelling, children cowering—all caucasians.

"God, this shit sucks," I say to Marvin.

"White folks' problems," he clucks, tilting his head to one side and shaking it like an old man. "Ain't nothin' but white folks' problems."

I decide to quit my job.

CHAPTER THIRTY-FOUR

"Jill Nelson, Jill Nelson. I'm glad to see you. Come on in." I follow a smiling Milton Coleman into his glass office. It is Tuesday, October 2, 1990.

"What's going on?"

"I'm all right." I pause for a few beats. "Milton, I feel that my position on the city desk has become untenable. There's no way for me to go back to doing the job I was doing. I've thought about what I'd like to do if I could have any job here, yours, whoever's, and there's really nothing I want to do but write a column. Both Mary Jo and Phil said in my evaluation that they thought I'd be good at it. Dorothy is going on fellowship and said she'd talked to you about my doing her column for a year, and that's what I'd like to do. If that's not possible, please consider me having quit, effective immediately."

The structure of that last sentence is a little awkward, but using the word "quit," not "resigned," is important to me. I've looked them both up in the old *Webster's Ninth*.

Resign: "to give (oneself) over without resistance; to give up deliberately; to renounce by a formal act; to give up one's office or position; to accept something as inevitable."

Quit: "released from obligation, charge or penalty; quite free of, released, literally at rest; to set free; to depart from or out of: to leave the company of; to relinquish, abandon or give over (as a way of thinking, acting or living); to give up (an action, activity or employment); LEAVE; to cease normal, expected or necessary action; to give up employment; to admit defeat: Give up."

I had initially planned to just quit outright, but then thought it'd be more diplomatic—as in, have fewer negative repercussions once I was gone—if I asked for the column, something by that time I didn't want and knew I wouldn't get, so management could feel, at least partially, that they'd rejected me and not the other way around.

Milton looks surprised and sad. "How did you come to this decision?" he asks. "Is it something specific?"

I laugh. "Lots of things happened, and you know about most of them, Milton," I say. "But I'm just tired of being here, of justifying myself every-day, of fighting with ignorant caucasians, of the whole trip. It's not any one thing or person, it's the institution. I was poor when I came here, but I had a good rep. Here, I've been disappeared. It's not worth it to me for the money. I don't think the *Washington Post* is interested in or ready for someone like me, or the type of writing I do, and it's not worth it any-more. I'm tired."

"I'm really sorry, Jill. If you leave, it'll be a real loss for the paper," Milton says. I believe him, but it's not enough. I know that like everyone else, when the shit hits the north wall, Milton has to cover his own ass. Sometimes he's covered mine, too, but I know now that the only one I can really depend on is me.

"Is there anything I can do?"

"No, Milton. And I wanna say that you've been great. I really appreci-ate your support. Without it, I probably wouldn't have lasted this long."

We talk for a few more minutes, then I say, "Well, I'm gonna go start packing up my desk."

"Hold off on that, let me take the column thing to the higher-ups."

"Why bother?" I grin.

"Because that's the way it's done," he says, and smiles.

At the door, we shake hands. "I'm sorry," Milton says.

"I'm happy." I smile. Then I go to my desk and start packing boxes.

That afternoon, Phillip Dixon takes me out for a last, long, written-off-on-the-*Washington Post* lunch at the Tabard Inn on N Street. We sit outside in the sun, eat, and talk. Like a concerned older brother—which he is, by one year—Dixon asks questions to make sure that I've thought out my decision, that I am not making a reactionary move, that I have enough money to live on for at least six months.

"So, how do you feel?"

"Great."

"What are you going to do?"

"Be happy."

After lunch I finish packing my boxes, then go and say goodbye to the few people I care if I ever see again. Very few, because most of my pals have temporarily escaped the *Post*, on fellowships, vacations, or maternity leaves. In my final act of political bullshit, I seek out a few infamous office gossips and tell them I've quit, I'm happy, goodbye. I leave it to them to communicate my side of the story to interested parties in the newsroom.

Then I walk to the front of the newsroom to say goodbye to Joyce and Margo, the sisters at the switchboard. When I tell them I'm quitting, they look shocked and saddened.

"Are you sure you're doing the right thing, baby?" Joyce asks me. I nod. "I guess you are, you sure don't look upset."

"I'm not, I'm happy."

"I'm gonna miss you," Joyce says.

"Me too, but I'm not dying. There is life after the *Washington Post*. We can still have lunch."

"Good."

"You know," says Margo, "You have a lot of courage. I admire you."

"I don't know about all that, I'm just doing what's best for me."

"What're you going to do now?"

"Be happy." It is my stock answer, a cliché, and it's true.

"Well, if you ever need anything, anything at all, you let us know," says Joyce.

"Thanks. I will. And thanks for always being in my corner, even when I was over in the magazine."

"That's all right, sweetie," Joyce laughs. "I liked you from the first moment I laid eyes on you."

"I'll stay in touch, you all do the same," I say, moving away. This is the only time all day I feel sad or sentimental, saying goodbye to the first people—and nearly the last—to look me in the eye at the *Washington Post*.

"Don't forget, if you need something, let us know," Margo calls after me as I walk back to my desk.

"Thanks."

Around five-thirty, Milton calls me into his office. My desk is packed, I've made my last subsidized telephone calls, and I've found two tall, good-looking young news aides in Hammer-style pantaloons to carry my boxes for me. I've even taken the liberty of typing a letter of quitting, er, resignation.

"Well, Jill," Milton looks embarrassed. "What do you have for me?" There is no mention of the column. I start to push it, ask him what the north wall had to say about that request, but then don't. Who cares?

I hand him my letter, we shake, I leave.

Finally, I go for my exit interview with managing editor Leonard Downie in his glass office on the north wall, a formality I'd rather avoid but, as Dixon points out, "You might want something from him sometime."

Our conversation is brief, cordial. I've always respected Downie, because even though I might not like or agree with what he says, he's been straight with me. I tell him so. He says he's heard I'm leaving and asks why.

I give my by-now-standard rap: I'm tired of fighting, I don't feel I've ever fit in here, I've spent most of my career working for myself, that's my norm, I'm simply doing what's right for me.

"Were there any specific problems on the city desk during the trial?" he asks. Ah ha, the loaded question. This is my chance to name names, throw bombs, wreak havoc. But I've had my fill of that for four years. Enough already.

"The whole trial experience was horrible. I think we missed important stories," I say. "But whose fault is it, and why? I don't know. Is it bad news judgment, stupidity, or racism? I don't know and I don't really care."

Downie asks me what I plan to do. I tell him I'll go back to being a freelance magazine writer, although I really don't know what I'm going to do except be happy. Then he asks me why I think I've had such a difficult time at the *Post*.

"It's like a friend of mine in New York, an ex-editor, told me when I was still on the magazine: 'You know what the problem is,' she said, 'Those people at the *Washington Post* can't imagine a black person like you.' I think she was right, Len." I turn away from him, look out the window at a sliver of 15th Street. "The sad thing is, I don't think I'm that hard to imagine. I think I'm probably more like the average African-American on the street than most people in this newsroom."

When I turn back to Downie he is twitching slightly and looking uncomfortable. Maybe he doesn't get what I'm saying, possibly I've gone too esoteric, could be he's bored. I doubt whether he's heard me loud and clear, but who knows? Who cares? I have absolutely no interest in either fucking with him or talking to him. It's over. We shake hands and I leave the *Washington Post* forever, free to imagine myself.

Now, that's my authentic African-American experience.

EPILOGUE

I quit my job because I wanted to be happy. But even in 1990 it wasn't easy to escape the plantation. Rumors flew concerning my departure. A woman from the *Daily News* even called and told me that a source at the *Post* told her I'd quit because I'd embezzled $17,000. I politely suggested that if that were the case, she'd be calling me in prison. Then I let it go. I figured I'd left to get away from that kind of stuff, so why get into it now that I was free?

I never intended to write this book, but one afternoon that November, digging up gladiolus bulbs for the coming of winter, I thought about my interview with Bradlee and burst out laughing. Then I went inside and started writing. Most of the gladiolus bulbs stayed underground and froze.

In August of 1991, I moved back to New York to spend more time with my family. Now, early each May, my mother and I go to the Vineyard, open the house up, and stay there until it's too cold to go swimming any more, usually toward the end of September. We talk a lot. My brother Ralph, my sister-in-law Susana, and my nephew Max come for the summer. Stanley is healthy, happy, and with us as much as his filmmaking permits. If you see a red convertible pull into the driveway, it's probably Dad. Lynn doesn't visit, but we know she'll always be a part of us, whoever or however she imagines herself.

Misu just finished her junior year at college and is a wonderful person. Michael and I remain close friends.

Most of all, I'm happy, and finally number one to myself. The me I imagine every day is a lot more interesting and loving than anyone—including me—ever would have expected. I'm not exactly sure what's next, but I imagine it will be authentic.